Lox, Stocks, and Backstage Broadway

LOX, STOCKS, AND BACKSTAGE BROADWAY

Iconic Trades of New York City

NANCY GROCE

A Smithsonian Contribution to Knowledge

Smithsonian Institution
Scholarly Press

Washington, D.C.
2015

Published by SMITHSONIAN INSTITUTION SCHOLARLY PRESS

P.O. Box 37012, MRC 957
Washington, D.C. 20013-7012
www.scholarlypress.si.edu

Front cover image: View down Broadway, New York City, Detroit Publishing Company
Photograph Collection, Library of Congress, Prints and Photographs Division.
Back cover images (left to right): Wall Street bull, New York City, photo by Carol M.
Highsmith, Carol M. Highsmith Archive, Library of Congress, Prints and Photographs
Division; Times Square station, photo by davis2k via freeimages.com, Image ID 354529,
all rights reserved; Empire State Building, Library of Congress, Prints and Photographs
Division; poster for a Federal Theater Project production of Shaw's *On the Rocks*, design by
B. Lassen, WPA Poster Collection, Library of Congress, Prints and Photographs Division.

Library of Congress Cataloging-in-Publication Data:

Groce, Nancy.
   Lox, stocks, and backstage Broadway : iconic trades of New York City / Nancy Groce.
     p. cm.
   Includes bibliographical references and index.
   1. New York (N.Y.)—Social life and customs. 2. Occupations—New York (State)—
New York—History. 3. City and town life—New York (State)—New York—History.
4. New York (N.Y.)—History. I. Title.
   F128.3.G76 2010
   306.09747'1—dc22   2009030706

974 (ordered under)
   ISBN: 978-0-978846-04-6 (cloth)
   ISBN: 978-1-935623-76-2 (pbk)

Printed in the United States of America

∞™ The paper used in this publication meets the minimum requirements of American
National Standard for Information Sciences—Permanence of Paper for Printed Library
Materials, ANSI/NISO Z39.48-1992.

CONTENTS

FOREWORD

I N 2001, I was honored to serve as the corporate chair of the thirty-fifth annual Smithsonian Folklife Festival. It was the largest exhibit about New York City ever mounted by the Smithsonian. One million visitors came to fete my hometown and celebrate its diversity. The festival inspired *Lox, Stocks, and Backstage Broadway*, the first book in many years to give an overview of New York City's traditions, cultures, and folklife. *Lox, Stocks, and Backstage Broadway* is written for people like you and me, who love New York City and its complexity, success, and poignancy.

The book is the culmination of a journey that is both intensely personal and universal. My family has been part of the New York story for three generations as builders, bankers, and supporters of cultural institutions. It is a story of immigrants welcomed by the Statue of Liberty as they came in search of a better way of life. They fashioned, and continue to shape, a dynamic city where the volume is louder, the pace faster, and the rhythms of life more varied.

Each New Yorker is an architect of the city's culture. As such, New Yorkers, both eminent and ordinary, serve as our guides in the behind-the-scene tour that follows in these pages. It is the quintessential New York story as told by the people who make Gotham what it is. And what would Gotham be without the lullaby of Broadway and all the people—both onstage and backstage—who make it sing? And what about the food specialists who feed Gotham's insatiable appetite for a "nosh"—the bagel and bialy bakers and the lox purveyors, who slice the smoked salmon so thin that you can see through it? Then there are the transit workers who move New York's millions through the arteries that feed the many hearts of the city. The subways they run used to be moving art galleries, resplendent with graffiti. Now the kids who used to spray paint trains in the Bronx have moved into the real art galleries that blanket the city with every form of visual expression. And of course there's the economic engine that drives the demand for so much of what those galleries offer—the business movers and shakers who inhabit the canyons of Wall Street. From high culture to high towers, Gotham never stops being a work in progress. Gotham's trades undergird every aspect of that work.

Gotham has come a long way. In 1788, New York was briefly the capital of the nascent United States of America. On March 30, 1789, George Washington was sworn in as the first president on the steps of New York's Federal Hall. Today, New York is the 24/7 crossroads of the world.

The "city that never sleeps" is also the city whose spirit never fails. When the World Trade Center was felled by terrorist attacks on September 11, 2001, an iconic symbol of the United States and of New York was destroyed. A simultaneous attack on the Pentagon damaged a symbol of U.S. military might. But the real strength of the United States remained untouched: our freedom and democracy. The symbol of that strength, our Statue of Liberty, continues to beckon the vast and varied tapestry of humanity that has always been the bedrock of both New York City and our nation. Let us savor all the flavors of Gotham as we peel back the layers of the "Big Apple." New York, New York: it's a wonderful town!

Howard P. Milstein
Chairman & CEO, Emigrant Savings Bank
Former Member, Smithsonian National Board

PREFACE

L OX, STOCKS, AND BACKSTAGE BROADWAY documents the men and women engaged in the iconic trades, occupations, and industries of New York City. From Broadway to Wall Street to the farthest reaches of New York's fabled subway system, and with numerous stops in between, the following pages celebrate the occupational skills, crafts, knowledge, and traditions that have helped to fashion New York into a legendary metropolis. More than a glimpse into the "rites and mysteries" of selected New York trades, the following pages introduce readers to a remarkable caste of artisans, workers, laborers, and artists—talented individuals whose jobs create, maintain, and nurture the very heart of Gotham.[1] Our featured narrators are contemporary New Yorkers from various classes, races, and backgrounds. In most cases, they are not celebrities outside their chosen professions, but they are typical of millions of other city residents whose voices are all too rarely heard in the deluge of materials written about New York City. Not only are they eloquent and knowledgeable in recounting their own stories, the history of their city, and the development of their individual trades, but their wisdom, humor, and humanity reflects the best of New York. Their words allow us a fascinating glimpse into the core of the Big

Apple. Wise, concerned, passionate, and often very funny, these are people who you will enjoy meeting.

This book is based on extensive interviews and research undertaken by the Smithsonian Institution's Center for Folklife and Cultural Heritage to document urban culture in the five boroughs of New York City at the turn of the millennium.[2] Over the course of several years, dozens of folklorists, anthropologists, ethnomusicologists, and historians armed with tape recorders and cameras fanned out across New York City to interview hundreds of artists, artisans, craftspeople, and other local experts who together weave the quotidian fabric of New York's urban life. They sought to document both the specialized and unique as well as the day-to-day aspects of city life that give New York City its vibrant character.

The talented and talkative people interviewed by these Smithsonian fieldworkers and the information they shared with us formed the basis of *New York City at the Smithsonian*, a major exhibition in summer 2001 at the annual Smithsonian Folklife Festival. For almost four decades, the Smithsonian Folklife Festival, a living exhibition held on the National Mall, in the heart of the nation's capital, has been a summer ritual in Washington, D.C. In summer 2001, over the course of the festival's ten days, more than one million museum visitors listened as several hundred articulate New Yorkers, invited to Washington as the Smithsonian's honored guests, talked about their city, demonstrated their crafts and occupations, and performed the music and dances that define, color, and enrich daily life in New York City. The stories and experiences of many of those who came to Washington as featured speakers on the occupations of New York are found in these pages.

The emphasis of the Smithsonian's New York City research program and the subsequent festival was on "rooted" traditions and regionally distinctive aspects of New York's urban culture. Of course, all cultures change, and change and modification of even the most deeply rooted traditions reflect a healthy, living culture. With this in mind, the many folklorists, historians, and urban scholars involved in the Smithsonian's New York City project prioritized dynamic and contemporary aspects of urban life over the antiquarian and quaint. Researchers sought to take "ethnographic snap shots" of life in today's New York. "Wouldn't it be wonderful," we agreed, "if we had an interview with the New Yorkers who painted shop signs, or baked bread, or built our landmarks, or traded on the streets of New York in 1700, or 1800, or 1900?" What was it like for workers and craftspeople to live and labor in New York in ages past? Unfortunately, until recently few scholars or researchers thought to ask "everyday people" about everyday lives. For most, it was easier to talk with fellow scholars or ask public pundits for their thoughts about "the people" than to talk directly to "average" New Yorker workers. As will be immediately obvious, the everyday people interviewed in the course of this project have extraordinary knowledge of their trades, deep understanding of their communities, and profound insights into their city. And being New Yorkers, they are not unwilling to share them. Listening closely to what they have to say provides an important window to the vibrant urban culture of the city.

The Smithsonian New York City Project was launched in 1999 not only to provide background material for the 2001 Smithsonian Folklife Festival, but also to create a body of interviews and recordings documenting life in New York at the turn of the millennium. Interview field tapes recorded in the city were augmented by several hundred hours of audio and video recordings of concerts, narrative talks, and public discussions held before small and large audiences at the 2001 Smithsonian Festival. Both the field tapes and the 2001 festival tapes are now housed at the Ralph Rinzler Archives and Collections at the Smithsonian Institution Center for Folklife and Cultural Heritage in Washington, D.C.[3]

The Smithsonian Institution, the national museum of the United States, is one of world's outstanding museums and centers of learning. The Center for Folklife and Cultural Heritage is a research and educational unit of the Smithsonian Institution promoting the understanding and continuity of diverse, contemporary grassroots cultures in the United States and around the world. The center produces the Smithsonian Folklife Festival, Smithsonian Folkways Recordings, Smithsonian Global Sound, exhibitions, documentary films and videos, symposia, publications, and educational materials. It also conducts ethnographic and cultural heritage policy oriented research, maintains the Ralph Rinzler Folklife Archives and Collections, and provides educational and research opportunities through fellowships, internships, and training programs. Unfortunately, prior to this project, its holdings of materials documenting the culture and traditions of New York City were modest. We hope that the New York City Project interviews will help to remedy this lacuna. We are delighted that the voices of the many remarkable people we interviewed during the course of this project are now part of our national record and will be available to researchers in years to come.

Finally, a word about more recent events that have had an impact on New York: most of these interviews were conducted prior to the September 11, 2001, attacks on the World Trade Center, which left nearly three thousand of our neighbors dead. A few days after those awful events, as national commentators intoned "we will never be the same," I spoke to the captain of my local fire house in the Yorkville section of Manhattan. "Things will go back to normal," he said as hundreds of neighbors stopped by to offer condolences and leave flowers and food at a fire house that had just lost nine of its members. "Of course, it will take a while . . . but things will be OK. It would take an awful lot to change this town." His understanding, insight, and faith in his city have been borne out. It will take a great deal more than a single event, however horrific, to change the cultural patterns and to shake the profound urban pride developed over four centuries by the people of New York.

INTRODUCTION

Unique New York:
Local Culture in the Global City

WHAT MAKES New York City unique? Distilling the essence of New York's cultural complexity, summing up its vitality, richness, and energy is a daunting assignment, one that calls for a good deal of hubris, or, in the local parlance, *chutzpah*. The New York I experience daily as a New York resident, a livable metropolis of discrete neighborhoods and overlapping communities, is rarely the one I see portrayed by the media, read about in novels, or hear spoken of by tourists. Nor do I hear the voices of the New Yorkers whose lives and labors help to shape New York's most distinctive trades and occupations.

This book, which is based on a multi-year research project that culminated in the 2001 Smithsonian Folklife Festival, gives me and some of my fellow New Yorkers a chance to describe how we see our city, to reveal some of its most colorful occupational traditions and trades, and to explain how New York can be simultaneously both a global capital and a hometown. It provides a platform to refute the tourist's refrain "I love to visit New York, but I couldn't live there." Like me, millions of New Yorkers would not think of living anywhere else.

1

At first, it might seem like an oxymoron to talk about the traditions or folklife of one of the worlds most modern cities, but in fact, daily life in New York would be impossible without a substantial body of shared urban traditions and of collective community knowledge, customs, historical memories, and cultural understandings. These traditions provide the basic ground rules that shape how New Yorkers interact with their families, their colleagues, and their fellow New Yorkers. From subway etiquette to local street food to verbal repartee to stickball games, these traditions create a shared urban culture that, in turn, creates a sense of community and gives New York City its unique sense of place. A subset of this shared traditional knowledge also shapes and governs the distinctively New York trades documented in this book.

A COMMUNITY OF COMMUNITIES

In addition to a shared urban culture, all New Yorkers also have one or more reservoirs of specialized traditional knowledge acquired from their ethnic or religious upbringing, working in a particular occupation, or living in a specific area of the city. The innumerable, multifaceted ways in which these factors interact are what make New York such a complex world capital. Of course, it would be impossible to cover all aspects of New York's culture in a single volume, but by highlighting some of the trades and occupations that are most closely identified with New York City, readers will be introduced to both the ordinary and extraordinary aspects of life in Gotham. Before setting off on our journey, however, it might be helpful to provide just a bit of background on the history, culture, and organization of contemporary New York.

What gives twenty-first-century New York a sense of being unique is not merely the myriad ethnic and interest groups that are found in the city, but also the complex ways in which they overlap and interact. The physical landscape of New York, the lack of space, the reliance on mass transit by people of vastly differing backgrounds, neighborhoods that are home to both the very rich and the extremely poor make it impossible for New Yorkers to ignore the influence of "others." From kosher Chinese restaurants to Irish hip-hop groups to Mexican pizzas, cultures from all corners of the globe have influenced one another in New York, in part, because of their physical proximity.

Over the past few decades, scholars have often observed everyday life in American cities through the prism of class, race, or ethnicity. This approach, while valuable, does not do justice to the kaleidoscopic complexity of how individuals act and interact in contemporary urban settings. New York City abounds with groups of people united by occupational, residential, recreational, or intellectual interests. Each one of these disparate interest groups forms a community with a discreet body of shared knowledge, history, and traditions, that is, a folklife of its own. These communities usually accommodate overlapping memberships; in fact, it would be hard to find a New Yorker who did not simultaneously belong to more than one of these urban communities. Depending on when you ask, the average New Yorker might identify herself by the ethnic group(s) into which she was born, the neighborhood she comes from (or lives in now), what she does for a living, or what she does in her leisure time. Thus, a Jewish Puerto Rican from the Upper West Side (who now lives in Brooklyn's Cobble Hill neighborhood), who works as a stock trader on Wall Street during the day and spends her evenings at Indian bhangra dances in Queens, can legitimately claim to be part of each of those separate communities. The number of choices available in New York is mindboggling. The sheer size of New York allows residents the freedom, and if they wish, the anonymity to endlessly recreate themselves. This vast social and cultural smorgasbord contributes to the allure of, but also creates apprehension about, the city.

New York has always been different. Unlike Boston, Philadelphia, Baltimore, and other East Coast cities, it began not as a refugee settlement for out-of-favor English religious sects, but as the Dutch trading colony of New Amsterdam. Soon after Peter Minuit obtained rights to Manhattan Island from the Canarsie Indians in 1626, visitors from Boston and Philadelphia condemned New York as a polyglot den of iniquity: a place where Mammon's money and trade overshadowed the word of God, where people of all nations and colors mixed freely, and where children were allowed to play in the streets even on the Sabbath.[1] Although New York has been the port of entry to more Americans than any other city—some historians estimate that one in four Americans has at least one ancestor who lived in Brooklyn—few Americans think of New York as a typical American city. Why? Perhaps it can be traced back to a deep-seated distrust of urban life. From the time of Thomas Jefferson and other framers of our Republic, through nineteenth-century reformers, to the rush to modern suburban housing developments, the ownership of land and renouncing of foreign ties to become "fully" American have always been the national ideal. Renting apartments, remaining in ethnic immigrant enclaves, and using mass transit have not. And if cities were inherently evil and filled with recently arrived, potentially sinister "foreigners," no U.S. city was more evil or more foreign than New York.

Today, New York City is a metropolis of more than eight million people. It consists of five separate boroughs—Manhattan (New York County), Brooklyn

(Kings County), the Bronx (Bronx County), Queens (Queens County), and Staten Island (Richmond County), of which only the Bronx is located on the mainland of North America. New York was initially established as the colony of New Amsterdam by the Dutch West India Company in 1624. In 1664, England took control and King Charles II appointed his brother, James, Duke of York (later King James II), proprietor of the growing city. A name change was in order and thus New Amsterdam became New York. In addition to honoring his brother, Charles renamed the neighboring counties "Queens" for his wife, Catherine of Braganza; "Kings" (Brooklyn) for himself; and "Richmond" (Staten Island) for James's country estate in Yorkshire. The Bronx was named for Jonas Bronck, a Swedish sea captain from the Netherlands, who settled there in 1639. (New Yorkers *always* say "*the* Bronx." Local folklore claims that "the" must be included because "people used to talk about going to visit *the* Bronck family.") Contemporary New York is barely a century old, dating back only to the Consolidation of 1898, which united Manhattan with the surrounding city of Brooklyn and smaller towns and hamlets scattered throughout Staten Island, Queens, and the Bronx. (Some Brooklynites still refer to Consolidation as "The Mistake of '98.")

New Yorkers rarely step back to think of their city as a whole; rather, they mentally compartmentalize the city into a series of more than four hundred neighborhoods that function almost as adjoining villages, each with a distinctive look, history, and character of its own. To residents of New York, the cafes of Manhattan's Greenwich Village or the tree-lined streets of Brooklyn's Park Slope are light years away from the pandemonium of Times Square, the suburban calm of Queens's Forest Hills, or the small-town feel of Staten Island's Tottenville. Cobble Hill in Brooklyn has very little in common with Murray Hill in Manhattan or Cyprus Hills in Queens. Watching sailboats gently ride at anchor off City Island in the Bronx seems a world away from the bustling boardwalk at Coney Island. Every day, millions of New Yorkers leave their neighborhood—and most New Yorkers will tell you (confidentially) that *their* neighborhood is the best—and travel across dozens of other neighborhoods to reach their jobs, visit their friends, pursue their education, or seek out entertainment. Manhattanites journey to what they refer to as "the Outer Boroughs" where the "b & t" (bridge and tunnel) people live; residents of Brooklyn, the Bronx, Queens, and Staten Island go to "The City," which, many of them believe, is overrun with snobs and tourists. By cognitively mapping out New York's hundreds of neighborhoods in this way, as a series of smaller, intellectually manageable communities, New Yorkers make their city more comfortable and less overwhelming.

THE NEW YORKERS

So who is a New Yorker? If you were not lucky enough to be born in New York, how long must you live in the city to become a "real" New Yorker? New York has always been a city of immigrants who, for the most part, have welcomed or at least tolerated other immigrants. Nowhere else on earth do more people from more varied backgrounds live together in relative peace. Perhaps because it has been decidedly multicultural from its earliest days, both twelfth-generation descendants of founding Dutch merchants and newly arrived Asian immigrants can call themselves New Yorkers with equal validity. (Personally, I think you become a New Yorker as soon as you can name all the stops on your subway line.)

New York's vibrant ethnic communities are what many tourists find most striking, perhaps because it is easier to notice the city's diversity than to appreciate its unity. Today, New York is experiencing a wave of immigration unparalleled since the 1890s. Almost 36 percent of New York's eight million residents are foreign born. According to the 2000 U.S. Census, the leading homelands of New York's newest residents are, in descending order, the Dominican Republic, China, Jamaica, Guyana, Mexico, Ecuador, Haiti, and Trinidad and Tobago.[2] There are enough Maltese, Estonian, and Cuban-Chinese New Yorkers to support their own social clubs and trade associations. Today's New York is a palimpsest of generations of New Yorkers who have gone before, leaving their cultural marks, however faintly or vividly, on the urban landscape. And this diversity of new and old immigrant groups is reflected in New York's workforce, the people whose stories and insights fill the pages of this book.

In addition to immigrants from other countries, the city has always been a magnet to other Americans who saw opportunities, freedom, glamour, and excitement in New York that were lacking in their hometowns. These "urbanites by choice" include several main groups: first among them are African Americans, mostly from the American South. The families of many contemporary African American New Yorkers were part of the "Great Migration" to New York and other northern cities during the first half of the twentieth century. Migrants were drawn by job opportunities and hopes for greater personal freedom and security. It should be noted, however, that New York has always had a prominent African American community. As early as the 1740s, 20 percent of the city's eleven thousand residents were African American.[3] Another great influx of migrants was (and is) composed of the economically competitive, educated, and artistically gifted people who have come to New York from the hinterlands of the United States seeking an alternative to what they believed to be the limited opportunities and social conformity of mainstream American life. Some stay for a few years, others stay for a lifetime. Their voices also enrich the culture and workscape of New York.

OCCUPATIONAL FOLKLORE OF NEW YORK

Just as amazing as the diversity of its people is the diversity of trades and professions that are practiced in New York. More than merely "practiced": New York is the global capital of finance, the arts, fashion, diplomacy, and media. However, none of these trades are abstract, disembodied entities that exist without New Yorkers, nor are they huge, monolithic industries. Even in a city as large as New York, workers from each occupational community are bound together by what scholars refer to as "occupational folklore"—a body of shared knowledge, customs, stories, practices, and traditions specific to their jobs.[4]

This book highlights some of the most interesting and regionally distinctive of these occupational communities. For example, take Wall Street. Actually, as in other aspects of New York life, there is no one Wall Street; rather, Wall Street is a series of smaller, overlapping work-related communities. Wall Street workers do share some common folklore—for instance, tales of the buttonwood tree, the wall (a wooden fortification that marked the northern boundary of seventeenth-century Dutch New Amsterdam), eccentric millionaires, and the Curb Exchange. But the tens of thousands of New Yorkers who work on "The Street" think of themselves as members of several unique occupational sub-communities, each with its own history, expertise, and traditions. Traders on the floor of the New York Stock Exchange (NYSE) have different stories and traditions from members of the New York Mercantile Exchange (The Merc). Members of the New York Board of Trade (NYBOT or "Coffee, Sugar, and Cocoa") use expressions and hand signals unknown to traders across the street at the American Stock Exchange (AMEX). As chapter 10 reveals, the distinctive traditions and histories of each of these organizations give each its own sense of identity, history, and culture, its own folklore. The Street quickly breaks down into numerous smaller communities made up of real people doing real jobs. Like other folk communities, Wall Street workers use orally transmitted stories, narratives, jokes, and generations of accumulated knowledge to do their work effectively and create a better workplace environment. In an industry where custom, tradition, personal relationships, and trust are highly valued, the impersonality of Internet trading is more than an economic threat; it is a challenge to a centuries-old way of life.

The theater, another of New York's major occupational communities, is the focus of chapter 2. Since the eighteenth century, the city has been the major hub of theatrical life in North America. The city's theaters followed the northward expansion of Manhattan's business district; by the turn of the twentieth century, the theater district established itself along Broadway at Times Square (42nd Street). Today, "Broadway" is synonymous with New York theater, and especially with musical theater. (Smaller theatrical companies throughout the city acknowledge Broadway's preeminence by describing themselves as "Off-Broadway" or "Off-Off Broadway.") Behind every Broadway show and its handful of star performers is an army of other workers: chorus members, costume makers, dressers, set and prop (property) builders, stagehands, managers, wardroom mistresses, curtain manufacturers, ushers, pit musicians, and lighting designers who ply their trades out of the limelight. In addition to a shared body of general theatrical folklore, each of these theater crafts has its own distinctive stories, skills, traditions, and customs. "It's like a small family around here," a fourth-generation New York stagehand once explained to me as we walked through the chaos of Times Square, oblivious to the tourists, traffic, and mayhem surrounding him.[5]

WHAT KEEPS GOTHAM GOING?

Although this book highlights New York's discrete occupational communities, it also documents some of the shared cultural traditions that bring city residents together. No New York institution does a better job of this than the city's Metropolitan Transit Authority (MTA), a vast system that serves as a common thread uniting the five boroughs and the hundreds of disparate neighborhoods. In the course of this book, readers will have a unique opportunity to hear the men and women responsible for running New York's famed buses and subways talk about their work and share their thoughts on "the system."

New York prides itself on being the most modern of metropolises, but an important key to understanding the "real" New York is to realize that, in many ways, New York is an old-fashioned city. Twentieth-century car-based culture has had less impact on New York than anywhere else in the United States. Trades such as water tower building, bialy making, and lox smoking are just a few of the older trades that still thrive in contemporary New York. We will hear what it is like to follow these long-standing, generational trades from some of their foremost practitioners. And we will hear from New Yorkers involved with much more recently evolved and evolving traditions, like the graffiti artists profiled in chapter 3.

No single book can contain all the voices of working New Yorkers, but *Lox, Stocks, and Backstage Broadway* will introduce readers to some of the more eloquent ones: everyday New Yorkers whose extraordinary skills, knowledge, and dedication are instrumental in creating the occupational communities and subcommunities that make New York special. What follows is a folklorist's view of urban occupational culture and urban history. It is heavily reliant on oral histories, narratives, and shared perceptions that rarely make their way into print. You are invited to listen to the voices of New York as they illuminate the past, decipher the present, and endeavor to imagine and shape their city's future.

URBAN FOLKLORE AND OCCUPATIONAL FOLKLORE

A Theoretical Street Map

L OX, STOCKS, AND BACKSTAGE BROADWAY* presents a workscape of some of New York City's most iconic occupations. The heart of this project, and the impetus for producing this book, is to share the eloquence and insights of some of the many New Yorkers who were interviewed in the course of the Smithsonian's New York City Project. The project itself was typical of many contemporary "applied folklore" projects.[1] Fieldworkers, the majority of whom were professionally trained folklorists, set out to identify and document individuals with specific skills and knowledge with the objective of selecting and inviting a subset of them to participate in the 2001 Smithsonian Folklife Festival in Washington, D.C.[2] Unlike days of old when folklore scholars left the comforts of their libraries and set off to "the field" to collect materials armed with complex theories to prove or disprove, the approach of our fieldworkers tended to be ethnographic and descriptive.[3] Our fieldworkers sought to document "expressive behavior" and examples of the "communicative process," but their time and energies were guided to a great extent by the pragmatic goal of organizing and producing a major public program by a specific date.

Although neither the project nor this book was heavily theoretical in nature, because the majority of researchers involved were folklorists, it might be useful to provide a brief overview of the relevant scholarly discussions and influential literature, the historical and theoretical street maps, if you like, that informed and guided us during our urban expeditions. The urge to divide, analyze, and parse specific aspects of culture, cultural performances, and expressive behaviors into disciplines is very much a peculiarity of academics. Non-academics tend not to worry about whether their actions fall under the purview of sociologists, linguists, folklorists, anthropologists, or oral historians. (In fact, the unsuspecting urbanite might blithely cross all these disciplinary boundaries merely by buying a hot dog from a street vendor.) Nevertheless, applying the lens of a specific scholarly discipline to complex cultural expressions can often provide a clearer focus and more nuanced understanding.

This study falls squarely between two important but historically underrepresented areas of folklore scholarship: occupational folklore and urban folklore. Folklore has always been a messy discipline.[4] At its heart, folklore is the study of culture, but folklorists are notoriously uneasy about having to define their field, limit their areas of interest, or explain how folklore differs from sister academic disciplines such as anthropology, sociology, or oral history. (Folklorists have been known to avoid the question by defining *folklore* as "what folklorists study.") Despite this latitude, from its inception as a field of scholarly study, most folklorists have been predisposed toward researching the rural and the pre-industrial. Inspired by nineteenth- and early-twentieth-century romanticism, with a large admixture of nationalism, most early folklorists concentrated on collecting and cataloging discrete items (beliefs, customs, folk songs and ballads, crafts, fairy tales, charms, etc.), which they viewed as static "survivals" dating back to older, more primitive stages of civilization.[5] They sought to rescue, or at least document, these precious ancient survivals, gleaning them into books and articles before they were swept away by the inevitable "progress of civilization." To many of the founders of the field, nothing presented a greater threat to folklore than the growth of urban culture and the industrialization of the work force.

Although a few pioneering American folklorists, such as William Wells Newell, collected folklore in New York City as early as the 1880s, their emphasis was very much on the survival of individual items brought to the city by rural or ethnic immigrants.[6] In the case of New York, nineteenth- and early-twentieth-century historians, newspaper reporters, local color writers, poets, and song writers did a vastly better job of documenting the city's urban culture than did folklorists.[7] But as the ivory-tower nostalgia and romanticism of

1920s academics shifted to the political activism of 1930s public intellectuals, definitions of *the folk* and approaches to folklore collecting began to change. In American folklore, much of this change was due to the inspiration of a Boston born, Harvard trained scholar named Benjamin A. Botkin (1901–1975).

As scholar Jerrold Hirsch has noted, Botkin was "one of the first American folklorists who did not view the modern world as a threat to the existence of folklore."[8] As a scholar, Botkin embraced the city and the complexities of urban life, the factory and other contemporary, non-rural places of work, and the provocative concept that folklore was not static, but continued to change and evolve to meet the needs of its practitioners. Writing in the introduction to his *New York City Folklore* (1956), one of a series of popular compilations of regional, historic, and occupational folklore that he produced later in his career, Botkin summarized his approach:

> The folk spirit or ethos of the city lies in this very spirit of change, which, from the point of view of a folklorist, is the most distinctive and central aspect of the city's unity-in-diversity. . . . Though change would seem to be inimical to the growth and preservation of folklore, it is inherent in the element of invention or fantasy which, supplementing the conservative factor of tradition, is the creative factor in the folklore process. For every item of folk fantasy that dies, a new one is created, as folklore in decay is balanced by folklore in the making.[9]

As a Harvard undergraduate, Botkin concentrated on literature and poetry, but was also influenced by Harvard's noted academic folklorist George Lyman Kittredge. During the early 1920s, he pursued a master's degree at Columbia University and also taught English at the University of Oklahoma. Botkin was drawn between Oklahoma, and later Nebraska, where he studied English and poetry for his doctorate with Louise Pound, and New York, where his circle included avant-garde artists, activists, and musicians, which included his cousins George and Ira Gershwin. In his early writings he sought to reevaluate how folklore functioned in the modern world and broaden the scope of topics that should be of concern to folklorists.[10]

What made Botkin more than an influential academic was his appointment as the national folklore editor of the Federal Writers' Project (FWP) in 1938, his later co-founding and chairing of the Joint Committee on Folk Arts of the Works Progress Administration (WPA), and finally, in 1941, his tenure as chief editor of the Writers' Unit of the Library of Congress Project. These posts gave him the authority to assign government-supported fieldworkers to document culture in urban, as well as rural areas, collect materials from African American and immigrant populations, and interview office workers, shopkeepers, and industrial laborers, as well as farmers and ranchers. If some FWP writers, like the creative writers in the Living Lore unit, sometimes overstretched boundaries by blurring the lines between folklore, popular culture, and creative literature, they also pioneered new approaches and extended parameters in the study of American culture. Working with other New Deal folklorists—including Charles Seeger, Alan Lomax, Zora Neale Hurston, Sydney Robertson Cowell, and Stetson Kennedy—these WPA-generated materials were "histories from the bottom up." The stories, oral histories, and songs sent by fieldworkers to WPA offices not only provided work for researchers in the depths of the Depression, but also gave ex-slaves, ethnic Americans, and urban workers "an opportunity to speak directly to their fellow citizens," and the WPA folklorists "assumed that in the act of listening, the audience would acknowledge that those speaking were part of their [shared American] community."[11]

Botkin's paradigmatic shift from approaching folklore as a static artifact to seeing it as a continually evolving set of expressions and behaviors used in negotiating the urban landscape has become so widely accepted by contemporary folklorists—including the ones involved in the New York City Project—that it is hard to imagine the shock and vitriolic backlash his work elicited from some of his contemporaries, especially a few academic folklorists who dismissed him as an un-scientific popularizer and denounced his publications as *fakelore*. "What got him in trouble with the academic folklorists," Bruce Jackson wrote in Botkin's obituary in the *Journal of American Folklore*, "was the simple and sadly elusive fact that his vision was so much broader than theirs: they were looking for texts that could be properly annotated and indexed; Ben was trying to document the soul of a land."[12]

Botkin left the WPA in 1941, and after heading the Library of Congress's Archive of American Folk-Song for several years (1942–1944), he settled permanently just north of the city in Croton-on-Hudson. During the 1950s, he published a series of immensely successful regional- and subject-specific folklore compilations, beginning with his 1944 best seller *A Treasury of American Folklore: Stories, Ballads and Traditions of the People*.[13] Botkin neatly summed up his commitment to urban folklore in the preface of his 1954 compendium *Sidewalks of America*, writing:

> For years American folklorists from the cities have been going into the Kentucky mountains and other remote places to gather folk songs and stories, while all the time folklore was all around them on the sidewalks

of America. To be sure, contemporary urban folklore is not always easy to recognize since it does not always fall into the conventional mold, and much of it is folklore-in-the-making.[14]

Despite Botkin's contributions and growing public interest in folklore and especially folk music, the 1950s and 1960s were bleak times for urban folklore studies. True, some pioneering folklorists, influenced by dynamic research in the fields of sociology and anthropology began to use the phrase *urban folklore*,[15] but by and large, folklorists accepted the prevailing anti-urban sentiments of an increasingly suburban United States. Years of neglect capped by civic unrest and soaring crime rates led many Americans and American scholars to view cities primarily in terms of pathology.

With a few notable exceptions, folklorists turned their attentions elsewhere. When urban folklore was addressed at all—for example, the 1968 symposium *The Urban Experience and Folk Traditions* held at Michigan's Wayne State University—folklorists chronicled the survival of rural and ethnic traditions in the city rather than address larger more synchronistic issues. In the subsequently published proceedings, conference organizer Ellen Stekert admitted this, noting that "traditions that have originated and developed in the urban milieu are explored only fleetingly."[16]

It was not until the late 1970s that folklorists began to take renewed interest in the study of urban areas. The impetus for exploration of urban cultural traditions came from two directions: The first was sparked by renewed calls by theorists for more attention to and sophisticated interpretations of how urban culture functions. The second was the rise of a generation of younger "applied" or "public sector" folklorists working for urban nonprofit art, cultural, and educational organizations—especially in Washington, D.C., New York, Chicago, and Philadelphia. These cultural workers in the public sector sought to identify and document urban folklore primarily to use it as the basis of concerts, lecture series, school enrichment projects, festivals, and other public programs.

Canadian folklorist Martin Laba drew attention to this renewed interest in urban traditional culture in an influential 1979 *Journal of American Folklore* article, which stressed the need for a conceptual basis in the study of urban traditional culture. "The discipline of folklore," he wrote,

> has yet to develop a theoretical perspective which is consonant with urban experience. Folklorists have failed to apprehend the city as a whole and continue to dissect the urban environment into ethnic or generic compartments for examination of items of folklore transplanted from rural to

urban settings. . . . [A] concept of the city as a whole with its premise that the city itself critically affects human expressive behavior demands that we investigate the manner in which urban experience is stratified and managed through folklore.[17]

Laba also called on folklorists to examine urban subcultures and their "networks of communication . . . [with] shared symbols and meanings, an esoteric language, cultural objects, a vocabulary of motives, and a mythology. Whether a cultural world is as broad and amorphous as a spectator sport," he argued, or "specialized as in the case of the strategic universe of an occupational group, it exhibits two constitutive properties: a scene and an expressive behavior within that scene."[18]

Barbara Kirshenblatt-Gimblett, involved with an active group of applied folklorists in New York City, also drew attention to traditional culture in the city in her 1983 article "The Future of Folklore Studies: The Urban Frontier":

> The city is thus not a museum of folk traditions brought to it from elsewhere, but a crucible in which expressive behavior is forged. From a theoretical perspective, the frontier lies in developing approaches to explore the relations of expressive behavior to the special conditions of urban life. Implicit here is the idea that cities are diverse and that historical and cross-cultural perspectives are essential to the study of urban folklore. . . . In addition to focusing our attention on the expressive life of cities, the study of urban folklore promises to reshape our thinking about folklore more generally.[19]

The article also provided readers with a solid overview of the enormous amount and varied forms of urban expressive behavior then flourishing in New York City. Some, such as children's street games or pigeon flying were old traditions; others, such as graffiti writing and break dancing, although based on older traditions, were still in the process of growth and transformation. All were a convincing argument for "tradition as a construction rather than an inheritance."[20]

Concurrent with the increasing amount and sophistication of folklorists' theoretical interest in urban America during the late 1970s was the emergence of a critical mass of "applied" or "public sector" folklorists living and working in the New York City area. Although the idea of public sector folklore was not new—many of the earliest collectors had not held university posts—what was new was the opportunity for employment at museums, arts councils, and cultural and educational organizations. Assisted by grants from the National Endowment for the Arts, the New York State Council on the Arts,[21] the New York City Department of Cultural Affairs, and other funding sources, the new generation of public sector folklorists sought to identify and document traditional culture not only for its own sake, but also to use as the basis of cultural programming. Many of these projects emphasized individual ethnic groups, which was a popular approach to exploring the "multi-cultural" population of the United States during the 1970s, but others began to address urban culture as a sum of its many parts.

In 1978, a group of New York folklorists traveling back from an American Folklore Society meeting in Salt Lake City began to wonder why they had to fly to the other side of the country to find out what was going on in their own urban backyards. By the time they landed, they had decided to call an informal meeting of interested parties. An initial meeting was enthusiastically attended by a small group of city-based academic and public sector folklorists, and soon folklorists and other researchers interested in New York's urban culture were meeting on a regular basis. In winter 1979, establishing themselves as the New York City Chapter of the New York Folklore Society,[22] a core group organized a major public conference to highlight the growing interest in urban life and the innovative research taking place throughout New York City.[23] Their landmark four-day Conference on Folklore in New York City took place May 18–21, 1979. As Barbro Klein, one of the key organizers noted:

> The Folklore in New York City conference represents the first major effort, since the WPA collecting efforts in the 1930s, to bring leading scholars together to explore the folklore of New York City and to engage the people of New York City in the exploration.[24]

Presented jointly by the New York City Chapter, the New York Folklore Society, and Hunter College, with the cooperation of numerous other organizations including the Balkan Arts Center (now the Center for Traditional Music and Dance [CTMD]), the Museum of American Folk Art, and the New York Visual Anthropology Center, the free public event brought together many of the leading folklorists of the United States and audiences of hundreds of interested New Yorkers.[25] The presentations were supplemented with walking tours and behind-the-scene tours of numerous New York cultural institutions. The event received substantial press coverage and was judged a major success.

Building on the 1979 conference, in 1980 the New York City Chapter presented another public conference on the Folklore of Urban Public Spaces; and

in May 1981, it challenged anti-urban disciplinary biases head-on by focus-
ing folkloric attention on what had become a notorious symbol for urban
decay by organizing a conference on the Folk Culture of the Bronx. Held at
Lehman College's campus in the heart of the Bronx, this event continued the
practice initiated in the two pervious conferences of presenting the voices of
community scholars side-by-side with those of academic and applied folklorists. (One memorable session was titled "This is Not Fort Apache, This is
Our Home: Students Document Their South Bronx.") The keynote address,
"Folklorists Discover the City," was presented by eminent Indiana University folklorist Richard Dorson, who earlier in his career had expressed doubts
about the existence of urban folklore. These conferences were among the first
scholarly events to focus attention on emergent urban art forms such as graffiti artists, break dancing, and traditional religious practices such as Santería
and Espiritismo. Between 1979 and 1984, the New York City Chapter also
presented a series of smaller events—lectures, symposia, and concerts—that
addressed topics as varied as urban fortune-tellers, ethnic restaurants, shared
public spaces, and pigeon flying.

Meanwhile, with the support of the New York State Council on the
Arts and the National Endowment for the Arts, borough folklorists positions were established at the art councils in Brooklyn, Queens, and Staten
Island, and public sector folklorists were employed at other cultural organizations. In 1986, the New York Chapter of the New York Folklore Society evolved into City Lore: The Center for Urban Folk Culture, which
under the directorship of Steve Zeitlin became the first full-time professional folklore organization devoted to urban culture. Among City Lore's
many accomplishments were presenting folk arts programming at the giant
Queens Festival (1981–ca. 1987) and major documentary projects on various aspects of New York culture that resulted in numerous highly praised
exhibitions, publications, and public events.[26] Other on-going City Lore
programs include Place Matters, which documents tradition and the built
environment; The People's Hall of Fame, which celebrates individuals and
organizations that maintain and enrich urban traditions; the bi-annual
People's Poetry Gathering; and the recently launched City of Memory, an
innovative interactive online urban "story map."[27]

City Lore's accomplishments in urban folklore were matched in the field of
urban ethnomusicology by the CTMD.[28] Established in 1968 by Ethel Raim
and Martin Koenig as the Balkan Arts Center, during the 1970s its directors
worked closely with the Smithsonian folklorist Ralph Rinzler to identify musicians and dancers from ethnic communities across the United States for the

Smithsonian Folklife Festival. During the late 1970s and 1980s, Raim and Koenig, both native New Yorkers, concentrated on fieldwork in metropolitan New York, working extensively with Eastern European Jewish, Italian, Puerto Rican, and Irish communities.[29] In the 1990s, CTMD launched an innovative fieldwork model it called Community Cultural Initiatives—a collaborative program designed to establish and nurture community-based artistic documentation and presentation projects. In recent years, CTMD has worked closely with numerous groups, including New York's Albanian, Arab, Asian Indian, Indo-Caribbean, Dominican, West African, Soviet Jewish, Philippine, Mexican, Peruvian, Chinese, and Ukrainian communities.[30]

Over the years, the fortunes of New York's community of professional folklorists have waxed and waned based on the availability of public and private funding; however city folklorists have never been at a loss for materials to collect and study. Many city folklorists, like those at City Lore and CTMD, as well as others who came to the city during the 1980s and 1990s, have had long-established and close relationships with the Smithsonian Center for Folklife and Cultural Heritage and the Smithsonian Folklife Festival. The 2001 Smithsonian New York City Project, which forms the basis of this book, was a continuation of collaborative research with the city's urban folklorists that had begun decades previously.

OCCUPATIONAL FOLKLORE

As with urban folklore, the approaches to studying occupational folklore, especially the occupational folklore of the urban United States, have changed dramatically over the years. Today, most folklorists would agree with folklorist Robert McCarl by defining occupational folklore as that "complex of techniques, customs, and modes of expressive behavior which characterize a particular work group."[31] As the eminent folklorist and workers' culture scholar Archie Green notes, this is a far cry from the discipline's original approach to workers' culture:

> When the American Folklore Society was formed in 1888, most founding members . . . understood their subject to be popular tradition (or vestigial items of literary, musical, and cognitive culture) belonging mainly to four sets of people: Native Americans, Anglo-Americans, Afro-Americans, Americans who retained non-English languages. . . . But early folklorists were not particularly drawn to on-the-job behavior, unless the job consisted of tasks such as crafting arrowheads or moccasins.[32]

Initial curiosity about occupational folklore developed through folklorists' interest in collecting work songs. Although early collections such as Allen, Ware, and Garrison's *Slave Songs of the United States* (1867)[33] included some work songs, Fletcher S. Bassett's *Legends and Superstitions of the Sea and of Sailors* (1885)[34] seems to have been the first American study to feature a single profession. Collections of songs from loggers, seamen, and cowboys and other "romantic professions" appeared in increasing numbers in the following decades.[35] "It was not until the mid-1920s," Green points out, "that the lore of an industrial group was seriously explored."[36] That groundbreaking research was undertaken by George Korson, a newspaper man and future folklorist, who was then working outside of academic circles. In *Songs and Ballads of the Anthracite Miner* (1927),[37] Korson concentrated on the songs, but in subsequent studies "he came to see the coal camp or mine patch as an enclaved . . . society with a rich and varied subculture, of which song was but a single aspect."[38]

Botkin, who did so much to broaden folklorists' approach toward the study of urban culture, also significantly expanded the trades, occupations, and work sites deemed worthy of folkloric study. During his tenure with the WPA's Federal Writers' Project, he and his colleagues documented occupational stories and traditions from stenographers, taxi drivers, burlesque performers, and sweatshop workers.[39] He was as intellectually comfortable accepting field reports about "industrial folklore" from the factory floor as age-old trickster tales from the backwoods.

Unfortunately, the widespread interest in and celebration of workers' traditions and working-class culture articulated by WPA folklorists and other political, scholarly, and popular sources during the Depression and World War II had little lasting impact on U.S. folklore scholarship. During the 1950s, and 1960s, most folklorists once again turned their attentions to rural handcrafts and traditional trades, leaving the factory floor, the union hall, the office, and professional "white-collar" occupations to historians, sociologists, and psychologists.

Things began to change in the early 1970s when the annual Smithsonian Festival of American Folklife Festival (the forerunner of the present-day Smithsonian Folklife Festival), under the leadership of folklorist Rinzler and the guidance of Green, began a multi-year series of festival programs celebrating American workers. From 1971 to 1976, the Smithsonian's "Working Americans" programs invited workers from contemporary occupations to demonstrate their skills, tell their work-related stories, and share their occupational traditions during the well-attended festival on the National Mall in Washington, D.C. Based on the research and programming activities of a nucleus of innovative folklorists, including Robert Byington, Green, Luis Kemnitzer, McCarl, Jack

Santino, and Peter Seitel, these Working Americans programs presented occupational folklore from such "unexpected" folk groups as meat cutters and butchers, bulk freight truckers, glassblowers, molders, carpenters and joiners, sheet metal workers, telephone operators, lithographers, and air traffic controllers.[40] Despite interesting festival programs on railroad workers in 1977, sleeping car porters and energy workers in 1978, urban fire fighters in 1979, and trial lawyers in 1986, during the 1980s and 1990s festival programs on occupational folklore were increasingly few and far apart.[41]

Outside of the academy, and straddling the disciplinary border between folklore and oral history, the publication of Studs Terkel's best selling 1974 book *Working: People Talk about What They Do All Day and How They Feel about What They Do* focused national attention on the power and eloquence of workers talking about their jobs.[42] Folklorist Alan Dundes and co-author Carl Pagter also explored new territory in white-collar occupational folklore with a series of popular "Xerox lore" compilations, the first of which, *Work Hard and You Shall Be Rewarded: Urban Folklore from the Paperwork Empire*, appeared in 1975.[43]

In the years that followed, the American Folklife Center at the Library of Congress undertook two large surveys of life in older industrial cities: The Lowell Folklife Project (1987–1988), which documented ethnic and neighborhood traditions of the residents of Lowell, Massachusetts, and Working in Paterson: Occupational Heritage in an Urban Setting (1994), which was an intensive four-month study of occupational culture in Paterson, New Jersey. Like the previous Smithsonian projects, these collecting projects broke new ground in the scope of occupations being studied by folklorists; however, few of the featured occupations were inherently urban in nature.[44] As folklorist Kurt Dewhurst correctly pointed out:

> To begin to interpret the nature of folk expression in urban work settings, we must understand that the intersection of urban folklore and occupational folklore creates a particular experience that shapes the life of the urban resident/worker. The individual urban resident/worker is a product of a complex combination of experiences that determine and contribute to formation of self.[45]

Over the years, as their fields of research expanded beyond the agricultural, the factory, and the mill to more diverse work situations, many folklorists began to use the term *occupation folklore* instead of the previously popular *industrial lore* when discussing the workplace.[46] Concomitantly, as folklorists shifted from thinking of folk groups in static terms and expanded their objectives beyond merely collecting and classifying items "of lore" to providing ethnographic descriptions of "the communicative process" and "expressive behavior," they have increasing preferred to use the term *occupational folklife*.[47]

Before starting our journey to meet New York's workers, here are a few contemporary suggestions about collecting information on occupational folklife that informed our fieldworkers. The first comes from McCarl, a key curator in the Smithsonian's groundbreaking Working Americans programs, who in his seminal 1978 article wrote:

> The techniques, gestures, oral expressions, and customs which comprise the occupational folklife of a particular work group are theoretical constructs which . . . provide a background against which specific work cultures can be investigated. In the actual work situation these elements are fragmented, inverted, and continually mixed with outside concerns of the a popular, familial, and ethnic nature (to name but a few) that interact with the work context by constantly borrowing from and adding to it.[48]

Despite the optimism in the 1970s and early 1980s about expanding folklorists' perspectives and developing new theoretical models for studying the complexities of urban occupational communities, the past two decades have seen only a modest increase in the number of publications and innovative research projects on urban groups undertaken by American folklorists. The field as a whole has failed to keep pace with sister disciplines such as ethnomusicology, cultural studies, and linguistics in addressing larger theoretical questions about how tradition, heritage, occupation, class, and history interact to shape the contemporary urban workscape.[49]

The Smithsonian's New York City Project was one of the largest attempts ever undertaken to document the folklore and traditions of an American metropolis. Although it resulted in a treasure trove of information and interviews, it is only the smallest of steps toward documenting New York's complex cultural scene. We hope the project will inspire other researchers to focus increased attention on the wealth of urban and occupational traditions thriving in the contemporary United States. We hope that the engaging narratives and vivid ethnographic descriptions that follow will serve not only as a lasting record of the diversity and vitality of Gotham's culture at the beginning of the twenty-first century, but also that the information generously shared with us by so many of our fellow New Yorkers will enrich our understanding of how urban folklife and occupational traditions continue to shape and enrich the modern urban landscape.

BACKSTAGE BROADWAY

"**B**ROADWAY" has become practically synonymous with theater: both with "legit" (legitimate) or "straight" dramatic theater and the colorful world of musical theater.[1] It is one of New York's most significant contributions to world culture, as well as one of the city's major industries. For more than a century, Broadway has been where young, talented, and ambitious performers from all corners of the United States come to learn their craft and (with luck) be discovered. Even with the rise of the Los Angles film industry, most actors still begin their careers and hone their craft in New York. "If you think you have a face the camera will love," one Broadway director tells young hopefuls, "try L.A., but if you want to work, you really want to work and be an actor, come to New York."[2]

The art and fantasy of New York's Broadway would not exist without the skills, knowledge, traditions, and hard work of thousands of New York theater professionals. Broadway is like an iceberg: audiences only see the principal actors, the "stars" at the very tip, unaware how many artists and artisans are working enormous behind-the-scenes hours in ateliers, fitting rooms, rehearsal halls, and workshops to make the show a reality. The world of backstage Broadway includes costume makers, dressers, set designers and "prop" (properties) builders, milliners, speech coaches, stagehands, stage managers, wardrobe mistresses, curtain manufacturers, ticket sellers, ushers, doormen, rehearsal pianists and pit musicians, heating and cooling engineers, lighting designers, press agents, electricians, porters, cleaners, and hundreds and hundreds of Broadway "gypsies"—chorus members who sing and dance their way from show to show. By the time an opening night curtain rises, hundreds of people with scores of different skills will have contributed to its production. It is their combined sorcery that creates the magic of Broadway.

NEW YORK'S BROADWAY: THE OPENING ACT

The history of theater in the United States is intertwined with New York City's history. New Yorkers have always been enthusiastic theatergoers, and since the eighteenth century, the city has been the hub of theater life in North America. Perhaps because of the tolerant beliefs of its Dutch founders, colonial New York governments never enacted the harsh legal restrictions that hampered the growth of the theater in cities such as Boston or Philadelphia.

New York's earliest theater district took shape around present-day City Hall in lower Manhattan in the mid-1700s. Coincidently, the city's first theater, the Playhouse on Broadway, was actually located right on Broadway between Beaver Street and Exchange Place (near Wall Street) in the early 1730s. Theatre Alley, now a dreary, unremarkable passage way between Beekman and Anne Streets on the east side of City Hall Park, is all that remains of the once fashionable Beekman Street Theatre, which opened in 1761.

As Manhattan expanded northward, the theater district followed: from the neighborhood around City Hall to the Bowery in the early 1800s, to Union Square and 14th Street in the mid-1800s, to Madison Square in the late 1800s, and to Broadway at Times Square and 42nd Street in the early 1900s. Of course, many theaters were located elsewhere in the city. Substantial theaters thrived in uptown Manhattan neighborhoods such as Harlem and Yorkville, as well as throughout Brooklyn, Queens, and the Bronx, but by the 1910s, the heart of the district was centered on Times Square. However, throughout present-day New York, observant strollers might notice supermarkets, lighting shops, or drug stores housed in what were once magnificent theaters—reminders of the city's rich theatrical history.

The American musical really developed in New York. The first modern musical was *The Black Crook*, a confused 1866 melodrama featuring a chorus of beautiful scantily clad woman in flesh-colored tights (shocking back then), who sang and danced to the astonished delight of New York's heavily male theatergoing audiences. Despite its significant shortcomings as drama, *The Black Crook* was a smash. (Instead of listening for "the pealing of bells," one Manhattan minister complained, the men in his congregation had become more interested in watching "the peeling of belles."[3]) Since then, more sophisticated musicals have graced the New York stage, including such masterpieces as *Oklahoma!*, *Show Boat*, *My Fair Lady*, *Guys and Dolls*, *Fiddler on the Roof*, *Lion King*, and *The Producers*. But Broadway is more than just musicals. Non-musical legit theater also thrives in New York. For a playwright, having a production "make it" to Broadway is the ultimate sign of success.

TIMES SQUARE

In 1904, when the *New York Times* moved into its new skyscraper at Broadway and 42nd Street, the newspaper's owner, Adolph Ochs, went to city officials and insisted that the adjoining intersection, Longacre Square, be renamed after his paper. After all, he argued, another square at Broadway and 34th Street had recently been renamed after a rival paper, *The Herald*. Ochs got his wish, but numerous nearby businesses and one Broadway theater still proudly retain Longacre in their names.

THE BROADWAY FAMILY

New York's theater workers form one of the most remarkable occupational communities in the United States: in part because of the talents involved and in part because they feel so passionately and talk so eloquently about their trade. "As far as I'm concerned," Broadway wig maker Linda Rice told us, "it's the smallest town in the United States. Once you've worked with a couple of people in New York, you usually work with them again and again and again. There might be a thousand of us, but we all know each other."[4] Another Broadway gypsy agreed: "It's one degree of separation in the theater."[5]

This feeling of being a family is heightened by the fact that many Broadway workers, on stage and off, are actually the children or grandchildren of theater workers. One of the secrets of New York is how much history and tradition continues to shape even the most contemporary industries, and this is certainly true of the theater. "Broadway community is pretty much a mom and pop business, very mom and pop," Broadway historian Helen Guditas insisted.[6] There remains a strong sense of a family business about it, despite the recent influx of large corporations. The world of New York theater might be, as one actor remarked, "one huge dysfunctional family," but it's still a family.

THE REAL CHORUS LINE: THE GYPSIES

For every Broadway star, there are dozens of dancers and singers who make a solid, steady living as members of the chorus. Chorus members proudly refer to themselves as "gypsies" because they move from one show to another. It's a grueling life. Broadway actors perform in eight full productions a week (six nights plus two matinees—one on Wednesday, the other on Sunday), and they are continually taking speech, singing, acting, and improvisation classes to polish their art. If a show is a hit, chorus line gypsies could be solidly employed for years; if it fails, they might be out of work by the end of the week. Many gypsies initially wanted to be stars but found being part of a chorus equally as satisfying. "You just go from show to show because people get to know you," retired gypsy Terry Marone explained: "I sort of fell into it by accident and I was always very happy where I was. They say everybody wants to be a star; but no, not everybody does."[7] There's camaraderie in working in a chorus line that is often missing when playing more highly visible star or principal roles. When we asked gypsies what they thought about the 1975 hit musical *A Chorus Line*, several said they thought it didn't convey the sense of community and cooperation that exists among Broadway gypsies. "I thought it was great entertainment," one said, "but in my opinion, the characters come across as too competitive, too cutthroat."[8]

Today, thousands of New Yorker thespians are members of Actors' Equity Association and thousands more nonunion stage actors live in New York, waiting to be discovered. Although young hopefuls occasionally walk off a bus and into the spotlight, in truth, it usually takes years of hard work, rejections, disappointments, and scrounging at poorly paid, non-theater jobs for rent money before someone makes it on Broadway. (Some New Yorkers contend that there are no waiters or waitresses anymore in Manhattan, only "pre-celebrities" waiting to be discovered. Temporary jobs with flexible hours, such as waiting tables

in restaurants, bartending, and office temp work, do seem to attract a dispro-
portionate number of "actors-in-waiting.")

Aspiring actors and working actors both consider New York a conservatory:
"You can learn anything you want to learn because this is where the artists are,"
acting coach Ruth Nerken pointed out.[9] Even when performers arrive in New
York with degrees from prestigious college theater programs, it still takes several
years of apprenticeship—taking classes, auditioning, making connections, and
performing for little or no money in "showcase" productions—before they land
their first job. And even after landing a show, as one gypsy reminded us: "Just
to keep your livelihood going you have to go to singing classes, you have to go
to dance classes, you've got to keep your acting up. So, if you're in a show, you
really have to work all the time. You've got to be so disciplined."[10]

All chorus line performers are expected to be able to sing, dance, and act,
but "in the business" most people order those three categories to reflect their own
personal strengths: "Like I'm a singer who acts and moves," one explained, "but
I don't use that dance word 'cause it's not my forte. But it's important to classify
yourself as passable in all of them, because you're asked to do everything. So I
consider myself a singer. I enjoy acting, and I dance—when necessary."[11] "When
I started out in the business," another gypsy said, "I came in as a dancer who sings
and acts. The longer I stayed in the business, the more I realized I didn't want to
dance that much, and that hard, and that long anymore. So I concentrated on my
singing. So now I project myself as a singer, who moves very well and acts."[12]

MAKING IT "ON BROADWAY"

So who makes it on "The Great White Way"?[13] Millions of Americans have
daydreamed about getting on a bus, coming to New York, and becoming a
Broadway star. Generations of Americans have grown up watching classic films
like *Stage Door* or *42nd Street*, where truly talented and virtuous young actors
are discovered and ultimately rewarded. (Usually at the expense of pompous,
nasty, and morally suspect older performers.) Real life is, of course, more complicated, but each year, thousands of hopefuls still come to New York determined to be among the handful that will make it on Broadway. "When you're
in high school," one gypsy recalled during an interview at the 2001 Festival, "all
the theater kids are like: 'Yeah, we're going to go to New York, and we're going
to live on ketchup soup, and live by the theater, and live with the rats. . . .' But
then they all went to business school, and they're all, like, accountants, and they
gave up on the dream!"[14] But she didn't; and today she has impressive theater
credentials to prove it.

Another gypsy said she often thinks of the advice her college acting coach gave her: "If there's anything in life that you can be happy doing, do it. Because this career you've chosen will take 100% of everything that you've got. . . . If you're not 100% devoted to this, then this isn't the career for you. But if you know in your heart that this is the only thing that you can do, that's what will keep you going."[15] Even today, when things are slow, she sometimes has to wait tables to make ends meet. "And that's a misery." On the other hand, she finds it inspirational to "have the worst job on earth when you are not doing this, because it makes you realize that you can't get lazy. You've got to keep going; you've got to keep auditioning."[16]

As many as a thousand people may show up to audition for a Broadway show, which is sometimes dismissively referred to in the business as a "cattle call." To work in a Broadway or Off-Broadway theater, performers have to belong to Actors' Equity, although nonunion actors can appear in showcases. Performers hear about auditions for upcoming shows through trade papers, through the grapevine, on the union's website,[17] or by checking the busy memo board in the "Green Room," a large meeting hall on the second floor of Actors' Equity's headquarters building at the corner Broadway and 46th Street in the heart of Times Square. In addition to Broadway shows, regional theater productions, summer stock, and "road companies"—i.e., traveling versions of major Broadway plays—are also cast in New York.

Each performer has his or her theories about what works best at an audition as well as when to arrive, how to dress, and how to behave. One told us that she always liked arriving early for an audition—well, not too early perhaps, but say, an hour into the session, before the casting director's eyes glaze over or they formed too definite an idea of who they want. Other performers will show up for an audition even if their "type" doesn't exactly match the type being auditioned, on the theory that the casting director might have a change of heart. Some actors get superstitious and insist on wearing their lucky sweatshirt or going through the same personal ritual before they audition. It is, to say the least, a nerve-racking experience. And more times than not, you're not selected. "It's hard," one gypsy admitted, "and if you stay focused on what you didn't get, or what you could've, should've, would've had, you'll go crazy—you'll have a nervous breakdown and you'll end up in an institution somewhere! You have to find reasons to keep going."[18] How does she do it? "I remind myself over and over and over again, there's nothing in life that I would rather be doing. When you get on stage, and the lights come up, and you've got people outside and you can feel their energy. . . . There's nothing in this world that's greater than that feeling of being on stage and seeing a full house!"[19] As in any other business, over time some performers build up solid reputations as chorus line professionals. Although they must still audition like everyone else, directors and casting people often prefer to hire them. This core group of several hundred performers makes up the nucleus of the Broadway gypsy community.

"LET'S PUT ON A SHOW"

"There are two things that everybody thinks they can do," one veteran performer said during our interview, "and one of them is act."[20] Professional performers, another pointed out, made it look so easy that audiences often don't realize how much work goes in to make it look simple. Chorus lines usually begin rehearsals at least four to six weeks before opening night. Union regulations limit the number of hours that the performers can be asked to spend in daily rehearsals to "seven [hours] out of ten" in the weeks leading up to the preview run; and "ten [hours] out of twelve" the week before previews open.

Rehearsals usually begin in a rehearsal space or dance studio, rather than in the theater, which is frequently still occupied by the soon-to-close play it will be replacing. Chorus members start by reading through their lines, "blocking" where they will stand, discussing how to move in dance numbers, and singing through the score. The performers are still "on book," which means someone is sitting in the auditorium or in the studio with a copy of the script ready to "feed" (remind) performers if they "go up on their lines" (forget). At some point before opening night, the director will demand that everybody be "off book" (have their parts memorized). Small and large changes continue throughout the rehearsal period, but at some point before opening night, the show will be "frozen" and no more changes permitted. There's a famous backstage Broadway story about how the director and choreographer of the musical *Gypsy* approached the legendary performer Ethel Merman right before opening night to make yet one more change. "Well boys," she said, "call me Miss Birds Eye, but the show is frozen!"[21]

Early in the rehearsal process, Broadway shows are visited by a representative of their local union, Actors' Equity, who checks that the performers know the union rules and regulations and that stages, props, and sets are safe and present no "extraordinary risks" for the actors. For almost thirty years before her retirement, the person who did this was Terry Marone, Actors' Equity's Chief Outside Representative. Few people could be better qualified than this ex-gypsy, who has "been in the business for 20,000 years" and appeared in the chorus lines of twenty-six musicals, including the original productions of *The Music Man*, *My Fair Lady*, *Kismet*, and *The Most Happy Fella*. Since joining Equity as a staff member, Marone has seen every Broadway production on either side of the Atlantic looking for risks that range from steeply "raked" (i.e., slanted) stages to overly high heels to the use of hazardous chemicals to produce stage smoke. We asked if she could recall some memorable moments. Well, she said, there was that time in 1972 when, as usual, she went to a first rehearsal to make sure all the cast members understood the union regulations. "It was a show called *Oh, Calcutta!* It was a nudie show; I mean they weren't nude all the time, but they were nude. And at the first rehearsal that I went to, guess what, they were all sitting in front of me nude! And all I kept thinking was, 'My god! My parents should see what I do for a living!'"[22]

Most of the people we spoke with were Actors' Equity performers who worked on Broadway, but many New York actors begin their careers in non-Equity Off-Broadway or Off-Off-Broadway theaters, often performing in showcase productions. In these venues, working hours are much longer and pay scales are much lower. During a showcase, a play will be constantly changed, refined, and hopefully improved. Performers appearing in a non-union showcase usually receive only carfare and a pittance of pay for several months of rigorous rehearsals. Actors do it for experience, credentials, and on the slim chance that the production will eventually make it to Broadway or at least make a profit during an extended Off-Broadway run. Edie Cowan recalled making about four hundred dollars over the course of a six-month-long showcase.[23]

Now an experienced and respected director and choreographer, Cowan had some thoughts about why some why some people make it on Broadway and others don't. Cowan, who began her career as a gypsy and appeared in the original companies of such classics as *Annie* and *Funny Girl*, felt that what distinguishes true Broadway gypsies was not only the excellence of their skills but their flexibility:

> When you're in a new show, you're always making changes. They need people who not only can sing and dance and act wonderfully, but they need people who can pick things up quickly. So the singers on a new Broadway show can practically look at the score and know their part. They're sight-readers. They can make changes and absorb them—there's no time to drill somebody. If you don't get it, you're out of there.[24]

Being in the chorus line means being part of a community, a theatrical family. "If you're working in an office," said one gypsy, "you're there from nine to five. You put your personal life on hold and you come in and do your work. But if you're in the theater, especially if you go out-of-town, you're sleeping in the same hotel, you're having lunches and dinners together, and you have drinks around the bar at night. . . . Everything about the theater breaks down those walls that people put up when they work in an office. In the theater, everybody knows everybody's personal life. And that's what makes it a family."[25]

"AND APPEARING IN TONIGHT'S PRODUCTION . . ."

In addition to learning their own parts, chorus line gypsies also have to understudy the lead or principal roles. Typically, they rehearse once a week with the other understudies, but they never know when they might have to go on. Cowan's story about what happened to her one night during the original production of *Annie* gives a good, actor-eyed sense of what it means to be an understudy:

> I was playing one of the Boyland sisters. I was understudying Lily St Regis, who is Rooster's girlfriend and does *Easy Street*; she's one of the villains. So in Act II, we sang our *You're Never Fully Dressed Without a Smile* number. We're on a treadmill. The treadmill rolls off the stage and the scene in the orphanage is coming on, and you're seeing Lily enter, like, maybe thirty seconds later. We roll off, somebody pulls me off the treadmill: 'You're on as Lily!' I exit stage right and I have to reenter stage left, so I'm running around backstage. I say, 'What happened to Barbara?' 'She collapsed! She fainted! You're on!' So we get over there. They were grabbing my hat off; they grabbed my Boyland sister's wig. The dresser is throwing the other wig on, the other hat. I had my Boyland sister's dress, which is long; they just pulled it up, tucked it in, threw the coat on—I don't think we had time to button it!—and sent me on. I thought, 'OK, this is what they're paying me for.' And we did the scene.[26]

In addition to the understudies, who substitute for the staring roles, every Broadway musical also employs one or more "swings," performers who fill in for chorus line gypsies who can't go on because of sickness, injury, or because they are suddenly asked to fill in for the principal *they* have been understudying. Most evenings, swings spend their time waiting in the dressing room drinking coffee and doing crossword puzzles—on hand just in case an emergency should arise. Although rarely seen by audiences, swings are highly respected by the gypsies. Actor and gypsy Tom Rocco explained why he thought swings had the most difficult job in the theater:

Now, in *Tommy*, we had two male swings and two female swings. . . . They didn't perform every night, but they had to be *ready* to perform every night. The two men covered the eight or nine chorus men and the two women covered the eight or nine chorus women. Now, my "track" [part] in the chorus had thirteen costume changes and I was in about ten or eleven scenes in the chorus. So the person who covered me had to know *all* of that. In songs, sometimes I'd sing the high part; sometimes, I'd sing the low part. So they had to know what part I sang in the songs, where I changed clothes, what costume to put on, who their dresser was for each number, where they had to go, and whether they had time to go the dressing room or not. For me *plus* for four other guys! And they had to go on at the drop of a hat![27]

Most Broadway gypsies look forward to spending at least part of their careers in a long-running Broadway show. Being in a long-running show such as *CATS* or *Les Misérables* ensures chorus line gypsies both greater stability and a livable income. "If you want to work in this business," one said, "sometimes it's better to be a good, competent gypsy, because you will work. If you're a star, work is limited, very limited. If you want a steady income and you have a good reputation in the business—that you do your work, you take direction, you're not a diva—you can have a good life and steady work."[28]

Making a living as a Broadway gypsy requires determination, skill, and frequently, luck. As one actor pointed out, it's one of the few professions left in the United States where you and all your co-workers really, truly want to be there. "There's nothing else that they can even think about doing," she said. "They come to New York because that's what they want to do, that's what they *have* to do. Everybody has this burning passion for it."[29] For seasoned performers, the reward of being a Broadway gypsy is found in being part of a theater family, and the applause and laughter of the audiences. Actually, reflected Cowan, "It's not applause that does it for me, it's the sound of laughter. People applaud after a number because it's expected of them, but they don't laugh unless it genuinely moves them. You can't control laughter, you can't force it. And to me, that's always been the most magical sound in the theater."[30]

THE GYPSY ROBE

No theatrical custom is more closely tied to New York's Broadway than that of the Gypsy Robe. For the past fifty years, no musical has opened on Broadway without the blessings of this magical garment, which brings with it luck, tradition, and a sense of community.

It all started on the opening night of *Gentlemen Prefer Blondes* in 1953. Just for fun, Bill Bradley, a chorus line gypsy, donned a muslin dressing gown and paraded around backstage, bestowing blessings on the production. The musical was a hit. A few nights later, Bradley sent the same robe to his friend, another chorus gypsy, on his opening night, speciously claiming that the garment had been worn for luck on opening nights during the 1920s by the beautiful chorines of the Ziegfeld Follies. His friend's musical, *Call Me Madam* staring Ethel Merman, was also a phenomenal success. To keep the luck rolling, the friend sewed a rose from Merman's costume onto the gown and sent it to *his* friend on a third opening night. Before long, it became traditional for the robe to be presented from one Broadway musical to the next on opening night. The wardrobe mistress or master of each show is expected to sew, paint, or otherwise decorate a section of the robe with mementos of their show before passing it along.

During the 1960s, official rules gradually evolved about how the garment was to be presented and who was to receive it. Today, the Gypsy Robe is handed on in a formal ceremony; one taken seriously, if not somberly, by members of the chorus. Half an hour before the opening night curtain, the stage manager assembles the chorus in a circle at center stage. Actors' Equity representative Marone and robe historian Gloria Rosenthal, both of whom have been instrumental in keeping the tradition alive and orderly, appear with the current Gypsy Robe winner, the reigning King or Queen of the Gypsies, and the robe. After a short speech about the tradition, the current King or Queen selects a successor—by custom, the gypsy with the most seniority in past Broadway productions—who then becomes the new king or queen of the gypsies. "It's exciting," Marone told us, and invited us to join her at a Gypsy Robe ceremony on the opening night of the Gershwin-based musical *Fascinating Rhythm*: "They come out with their hair up and their old clothes on—getting ready for opening night. I get them in a circle. And I'll say something like, 'After all those rehearsals at 10 out of 12 and 7 out of 8 ½'—those are the rehearsal hours—'and so many weeks, it's opening night on Broadway!' The winner's name is announced, "So, big hoopla! And they all jump up and down. 'Oh, I got the robe, I got the robe!' Then they have to put the robe on and walk around the circle counterclockwise three times, with everybody touching the robe for good luck. Then they have to go to every dressing room and bless the dressing rooms with the robe."[31]

Each robe lasts for fifteen or twenty shows before there is no more space for additional decoration and then it is retired. Today, there are more than two dozen robes, most of which are kept in the Times Square offices of Actors'

Donated to the Smithsonian National Museum of American History during the 2001 Smithsonian Folklife Festival, this Gypsy Robe documents Broadway's 1995–1997 seasons. *Rent, Titanic, The King and I, Big, and Once Upon a Mattress* are among the shows celebrated on its panels. PHOTO COURTESY SMITHSONIAN INSTITUTION.

Equity for safekeeping, although several have recently been donated to the Smithsonian Institution, the New York Public Library, and the Museum of the City of New York. More than stunning visual objects, the Gypsy Robes encapsulate the history of five decades of American musical theater. Whether a gigantic hit or a massive flop, if a musical opened on Broadway, it has left its imprint on the Gypsy Robe. "They're the only thing that the chorus really has," continued Marone. "We always say to the stars: 'Sorry folks. You've got the Tonys, the [Drama Critics'] Circle, and all these different awards, but you don't have this one. This is just for the chorus!'"[32]

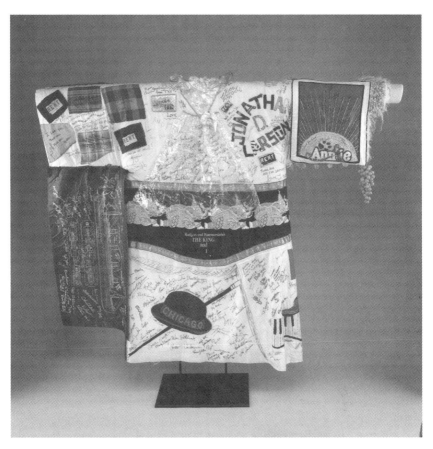

Elaborate back panel of the Smithsonian's Gypsy Robe. PHOTO COURTESY SMITHSONIAN INSTITUTION.

So on April 25, 1999, half an hour before opening curtain, we found ourselves center stage at the Longacre Theatre on West 48th Street with Marone, gypsy David Clemmons, who had received the robe a few days before for *The Civil War*, robe historian Rosenthal, and various and sundry theater dignitaries. Clemmons announced that Tim Hunter would be the next "King of the Gypsies" to the wild applause of the chorus line and other members of the cast and crew, who stood just outside the gypsies' mid-stage circle. The new king donned the robe with great pride, made three dignified counterclockwise passes around the circle, and joyfully set off to bless the backstage dressing rooms. The rest of the cast dispersed to finish their preparations and nervously await the opening curtain. So did it work? Well, neither *Fascinating Rhythm* nor *The Civil War* enjoyed great reviews or extended runs, but that probably didn't make the ceremony any less important for those who took part in it.[33]

BROADWAY CRAFTS: CONSTRUCTING ILLUSIONS

The actor who "struts and frets his hours upon the stage" would have to do so on a bare stage and in street clothes if it were not for the skills and knowledge of an amazing community of backstage artists, artisans, craftspeople, and theater workers. The offstage contributions of directors, producers, agents, and playwrights are widely credited, but equally impressive contributions by scenic, costume, and lighting designers, carpenters, stagehands and property crews do not always receive the credit they are due.

The New York theater industry supports a large network of highly specialized local workshops and ateliers that produce the scenery, wigs, props, costumes, and other two- and three-dimensional objects needed for every Broadway production, as well as by opera companies, movie shoots, television shows, road companies, and regional theaters throughout the United States. Although many of the city shops are small ateliers, combined they make up a multimillion-dollar industry and employ hundreds, if not thousands of people in the New York metropolitan region. As is true with the performers who appear in front of the curtain, those who gain renown in the world of backstage crafts tend to be the crème de la créme of their professions. Long years of apprenticeship, study, and effort are required to make a name for one's self as master craftsperson on Broadway. Costume and set designers are credited in Broadway playbills, but the artisans who actually produce the objects that impress and dazzle theater audiences are rarely acknowledged. It is their skills that help performers to weave the spell; their artistry that creates the "suspension of disbelief" that enmeshes theater audiences.

Production on a Broadway show begins when, after consultation with a show's director and producer, its costume and set designers send out sketches to several local production shops outlining "the look" they want for a show. The shops then submit bids and contracts are awarded. But it's not always that straightforward. As one craftsman complained: "Some designers let you know exactly what they want a costume to look like, right down to the number of polka dots in a ruffle on the bottom tier of the skirt. But others come in with a sketch on a brown paper bag or crumpled cocktail napkin. And you go 'Huh? What *is* it?'"[34]

Not infrequently, it has been the skill, imagination, and know-how of uncredited backstage craftspeople who have made the reputations of noted stage designers and saved entire productions from impending ruin. "I find it a blessing when I can work with a designer who has a sketch," make-up artist Scott Sliger told us, instead of one who says "Kind of like this, and kind of like that. It makes my job much easier and the whole thing flows a lot faster."[35] Many designers do work closely with the craftspeople. Gary Brouwer, one of Broadway's foremost milliners (hat makers), is often called upon to help design the head pieces that he will also produce: "There's a lot of designers—they know you, you know them. It's a meeting of the minds almost. If they do sketches, they're very vague. You make a sample, you make a mock-up, and you talk about it."[36] Wig maker Linda Rice, whose credits include making the wigs for *Saturday Night Live*, will defer to costume designers, "Because ultimately, they are my boss, but they might not know how to do these wigs. They might say, 'Well, I want red,' and don't realize that there are fifty-five different shades of red. So then it's up to me to help the costume designers realize what's in their head."[37]

A widespread complaint among Broadway craftsmen is deadlines. "I think speed is one of the major musts in our business," one confided. "The first question you always ask is 'When do you want it?' And then you hope for the best. Sometimes it's the worst."[38] Brouwer recalled finishing a hat for a performance at the Metropolitan Opera in the back of a taxicab that was going sixty miles an hour up Tenth Avenue because "Mr. Pavarotti had to go on stage and can't do it without a hat!"[39] Noted costume maker Barbara Matera agreed: "Sometimes the designer is very well prepared and has got all his stuff together and maybe you have six or eight weeks to think about it—which is great because you do really need the time. Another time, they'll say that they haven't designed it yet, and there are four weeks until the dress rehearsal! Sometimes the rush is good. You know, ideas get going and there is not too much time for people to be laid back about 'it could be this or it could be that.' We always say that costumes take as long as we have to make them."[40] According to one prop maker: "They never, ever give you enough time. It's always last minute. They could save so much money by doing it early, but they just *don't*. Drama, crisis, tension—you have to thrive on it!"[41]

So where does all this backstage magic take place? Scattered throughout metropolitan New York are scores of small, medium, and large workshops that cater to the very specialized needs of Broadway theaters. Years ago, these workshops tended to be located close to Times Square, but today most have relocated to industrial loft buildings in unglamorous sections of Brooklyn, Queens, the Bronx, or the lower Hudson River Valley where more room is available for less rent. None are open to the public, but when our interviewers entered through deceptively drab doorways, it was immediately obvious that these are not average offices.

"LOOKING THE PART": BROADWAY COSTUMES

Matera's bustling theatrical costume shop in Manhattan's Flatiron District is such a place. Interviewed before her untimely death in 2001, she was modest and self-effacing master craftsperson who was greatly respected and genuinely admired throughout the Broadway theater community.[42] Trained as a theater costume maker in her native England in the late 1940s and early 1950s, Matera moved to New York in 1966 to work in the famous theatrical costume firm Brooks Van-Horn. She quickly earned a reputation as an exceptional craftswoman and soon left to establish her own shop in her small 86th Street apartment. "We had no room. Our first cutting table was a big sheet of plywood on top of a grand piano."[43] When one of her roommate/partners slept late, the woman who did beading and embroidering used to set up her work frame over his bed and would be hard at work when he woke up! Word spread that Matera had opened her own shop and soon she was producing costumes for such Broadway legends as Mary Martin and Gwen Verdon.

Today, Barbara Matera, Ltd. employs between sixty and—"if we get really busy"—one hundred artisans. Working from sketches submitted by a show's designer, Matera's staff produces exquisitely made and superbly fitted costumes for plays, musicals, operas, ballets, and circuses. Occasionally, the shop undertakes some special jobs—like a beautiful, sequined presidential inaugural gown that First Lady Hillary Clinton wore to her husband's first inaugural ball in 1993. Matera's workshop is crowded with bolts of sumptuous fabrics, rolls of multi-hued ribbons, and shelves of luxurious trimmings; cabinets brim with boxes of luminous beads and table-top containers sprout exotic-looking feathers. Throughout the loft, scores of drapers, fitters, cutters, dressmakers, and tailors work to complete costumes for a score of upcoming performances.

Among the more specialized jobs are the beaders—who hand stitch beads and sequins on to stunningly elaborate costumes; hand embroiders; and "swatchers"—two or three employees who scour New York's fabric stores collecting cloth samples for approval by the show's designer. "There are tons of fabric[s] in New York," Matera explained, "but it's not just one place; it's downtown, midtown, and uptown. If you haven't been to them, the designers are really just haunted."[44] Matera buys good fabrics, sometimes paying over one hundred dollars a yard for high-quality silks and brocades because given the

Judith Marsh, a beader in Barbara Matera's costume shop, adds final touches to an elaborate bodice that doubles as a flying harness for performers in the *Lion King*. PHOTO BY NANCY GROCE, COURTESY SMITHSONIAN INSTITUTION.

wear and tear of the theater, "cheap doesn't last." Matera's costumes start at several hundred dollars but can easily run into the thousands.

While the designers finalize fabric choices for each costume, Matera's staff is hard at work draping mannequins with paper prototypes, cutting patterns, and doing preliminary fittings on actors and actresses. When the actual costume is produced, the actor returns for a final fitting. "The actor comes first," Matera insisted: "The designer—it's fine that he has designed this beautiful thing, but if the actor is uncomfortable, or can't move, or he really hates it, I think the designer has to go with that."[45] Most Broadway actors are modest and matter of fact about coming in for their fittings, which take place in Matera's semi-private front office equipped with several small, curtained-off changing cubicles. She admitted to having to deal with the occasional prima donna who needs total privacy, or big stars who will summon her or her staff to their hotel rooms and then keep them waiting for hours before they deign to make time for a fitting, but those seem to be an exception. In fact, although she was discrete about naming names, her most challenging clients seem to be Hollywood rather than Broadway stars. Like many other Broadway workers, she pointed out that the occupational culture of the New York theater is not the same as that of the Hollywood film industry. Broadway

Tim Blacker, a craftsman at Barbara Matera's shop, readies an ornate costume for its debut at the Metropolitan Opera. PHOTO BY NANCY GROCE, COURTESY SMITHSONIAN INSTITUTION.

is unnerving for many Hollywood stars: "There are no cuts and you have one chance to do it in front of an audience and that is that—and you have to do it night after night after night. So there's a lot of pressure on them when they come to Broadway."[46]

On the day that we interviewed her, dozens of completed tutus hung overhead awaiting shipment to a southern ballet company; at a nearby workbench, a craftsman attached glimmering trimmings to an armored breastplate that was about to make its debut at the Metropolitan Opera; across the aisle, several dressmakers sat at a row of sewing machines stitching outfits for the soon-to-open musical *Sussical*; and at the far end of the loft, a beader put the final touches on an elaborate bodice that would double as a flying harness for dancers in the *Lion King*. Many of Matera's craftspeople come from South America and Eastern Europe; most had been with her for fifteen or twenty years. As we left, Matera turned her attention to a discussion about her next project with a designer from a nationally renowned circus. Their elephants needed proper attire for next season's production, so what would be the best way to measure the pachyderms?

Do Matera's workers ever see their costumes on the stage? Sometimes. Often, when actors came in for their final fittings Matera would ask them walk through the workroom so her employees could see their handiwork. What do they think? "Oh, they love it! They all stand around and they applaud!"[47]

THE PROPER TOPPER

If Matera's shop is one of largest backstage Broadway establishments, Brouwer's theatrical millinery shop in Long Island City is one of the smaller ones.[48] Brouwer, a tall, elegant man with a wicked sense of humor, trained as a fashion designer in his native Holland before coming to the United States in the mid-1950s to work in the fashion industry. In 1962, he got a call from Eve's Costume, a family-run costume shop, which had been supplying costumes for New York theaters since the mid-1800s. They asked him if he was interested in making some hats for the stage. And? "And I said, 'Oh, do they wear hats in the theater?' I was totally unaware of it, because I'd done strictly fashion. And so I started there and the first show they asked me to do was a big special on TV with Lucille Ball and Henry Fonda. I remember that very distinctly because Lucille Ball was intensely happy with the huge hats I had made for her. She said, 'Those are the best hats I ever had; Hollywood couldn't touch it!'"[49]

Brouwer went on to become a legend in theatrical millinery, making hats for Broadway shows, operas, ice capades, circuses, Radio City Music Hall spectaculars, Las Vegas reviews, television specials, variety shows, movies, and regional theaters. He is particularly renowned for his elegant turbans, including the one worn for many years by Johnny Carson as "Carnac the Magnificent" on the *Tonight Show*. During his career, he oversaw both large shops and small ateliers and has been involved in more productions than he can remember. Some Broadway shows require hundreds of hats—like the 2001 revival of *42nd Street*, for which Brouwer produced 450 hats. And then there is the Metropolitan Opera: "The chorus alone is sometimes eighty people, and they all wear hats! If they run out of music: 'let's put another hat on!'" Then there's the circus: "Talk about an avalanche of hats! There's nobody in the circus without anything on his or her head!"[50]

Broadway milliners provide "an avalanche of hats" for theatrical productions throughout the United States. PHOTO BY NANCY GROCE, COURTESY SMITHSONIAN INSTITUTION.

One of the things he likes about working for the theater, Brouwer said, is that his hats are already sold before he makes them. "In fashion," he said, "you have to make a hat and hope it sells."[51] Costume designers often come to him with only a vague idea: "It's totally verbal. There are not even sketches. If anything, I make a sketch and say, 'Well, what do you think about this? Does it look good?' Of course, they trust me."[52] Brouwer's hats can costs up to several thousand dollars, and some—like those he designs for Las Vegas show girls—include an impressive combination of electric lights, feathers, and frills that stretch the definition of "hat" to its outermost limits. Working at a small workbench in a spare white loft, Brouwer uses handcrafted wooden hat blocks, buckram, a rainbow of felts, fabrics, feathers, ornate trimmings, and boundless imagination to make his fabulous creations. Occasionally, he will don a half-finished hat and peek into a narrow dressing mirror affixed to the edge of his workbench—just to make sure he's on the right track. "To me, it's almost like carpentry—because of your hands, what you're doing, you're not going to have flat wood. You build something out of it. The same thing with millinery, you buy yardage. It's all flat on the table. You need a pair of good hands and a very good eye for proportion. By the time a milliner is through with it, it all stands up by itself. It's sculpture."[53]

"YOU LOOK MARVELOUS"

Of all of the backstage Broadway people we interviewed, Brooklyn-born Bob Kelly was one of the most colorful, and not just because he is a legendary make-up artist. Actually, Kelly started out as a wig maker—a trade his Irish grandfather learned before coming to New York in the 1870s and going to work for such fabled theaters as Tony Pastor's Music Hall and the old Academy of Music on 14th Street. Kelly didn't get a chance to work with his grandfather, who died in 1938, but when he returned from World War II, he was intrigued with the trade and decided to apprentice with a shop that made wigs for the Metropolitan Opera: "I said, 'Gee, why don't I try it?' And when I got into it, I fell into it fairly easily, like it was born in my hands."[54]

Dressing and curling wigs backstage at the Met led him into make-up: "They're doing make-up on themselves, and all of a sudden, someone asks you to pick up a pencil and draw a line here, or do this there. Nobody sat down and taught you. Before you know it, they thought I was a make-up artist. I wasn't, but somehow that's the way you pick it up. My hours were horrendous—six days a week from 10:00 in the morning until 12:00 or 1:00 at night. No overtime, it wasn't heard of in those days. But it was really a great experience. You work and work, but what you learned was yours forever."[55]

During the 1950s, Kelly's reputation as a make-up artist and wig maker blossomed. Although he claims that he was still learning—"I had Max Factor's make-up book and I'd go into the make-up cabinet and read the book fast!"[56]— by 1958 he was accomplished enough to open his own shop. It was the city's heyday as a center for television broadcasts and Kelly's clients included *The Steve Allen Show*, Sid Caesar's *Show of Shows*, *The Hallmark Hall of Fame*, *The Jackie Gleason Show*, *You Are There*, and *Captain Kangaroo*. A few years later, working with friend and chemist Dr. Paul Fisher, he began manufacturing his own brand of theatrical make-up in a small Brooklyn factory. His firm, Bob Kelly Cosmetics, was an enormous success, especially after he had the brilliant idea of marketing a basic theatrical make-up kit to high schools, colleges, and amateur thespian groups throughout the county. (Anyone who has ever performed in a local theater group has undoubtedly used Kelly's products.) Looking at an enormous wall of signed celebrity photos in his workshop, we noticed that each had some variation of "Thanks, Bob!" impressively scrawled across it. "Yeah, I knew them all," he said, launching into another story, this time about doing make-up for the Beatles the night they appeared on the *Ed Sullivan Show*.[57]

Today, more than a dozen wig makers or "ventilators," wig designers, and make-up artists work out of Kelly's jumbled shop on the upper floor of an old office building just off Times Square. "It's sort of a League of Nations here," Kelly said looking around his workroom, "we have Orientals, Polish, Irish, Italian, a couple from Cuba, from the Dominican Republic, we're all mixed up."[58] Most of the ventilators are Asian women, who sit facing each other around worktables in the main room. Most have been with Kelly for years; some for decades. "I am probably lucky, nobody ever quits. They don't get rich working with me, but at the same time, they don't get aggravated to death."[59] In an adjoining room, he showed off several private barbershop-like cubicles, fitting rooms for non-theatrical clients who wish to remain anonymous. He offers a few words of wig wisdom: "If someone tells you they like your wig, it's a crumby wig. No one is supposed to know you're wearing one"[60]; however, he demurred when asked for his tonsorial assessment of any particular celebrity. Taking a puff from his ever-present cigar, he talked about his plans to open a theatrical make-up school in New York: "There are none here on the East Coast; they're all on the West Coast. After all, at seventy-seven, you got to look forward to something. I might live to one hundred, and then what am I going to do?"[61]

WIGS, WIGS, AND MORE WIGS

One of the prominent craftspeople working out of Kelly's shop is wig designer Linda Rice. Like many backstage Broadway artisans, Rice initially wanted to perform, but while helping out backstage in a regional theater to earn a "walk on" spot, she had a revelation: "I looked around and said, 'This is so cool! What am I doing wanting to be on the stage?' So I started concentrating from the neck up."[62] As part of her job doing costumes and make-up in regional theater she began ordering wigs from Kelly's shop in Manhattan: "And these beautiful beards and moustaches would come. I said, I have to go there, I have to find this man."[63] So in 1984, Rice moved to New York to work with Kelly.

Theatrical wig making begins with a tiny specially made polyester-nylon mesh, which is fitted to a performer's head and hairline. Thousands of individual microscopic hairs are then hand tied to the mesh. "Anybody who knows what a latch hook rug is—it's the same idea of knotting; only you're doing it in microscopic form with individual hairs instead of yarn. Once you learn the basics of wig making, it's just about practice, practice, practice. The more you hand-tie individual hairs into this silly little net, the faster you're going to get."[64] It takes about fifteen hours to complete each wig, and they can cost anywhere from $1,200 on up, depending on the length and complexity of the hairstyle.

Rice has designed and produced wigs and overseen hair and make-up for numerous Broadway plays, but for the last decade or so her primary job has been as the designer and producer of wigs for NBC's comedy review *Saturday Night Live*. When doing a Broadway show, the wig makers are usually brought in four to six weeks before a production opens. When Rice worked on *Beauty and the Beast* in 1993, for example, she was given three months, "Because we had to build wigs for clocks and candles. And we had to build the Beast, which had fifty-nine pieces of hair on his body!"[65] But *Saturday Night Live* is another story: "I have forty-eight hours. We get our sketches 12:00 midnight Wednesday at the starting gate, and we work for two days solid without any sleep building the wigs for a 12:00 noon rehearsal on Saturday. With *Saturday Night Live*, what you see is what you get. At 11:30 Saturday night, if somebody's pants fall down, the entire nation knows it. There's no time for editing. There's no lag time. It's one of the few live shows, other than news broadcasts, left in New York."[66]

When we interviewed Rice in her New York shop one Friday morning, she was on the homestretch of completing more than a dozen wigs and beards that would be needed for that week's *Saturday Night Live*. She was overseeing an "army" of eight ventilators, who were busily hand tying individual strands of hair to mesh foundations; in the far corner, a "blender" was mixing strands

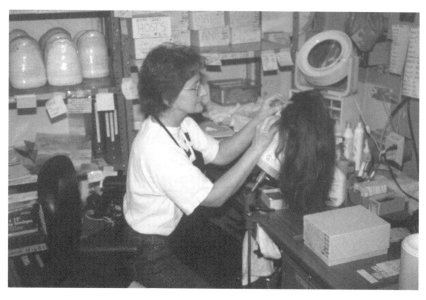

Master wig maker Linda Rice, working in Bob Kelly's Times Square studio, ties thousands of microscopic hairs into specially made custom-fitted polyester-nylon mesh to complete a single stage wig. PHOTO BY ANDREW DAVIS. COURTESY SMITHSONIAN INSTITUTION.

of different hair colors to create just the right shade of dirty blond for a particular sketch, and in the next room, a stylist was putting the final touches on a recently completed hair piece. Meanwhile, Rice was studying a recent photo of Russell Crowe, trying to decide whether to copy his current rather stubbly beard or go with his previous *Gladiator* look—Crowe was obviously going to be a *Saturday Night Live* target this week. When she got a chance, she said as she tied reddish hairs to the net, she hoped to redo *Saturday Night Live's* George W. Bush wig because the old one was beginning to look dated. "The president has become grayer since taking office," she said, "They always do."[67]

Like all Broadway craftspeople, Rice takes considerable pride in her work, but like many good back-of-the-house craftspeople, she gracefully accepts that she is part of a larger whole. When asked if she got attached to her wigs, she replied: "Never! When you work on *Saturday Night Live*, things get cut all the time. So, no, I'm not married to anything. You want it blond? Fine. Where's the bleach? You have to understand, we *service* performers. So when I'm doing hair on somebody, or I'm putting a wig on somebody, I am servicing the performer, just like a waitress in a restaurant. And, we only need one diva in the make-up room."[68]

"After I've designed everything I want, I just fill in all the gaps where we're slowing down in a particular area of the production line," she added, apologizing that she couldn't really stop to talk with us.[69] "Nobody sleeps. I'm lucky if I have about three hours of sleep from Wednesday afternoon until about 7:00 or 8:00 Saturday night." Does she fit her creations on the *Saturday Night Live* actors the night of the show? "No! I'll build you your wigs. Don't ask me to put them on at 1:00 in the morning on Saturday—'cause I can't see straight anymore!"[70]

MAKING IT LOOK REAL

When a Broadway curtain goes up, the first thing to catch the audience's attention is the scenery. Sometimes, the scenery and on-stage "props" (properties) are more entertaining than the play or more dynamic than the performances. Credit for designing and realizing stage sets goes to visionaries like Nino Novellino, whose shop, Costume Armour, Inc., is located in the Hudson River town of Cornwall, about an hour north of New York City.[71] For more than twenty-five years, Novellino and his employees have provided props for such classic Broadway productions as *CATS*, *La Cage aux Folles*, *Phantom of the Opera*, *Into the Woods*, *Starlight Express*, and *Miss Saigon*, as well as myriad television shows, parades, films, ballets, and operas. Using an array of skills, prop makers artfully

Head of Apollo Belvedere being crafted in Costume Armour's workshop for the 2001 Broadway production *Invention of Love*. Design by Bob Crowley; sculpture by Nino Novellino. PHOTO COURTESY COSTUME ARMOUR.

transform everyday materials into objects that help actors tell their story and assist theater audiences to believe in the story being told. Between the time that a set designer sketches out his or her idea for a production's "look," and an audience beholds what is behind the rising curtain on opening night, all parts of the set have be "realized"—measured, built, sculpted, painted, sewn, molded, or otherwise created and then approved by the show's director. Some of this work is done by set and backdrop painters, but all three-dimensional objects are created by "prop shops."

A New Yorker by birth, Novellino trained as an artist and sculptor at Brooklyn's Pratt Institute before learning the art of prop making in a theatrical prop shop in the Bronx in the mid-1960s. With the help of his wife, Mary, Novellino's firm became one of Broadway's largest and most respected prop producers. Today, he employs scores of artisans, including carpenters, painters, sculptors, and several full-time armorers like Brian Healy. Healy, a jovial, thoughtful young man who learned to make armor at Renaissance fairs, readily admits that career opportunities for armor makers in the contemporary United States are somewhat limited. So he was overjoyed when one of his friends told him about a help wanted ad for a theatrical armor maker at Costume Armour. "I went for an interview and Nino said, 'What kind of sword would you make for a seventeenth-century musketeer?' And I said, 'Oh, for that, you'd want a rapier with . . .' and I drew them a sketch. And he said, 'You're hired.'"[72] So now, Healy spends his days making and hand finishing shields, breastplates, gorges, cuirasses, and other bits of armor as well as menacing-looking weapons that will appear in theatrical productions, operas, and spectacles throughout the United States. Most of the armor is actually made of high-grade plastic, which has been carefully molded, polished, and painted. From only a few inches away, it looks convincingly real. Some armor is produced for stock productions—the shop does a surprisingly large business supplying Roman armor to churches for Easter and Christmas pageants. Others suits are custom-made for specific performers. This is especially true in

Prop maker Brian Healy of Costume Armour stands amidst miniature Nazi paratroopers created for the 2001 Broadway musical *The Producers*. Design by Robin Wagner. PHOTO COURTESY COSTUME ARMOUR.

the case of generously proportioned opera stars, who not only have to fit into their armor, they also have to be able to breathe while wearing it.

In another area of Costume Armour's huge facility, located in a rambling nineteenth-century mill that once housed a rug factory, artisans assemble wood and Styrofoam forms. When the Smithsonian documentation team arrived on a rainy autumn day, more than a dozen people were hard at work on a stack of huge books, two larger-than-life sculpted heads of a Greek god and goddess, and several iterations of a miniature cathedral—all of which would then be covered by paint, cloth, leather, mirrors, or whatever else was necessary to make them look persuasively real to theatergoers. We walked carefully between a giant chandelier from *Phantom of the Opera*, which hung a few feet off the ground waiting to be refurbished; an elaborate eleven-foot tall marbleized church altar alive with saints, angles, and cherubs, which had just returned from the Broadway run of *The Sound of Music*; a nearly life-sized coach-and-four left-over from Stephen Sondheim's *Into the Woods*; and several giant knives, forks, and garbage can lids from the recently closed Broadway perennial *CATS*.

In the next room, we watched as one of the craftsmen manipulated the shop's huge Vac-u-Form machine. Originally specially built for the 1964 New York World's Fair, the room-sized contraption turns large sheets of anonymous plastic in three-dimensional walls, columns, carriages, trees, statues, or anything else that can be imagined and sculpted. It was obvious that, with the addition of a little paint, the objects being molded would be drawing "oohs" and "ahs" from theater audiences in the not too distant future. Surprisingly, even readily available everyday items as bathtubs, sinks, and toilets are usually recreated for Broadway shows because the real items are too heavy to be quickly, easily, or quietly moved on and off stage between scenes.

We left the same way we had entered, through a long, dark hallway that Novellino and his staff have transformed into a Gothic dungeon—complete with looming rock walls, ancient wooden doors, torches held aloft by shapely disembodied arms, menacing iron chains, and more than your average number of gargoyles. Of course, it's all fake—props made by Costume Armour's workers. But what better way to set the stage for a shop devoted to illusion?

"THE SHOW MUST GO ON"

One of the remarks that came up time and again when interviewing Broadway workers was how much they loved being called upon to do something new, to meet the different challenges presented by every new show, every performance. Yet paradoxically, if a show is a great success—which everyone devoutly hopes it will be—things can become rather routine. Isn't it hard to do the same show night after night for months on end and keep it fresh? We asked some of the chorus line gypsies. "I love performing, and I never ever 'marked' through a performance," Broadway gypsy Cowan said with pride. Marked? "Marked—that means not dancing full out. They get in a long run and they think nobody's noticing and they just phone in the performance. They're not really there. I *never* did that."[73]

Occasionally, directors or producers will replace all or part of the cast of a long-running show to freshen up the production. Needless to say, this approach is not terribly popular with the performers. Cowan said she had no problems "staying" with a show like *Annie*: "I was in the moment. Another actor would read a line differently and it would make you respond differently. Or I might do it a little differently. And sometimes you would find new things in a show. So I never got tired of doing *Annie*. My feeling—and I'm tough about this—is if they're marking they should get out of the show. When people are paying as much money as they are for tickets, they deserve to see a fresh show."[74]

What about the props? The craftsmen explained that once costumes or props are delivered to the shows, it becomes the responsibility of the wardrobe mistress or prop master to take care of the objects. The backstage workers in charge of wardrobes and props must make sure that everything is ready the next time the curtain goes up. This might involve replacing buttons, mending rips, ironing and cleaning costumes, or fixing and repainting damaged props. "After the opening night, it's curtains for me," hat maker Brouwer told us, only half jokingly. "I leave. And then hope that the wardrobe person will take care of my hats." "Unfortunately," continued Brouwer somewhat fatuously, "they only have one color thread—heavy orange! Even if the show is in black and white, it's *always* heavy orange. So whatever they repair, there is a big, heavy orange spot somewhere. I don't want to know about it!"[75]

Wig maker Rice will periodically revisit the shows she has worked on "because little by little the hair dressers will start adding too many rollers or not enough. So the thing you designed that started out as this gorgeous curling wig that had all this detail, by the time you get there three weeks later, it's a bun in the back of their head!"[76] Actually, anticipating that things might deteriorate over time, as well as assuming that there will be a gradual turnover in backstage dressers, hair, and make-up artists, each show compiles a "Bible" at the beginning of its run—a photographic reference book detailing how each character should be dressed, made-up, and coiffed. In addition to making sure everything is in good working order, everything has to be put back in exactly the right spot so the actor can find it the following night in the midst of a performance. A chair that starts out upstage right in Act One and winds up being smashed downstage left in Act Three must be reassembled and returned to its original position. Making sure it gets there is the job of the company's prop person or stagehand.

WAITING IN THE WINGS

When the curtain goes up, it's like the ship is pulling away from the dock. You want to keep it floating, you want to keep it going in a straight line—'cause when it sinks, it makes everybody look bad. And the things you do to make it so you don't bring the curtain in!
—John Loftgren, Broadway Stagehand

The ultimate backstage job is probably that of stagehand. To find out what it is like to work as a Broadway stagehand, we spoke with Broadway stagehand John Loftgren, who also builds scenery and props and "loads in" (sets up) new productions.[77] Loftgren is a third-generation New York stagehand; both sides of his family have been involved with the New York theater since the 1880s, and his great-uncle Phillip Lennon helped found the International Alliance of Theatrical Stage Employees, Local One, the stagehand's union. "I knew when I was eight years old that this was what I wanted to do," he said with pride, and estimated that over the years he has worked on "about one million shows."[78] When he first started in the business, everything was made out of wood and canvas. Now everything is aluminum, steel, and plastic. "All the rigging used to be ropes, now it's all on cables. Now it's hydraulic, electronic. I program the computers to run the scenery."[79]

On Broadway, it's often said that theater is the most dangerous civilian occupation in the United States. Loftgren, who lost a friend in a fall from a catwalk, agrees: "What a lot of actors don't realize is that stagehands are technicians. And you're doing some very critical things. Lots of time, really boring, but a lot of time really critical. Like *Beauty and the Beast*—there's eighty thousand pounds of scenery hanging over that stage. Eighty thousand pounds! And it's moving! And especially when you're doing a load-in, you've been in the theater from 8:00 in the morning to midnight for, say, three months. So by the time the actors get there, they've been in the rehearsal studio and what they do is a lot about art. There's sort of a philosophical conflict going on there. The actor is into a creative, physical, mental mode, and the stagehands are into exhaustion—and trying not to get people killed. It's very serious stuff."[80]

Loftgren's favorite musicals include *Sweeney Todd*, *Crazy for You*, and almost anything by Stephen Sondheim, but he rarely sees a play from the front of the house. He worked *Beauty and the Beast* for years before he saw it from the audience's perspective: "It's completely different from out front," he told us. "Backstage, you hear what's going on, but you're involved with making sure that these pieces are exactly here, and that piece of scenery's there, and that person's standing here—everything is as choreographed as it is on stage. And I'd seen this show, maybe, five hundred times, and I was training somebody to take my place while I went on vacation. He was really good, so I didn't have to watch him anymore. And I went out front. Now, I put Chip—the little kid that you can only see his head—I put him in all of his illusions. So I have no illusions. Literally! That's why we don't tell people how the magic works, because then it wouldn't be magic. And I help the Beast to do the transformation where he actually flies up in the air, spins, and changes from the Beast into the Prince. I know exactly how and when it happens. And when I was out front, I couldn't tell! I was looking right at it and I couldn't see it! And when Chip came out at the end and said to his mother, 'Do I have to sleep in the cupboard tonight?' I was, like, choked up. And then I was, like, 'Damn, they got me!'"[81]

Loftgren has great respect for actors. "They're the ones that have to be out in front of the audience. It takes a tremendous amount of training and commitment. I give them all the credit they deserve. And I demand respect from them, too."[82] Most of the time, stagehands and actors get along reasonably well, but occasionally animosity can build up. "I've seen stagehands make it difficult for actors. Not by sabotage or anything, but I've seen them make it very difficult." Had it ever happened to him? "In fact, one actor was busting my chops and I told him, 'You never screw with your prop man, *ever*. And I'll prove it to you. When you're out there in front of those two thousand people, I'm going to break two of your balloons'—he had a whole thing of balloons in his hand—'and when they break, you can look at me and I'll be standing there with my arms crossed.' Sure enough, at the end of the scene, Bang! Bang! And I'm standing in the wings with my arms crossed!" How? "Everything this actor did was precise; every move was calculated and timed. So I noticed that at the end of this scene, when he turned to the music, his balloons always touched the same parts of the set. So I taped little pins to those parts. And the best thing about it, the balloon exploded with the downbeats of the music. Bam! Bam! It was perfect!"[83]

SHOW TIME!

For some craftsmen, working long hours backstage is enough: "I never go to a Broadway show," claimed milliner Brouwer, "I see too much commotion before it opens . . . the mystery's gone."[84] Wig maker Rice feels differently: "In terms of being an audience member, I'm a big sucker! I love Broadway and I go as much as I possibly can afford it."[85] And when she goes to shows she hasn't worked on, does she stare at the wigs? "You know," she said, "I don't care. Yeah, if the hair's hanging down around their knees maybe I might notice. But because I work so hard at what I do, I love it—just entertain me, give me a good time!"[86]

Both those who work backstage and those who perform in front of the curtain have a profound belief in the magic of theater. They talked passionately about the unique ability of live theater to interweave text, movement, costumes, sets, music, and acting in a darkened space to create a shared emotional response. About how good theater can transform hundreds of disparate people into a single spellbound audience. About how, with its immediacy and power, theater is unlike any other form of entertainment. "We'll always be around no matter how many computers and videos and movies come out," acting coach Ruth Nerken said confidently, "They don't replace the theater, they can't."[87]

URBAN PROFILE: TATS CRU

Graffiti Artists and the Urban Canvas

URBAN CULTURE is rarely static, and often it is not easy to compartmentalize. Folklorists tend to distinguish between "traditional culture"—customs, practices, and cultural expressions that exist narrowly over long periods of time—and "popular culture"—fads and fashions that flourish over a much great geographic area or among a much larger group of people but exist for shorter periods of time. But culture is messy and the lines between popular and traditional culture are often quite blurry. Graffiti is a wonderful case in point.

Like many underground urban art forms, graffiti "writing" had been percolating on the streets of the South Bronx, Brooklyn, Queens, and northern Manhattan primarily among Black and Latino teenagers for some time before most New Yorkers noticed it the mid-1970s. And then, suddenly, they couldn't help but notice it: Huge colorful murals, bold lettering, and a distinctive style done by "crews" of graffiti writers in the subway yards in the dark of the night began rolling through the city on the sides of train cars. Within a few short months, it seemed to be everywhere.[1]

The appearance of graffiti on New York's subways at the height of the city's economic and social woes created a huge public outcry. City officials and social pundits condemned it as vandalism, as well as a graphic reflection of the breakdown of urban order and morality. The Metropolitan Transit Authority (MTA), which was concerned that the visual disorder compounded the high crime rate that was already scaring away subway riders, launched a high-profile and ultimately successful anti-graffiti campaign.[2] Meanwhile, the visual vibrancy of the graffiti style combined with other grassroots arts forms such as MC-ing, DJ-ing, and break dancing ("b-boying" and "b-girling") coalesced in New York in the 1970s to form the basis of hip hop and, later, rap culture.[3]

The romance of the early days of graffiti, when crews of writers would evade police and transit cops, sneak into subway yards and tunnels, and "bomb" cars with stunning murals, is nostalgically remembered by some; however, the real history is a bit more complicated. By the early 1980s, many of the most talented graffiti writers were already finding it more rewarding, as well as more lucrative, to work "legitimately" for advertising agencies, graphic design firms, and art galleries. As the trains became cleaner, and galleries throughout the world began to lionize some of the writers, many of the New Yorkers who initially condemned graffiti began to recognize that it might have some merit as an art form. Some property owners and city agencies even began to commission the "vandals" to paint graffiti style murals and memorial walls on buildings throughout the city.[4]

A generation after it first appeared, graffiti is still very much alive but in transition. No matter what personal views about it may be, it is an indisputable part of the New York cultural landscape, and the Smithsonian was anxious to document what graffiti writers had to say about themselves and their craft. To this end, we were delighted to be able to interview Tats Cru, a respected trio of graffiti artists who grew up together in the South Bronx. Wilfredo "Bio" Feliciano, Hector "Nicer" Nazario, and Sotero "BG183" Ortiz met each other in art classes at James Monroe High School. Today, they make their living as full-time graffiti artists: accepting commissions for murals and graphic designs, touring and lecturing internationally on graffiti, and—because they are anxious to "give back"—teaching local kids at The Point Community Development Center on Garrison Avenue in the Bronx. They spoke with folklorist Elena Martinez about their art and the world of graffiti.[5]

Like most graffiti artists, when the members of Tats Cru began writing as teenagers, one of the first things they did was to adopt "tag" names. We asked how they decided what to call themselves and were surprised to learn that it had more to do with how "the letters work together" design-wise than anything else:

My name is Bio. Bio is my artist name, I am really Feliciano Wilfredo. I was born and raised in New York City. I started in the late '70s, early '80s. My name I actually got from a friend of mine; everyone goes through different names when they begin. I used to write 'VIO.' One day, a friend was, like, why don't you try this name, letters. Why don't you try it with a B? And I kind of liked the B, [so] I stuck with the name BIO. After a while, you sort of stick to a name, you get it up in a few spots and you're, like, this is the name I am going to stay with.[6]

Did you select "BG183" because of your street address?" we ask Ortez.

No, just because it sounded good because at that time a lota graffiti artists used street numbers, or the day they were born, or the year. But, I just used it 'cause it just sounded good together. . . . I used to like 'Bring,'— 'cause I used to bring stuff to people. And that was my name, Bring. So what I did to make my letters much faster—because during that time you had to really write quite quickly—was I took the first letter and last letter and put it together: B.G. But people still knew me [as] Bring. Then, I guess messing around with it, I felt like maybe a number was necessary. So, I came up with a number, 183. And so, I just kept it BG183 and I ran with it.[7]

Bio recalled, "[w]e started in the early '80s painting subway trains."

We were doing graffiti on the subways and our whole thing was just to get our name out there to be seen, to show our artwork. It wasn't so much that the people knew who *you* were per se, but they knew of your artwork because all these murals or images had a tag [name] but no face to it. You never knew who was putting it up, but you would see the name and recognize the art. . . . Brooklyn, Bronx, Queens, even in the hand-style of the writing you would be able to tell where this person is from because of the style. There are certain elements in it that are particular to a certain area. So, you can tell: 'oh, it looks like he is from Queens or from Brooklyn.'

We were doing our names on the outside [of subway cars] but colorful. We were doing what you call "pieces": you know, a few colors, designs, abstract style for the lettering. But the focus was on your name because the idea was the more you got your name out there, the more famous you were in that movement.[8]

For the young teenagers on what were then the very tough streets of the South Bronx, the idea that their names would be on a subway train for the whole city to admire was irresistible. "That was the best thing about it," Bio explained, recalling the graffiti scene in the 1970s and early 1980s:

> You were painting in the Bronx and, like, in a [train] yard. And the train would travel from Bronx to Brooklyn, from Brooklyn to Queens, and Queens back to Manhattan, so it was like a canvas that was showcased for everybody to see. [Riders] only had to get on the train and they had a free mural. . . . [Graffiti] really started back in, like, '69. We heard it started with a regular tag [i.e., just a name] and then somebody added more colors to it. When we got involved in the early '80s, there were already murals being done on these trains.[9]

Like many neighborhood kids, Bio, Nicer, and BG took their inspiration from a few pioneer graffiti artists such as Cornbread, Cool Earl, and Taki 183. According to Bio:

> Yeah, definitely, they were our inspiration. I mean, when we were young kids we saw these colorful trains coming by with cartoon characters and a name. . . . Yeah, you know, you were blown away by this whole thing. You didn't know who they were, but you would see their work and be, like: 'Oh man, I want to be like that!'. . . And there were so many people writing at the time that you would take ideas from each writer and try to develop your own style—you know, take bits and pieces from there that you liked; the colors from here; then over the years you will come to develop your own style. . . . They slowed down and then we started coming up—passing of the torch, so to speak.[10]

BG183 has been interested in art as far back as he could remember:

> I've been drawing since I was really small. I got into finger painting, to black and white ink, doing the acrylics, painting cartoon characters, such like Spider Man, Captain America or Superman. From there . . . [it] was aerosol graffiti art—and that you had to learn through your next door neighbors or this kid next to you in your class. That is how you picked up graffiti, because it was always there for you. Like, you took the subway trains and you'd see it then.

After a while, you get hooked on it, and you're, like, wow, you [won-der] how it got done? Maybe they got on the side of a train and held on and they painted their name? You really wanted to know more. The more you got into it, the more you thought: I want to continue doing it. . . . After school, you did your homework, then you went outside. . . . Now you'd have a chance to paint your artwork outside on the streets! It was like a twenty-four hour thing. . . . It didn't have to stop, you could go painting at, like, 2:00 in the morning! . . . You didn't go to school; but you painted. . . . You were doing something illegal, but out of trouble. We saw it was nothing really hurting anyone. . . . [It] became like a rush. . . . Cops would chase me, but it was like you had to put your name up, no matter where it was. You did deface private property, but you thought that was the only canvas around in your neighborhood. You know we were poor, we grew up poor.[11]

MEMORIAL WALLS

By the late 1980s and early 1990s, the urban landscape was changing for graffiti artists. The diligent efforts of the MTA, which aggressively painted over or cleaned off graffiti on the subways, and the appearance of the "Vandal Squad," which regularly arrested graffiti artists, as well as the repair of fences around train yards, made getting to the trains and having your work seen for any length of time on "moving canvases" much more difficult. New city regulations also made it illegal to sell aerosol paint to minors and mandated that shops had to keep aerosol paint in locked cabinets, which significantly cut into the amount of paint that could be easily "racked"—i.e., shoplifted—by enthusiastic, if not entirely law-abiding writers.[12]

At the same time that writing on the trains was becoming more challenging and less acceptable, two other avenues opened for graffiti artists. The first, which went hand in hand with the explosion of hip hop culture, was an international fascination with New York graffiti. Many street-trained artists suddenly found that advertisers, graphic art studios, clothing manufacturers, and record labels would pay top dollars for their talents.

Although the hip hop movement was a way out for some artists, the crack epidemic of the late 1980s and early 1990s, as well as the increasing impact of AIDS throughout New York, left many New York neighborhoods devastated. In response, it became fashionable for relatives and friends of a deceased person to commission a memorial mural or "wall" in their honor.[13] Graffiti artists, because of their style and their neighborhood base, were hired to paint these murals. Bio recalled how Tats Cru became one of the best known crews for doing memorial walls:

> I would say from '94 to about '98 [there was] a flood of memorial walls. We may have done over one hundred—just memorial walls! We were doing like two, three a month. I think it was just a reflection of what was going on in the city at the time in the neighborhoods. . . . There were a lot of drugs, a lot of violence, a lot of stuff going on, and memorials came as the result of that. Most people confused the situation [and thought] that memorials walls were all gang members or drug related, glorifying drug dealers.
>
> We did murals for guys who were involved in that sort of thing, but . . . the whole concept [started when] we were painting and someone came to us and said: "Listen, my brother just passed away. Can you take a tag for him, you know, on your wall write 'rest in peace?'" . . . So you write the person's name and 'rest in peace'—simple enough. Then the next time we did one, we did a heart and a ribbon, put the guy's name, and the year he died. As time went on, they started becoming more and more complex memorials. . . . So, it sort of went from this little tag in the corner to, now, the whole wall is dedicated to this individual.
>
> In the beginning, it was just for people we knew—friends or close friends of relatives. Afterwards, we started doing walls for people we didn't know. Other people would see the work that we did, and come to us and say: 'Listen, my cousin passed away, or my brother-in-law just was killed,' or whatever. And we would be sitting down with these people we've never seen in our lives, never met this person, don't know anything about them. And we would sit down at a table with the family, [and] they would describe to us how this person was, what he was like, how they want him remembered, what were his hobbies, his likes, this and that, just so we could personalize this wall. . . . We were putting up poetry; they would give us photos; they would give us dates—you know, dates when he was born, dates when he died. Family members would write a few words . . . thoughts to express [themselves]. . . .
>
> We would design this whole mural and put it up, and it sort of became a way of the grieving process for them. Family and friends would come out while we were painting. . . . The funny thing is we don't know these people when we started out [but] by the time we finish the murals, we practically knew the persons' whole life story. As we're painting, the

friends and family are behind us talking, not directly to us, just aloud, just reminiscing about relationships that they had with the person. 'Remember the time when we went and did this or did that?' and you're painting, and you're listening, and sometimes you just break down and start crying. But by the time that you finished each wall, it was like you had more of a sense of who this person was.

It was crazy . . . for us it was a real emotional thing, because a lot of times, we would be doing these walls right when the emotions were still strong; when the person had passed away a week, two weeks ago. People are crying. . . . You're trying to paint, and you're listening to all this, and you're like 'wow'—it gets to you after a while. Memorial wall painting is definitely different—different experience than any other work we've done. It involves real people, involves emotions, it is just significant of what is happening around.[14]

As it had a decade earlier when graffiti artists used subway trains as their canvasses, the use of public wall space—albeit usually with the consent of the building owners—drew negative reactions from many people in the community, who felt the art works were glorifying drug dealers and others who were not positive role models for the neighborhood:

We had problems with the community board for some of the murals we've painted. We painted one image where the guy sold drugs for a living. His mother wanted us to paint him with machine gun, gold chains, a Lexus in the background, a woman actually looking like a prostitute standing on the corner! . . . She didn't want to hide the fact that her son led this lifestyle . . . that it led to his death. She wanted to show the kids in the neighborhood: Look this is the lifestyle my son lived; this is guy you're looking up to; and this is what you can expect as a result of living that lifestyle.

It got painted, but we had the community board after us for about a year to change it. [They were] fighting with us: 'You can't be glorifying drug dealers!' . . . But they are missing the whole message. . . . Why should we try to hide the facts when his own mother wanted people to know? And she wants to show them—maybe, if it is just one kid [who thinks] 'I don't want to end up a painting on a wall,' then it served its purpose.[15]

And, Bio added, as New Yorkers who had grown up in a tough neighborhood themselves, they were reluctant to be too judgmental:

Tats Cru's vibrant mural adorns a wall in the Graffiti Hall of Fame located in a Spanish Harlem schoolyard at Park Avenue and 106th Street. PHOTO BY NANCY GROCE, COURTESY SMITHSONIAN INSTITUTION.

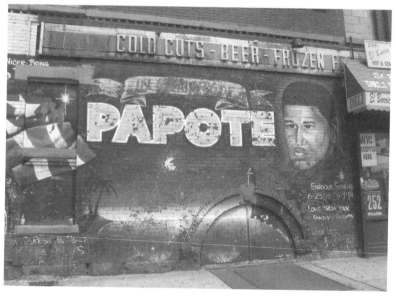

One of Tats Cru's early memorial walls continues to remind friends and neighbors of "Papote" on the corner of Lexington Avenue and 115th Street. PHOTO BY NANCY GROCE, COURTESY SMITHSONIAN INSTITUTION.

Tats Cru created murals with patriotic themes during the New York City program at the 2001 Smithsonian Folklife Festival. PHOTO COURTESY SMITHSONIAN INSTITUTION.

We felt these were not movie stars; they were not famous people. But they were loved, they had friends and family who loved them, so there was no reason why they shouldn't be remembered in the neighborhood. Who's to say why that type of thing is only reserved for the famous or for the rich? So, that's why we were out there doing what we had to do, regardless of what anybody was saying.[16]

Nevertheless, painting memorial walls started getting to Tats Cru. At one point, "BG was like, 'I don't know how many more of these walls I can take!'" In those days:

You [were] seeing all this, a lot of times young kids, guys your age, Latino or whatever, and you are seeing these are hard people . . . definitely hard people out there dying and going through these things. People were starting to recognize us and it was like, 'the memorial wall guys.' We would drive over to a neighborhood and everybody was, like, 'What are you doing over here, nobody died!'[17]

Fortunately, by the late 1990s, a drop in violence and fewer AIDS deaths made memorial walls less common, although a significant number were painted in the aftermath of the World Trade Center disaster in 2001. As a reflection of the newfound community respect that graffiti artists had won for their art during the previous decades, many of the 2001 memorial murals were commissioned by neighborhood improvement coalitions, business people, and fire houses.[18]

Today, Tats Cru is "thinking more on the commercial side. I mean we still do a few memorial walls a year, but it is not the main part of what we do." The acceptance of graffiti as a respected art form, both at a community and international level, is a source of pride. When Elena Martinez interviewed BG183 at Tats Cru's office and workshop in the Bronx, he told her:

> I was born and raised in the South Bronx, you know, all my life here. I still live four blocks away from here. . . . Now, when I walk by, I see people dig the graffiti art. We've painted every mural on the block. It feels good—people are labeling you an artist in the neighborhood, not like a vandal graffiti artist; someone that did bad. Now people will open [their] arms: 'Can you paint my house?'[19]

Tats Cru's complex and visually compelling pieces can now be seen throughout the city as well as in prestigious galleries and museums. They have toured internationally and are sought after lecturers at universities and art schools. We asked them if they thought that graffiti had been fully accepted and if their parents now approve of graffiti as their profession. "They have no choice at this point," said Bio:

> I mean, they're just like everyone else. They were like: 'What's wrong with you? Are you crazy painting on trains; writing your name on a wall; what is wrong with you?' Most people told us we were crazy. Even when we first . . . [started] painting legitimately for businesses and companies, we would still have police coming to harass us: 'Listen, you have to pack it up, I don't want you painting when I am on beat here.' We're like: 'What are you talking about? We're doing this with permission!' 'I don't care, I don't want to see this going on while I'm here.'
>
> Over the years it's gotten a little bit better because of all the publicity we've gotten, and we've been able to explain our point of view. But you still have a lot of people who don't see, or who don't take the time to realize that there is a difference: It is not the same as tagging your name on the side of someone's van to creating a one-hundred-foot mural with an idea and a theme. . . . So, every chance we get, we try to explain to people.

[Graffiti] can be a legitimate art form, a viable art form. Someone who chose to follow it can actually make a career from it. But there are still people who just don't agree because [of the way the] media has portrayed it for so many of years. They are just stuck in that thought process, they don't either have the time or just don't care to see beyond that. When they hear graffiti, it's vandalism, no respect for the law—that's the stigma that comes with it. Our whole thing is trying to change that perception.[20]

In addition to their commercial work, Tats Cru members are also actively involved in teaching art classes for neighborhood kids at The Point, a well-known community arts center in the south Bronx:

They come down and we give them papers and markers, and have them represent their name on paper. We teach them they don't really have to go bombing anymore out in the street. We show them that they could go to local stores, local landlords, and ask permission [to paint a mural]. And nine times out of ten in the Bronx, they will open their doors for kids out here to paint.[21]

URBAN PROFILE: LOCAL 28

"The Tin Knockers"

We build the lungs of the city.
—Nicholas Maldarelli

O NE OF THE GOALS of the Smithsonian's New York City documentation project was to create a historical record for the Smithsonian archives of artisans involved in a few of the many traditional construction crafts that have shaped New York's built environment. We have no shortage of architectural drawings, laws and codes regulating construction, tax records, pronouncements by architectural pundits, and dedication speeches by long-winded politicians. It would be wonderful if we also had first-hand accounts from, say, the surveyors who laid out the 1811 Grid Plan explaining how Manhattan Island looked as they worked their way uptown plotting out streets, blocks, and avenues, or could know the thoughts of the stonemasons who pieced together the giant piers of the Brooklyn Bridge in the 1880s, or could hear an interview with the iron workers who "topped off" the 1047-foot Chrysler Building in 1929 to create (at least for a few months) the tallest building in the world.

With this in mind, we sought out the members of Local 28 of the Sheet Metal Workers International, an old union that proudly points out that they are the ones who put the roofs on even the tallest skyscrapers.[1] The union had come to our notice when urban photographer extraordinaire Martha Cooper photographed their impressive float in the 1999 Labor Day Parade. The float, a stunning reproduction of the Manhattan skyline that features dozens of models of the city's most prominent buildings, was constructed from galvanized metal, "which is our main metal that we use in duct works."[2] In addition to the trailer-bed-sized miniature New York skyline, the union also exhibited a six-foot-tall traditional "tin man." Both had been made by apprentices at Local 28's training center in Jamaica, Queens. The float and the tin man were later brought to the Smithsonian Folklife Festival, accompanied by a delegation of apprentices and members of this dynamic union. In preparation for their visit, folklorist Elena Martinez from our sister organization City Lore: The New York Center for Urban Culture recorded a wonderful interview with Nicholas Maldarelli, a respected union leader, who had been given the responsibility of overseeing Local 28's training facility.[3] In fact, although he modestly neglected to mention the fact during his recorded interview, the school had been named the Nicholas Maldarelli Apprentice Training Center in his honor.

Elena began by asking Maldarelli to tell a little about himself. Like many other members of the union, he came from a family of "tin knockers":

> I'm a third generation in the sheet metal union. I started in 1953, January of 1953. I had a four year apprenticeship. . . . When I got out of my apprenticeship, I became a foreman. . . . I was super of the biggest shops in New York City. I was instrumental in supervising the erection and fabrication of the duct work in most of the office buildings in New York City. When I say most of the office buildings, I did an awful lot—I did my share of them. Jobs like One Liberty Plaza, I worked on the Twin Towers, I did the Meadowlands sport complex, I did Mount Sinai Hospital complex, and about fifteen other huge office buildings—sixty stories or larger.
>
> I was picked by Arty Moore, I guess around 1989, who was at the time the president of Local 28 . . . to be an instructor here at the [apprenticeship training] school. To show the kids, the apprentices, how to, you know—to give them what I know. At first I was a little hesitant about it, 'cause I was running big [jobs] out there. But after the first six months working with the apprentices of Local 28, and seeing what type of young people were coming into this Local, I really loved it. I loved teaching them; I loved watching their faces glow when they got the question right.

. . . It was a great feeling to give back what I knew; to pass it on to these young people.

I used to do a lot of artwork before I came into Local 28. And I started putting my artwork to metal, which I did when I became an instructor. They used to give me different difficult tasks, like making something for the Cardinal on St. Patrick's Day. And I would have to think of something to make: we made some challises for him and cups that he treasured. I did the whole St. Patrick's [Cathedral] in copper—you know, made a picture of that. Down in Washington, the International's President—we gave him a whole skyline of New York City made in copper. And various other little copper projects—and I did this all with the help of the apprentices. I used to come up with the idea, and I assigned each apprentice a certain part of the project. And they would love making these things representing Local 28 and giving them to special people. There's also a couple of pieces that are in museums, but the point I'm trying to say is that it wasn't actually me. I might have had the ideas, and I showed them how to do it, but it was the actual apprentices themselves that made the projects. Like these buildings . . . for the float. They came out pretty good.[4]

Members of the trade go by various nicknames: "tin knockers," "tin smiths," "tinkers." "Yeah, it's still us and we're proud [of them]." In addition to tin, tin knockers traditionally worked in a variety of metals, including copper, stainless steel, brass, galvanized iron, black iron, and lead. "Even Paul Revere—he was a tin knocker. You know, 'the British are coming?'—he was a tin knocker, so we're proud of him, too."[5]

Local 28 is particularly proud of its history. Its web page traces metal and metal smithing back to the prehistoric times and contains a good deal about medieval metalworkers craft guilds, as well as the complex history and importance of their local in New York and their union within the larger U.S. labor movement.[6] One of Maldarelli's favorite topics was the skill and contributions of Local 28 artisans:

Our men worked on the gargoyles in the '20s and '30s. . . . When the Chrysler Building was built [in 1929] our sheet metal workers put up those stainless-steel gargoyles. . . . We do stainless-steel work in kitchens all over New York City; big kitchens [with] all those beautiful stainless-steel hoods and stainless-steel tables—all done by the sheet metal workers! On some roofs we do a lot of lead work where they require a lead-coated copper. It's copper dipped into lead . . . that will last for two hundred years

One of the Chrysler Building's famous steel gargoyles, which were inspired by hood ornaments on Chrysler automobiles and crafted by members of Local 28. PHOTO BY GRAEME NORWAYS/ STONE COLLECTION/GETTY IMAGES.

or more, maybe even longer than that. Our jurisdiction is really quite a lot. We have a five-year apprentice program [and] it takes five years. They get as much study as a doctor does. So they're well worth their salary when they come out![7]

New York's sheet metal workers first unionized themselves in 1863. Although the union went through various permutations, Local 28 proudly traces its charter back to 1915. Today, there are close to 6,000 active union members, about 1,600 retirees, and 450 apprentices. Its jurisdiction includes metropolitan New York, including all of Long Island, and the five boroughs. "We did, at one time, have Jersey, and we kind of gave Jersey back to Jersey."[8]

Today, sheet metal workers work primarily on heating and air conditioning in buildings. "Our trade is very artistic," Maldarelli told us with pride:

We are the most highly skilled craft in the whole building industry. We are the only ones that still that take a piece of raw metal and shape it into products. Some of our duct works are pieces of art. . . . If you would see what we call a 'drop elbow' fitting and stuff like that, I mean, you could put some of these pieces in a museum. It's all laid out from a flat piece of metal. . . . It's like building a suit, but they do it out of metal. Each piece is cut, each piece is laid out, each piece is figured before it's even bent or rolled or shaped. So, a sheet metal worker is really an artist.[9]

But their trade's contributions are not limited to duct work:

Those beautiful copper roofs, the gold roofs you see up there? All done by sheet metal workers! It's all our work. . . . All those beautiful buildings that have these glows at night when they light them—all of that was all done by Local 28! We also do siding, not all of it, but we do a lot of the metal sidings that goes on these buildings. We do a lot of architectural details—church steeples, crosses; all those crosses that you see up there are all done by the sheet metal workers.[10]

We asked who came up with the idea of creating the union's New York skyline float, complete with miniature sheet metal buildings, for the Labor Day Parade:

We decided to do the whole the whole skyline to represent us. . . . All those buildings, without us, couldn't exist. You can build a building, [but] what good is it—these here are all sealed buildings! There's no windows that open up on these buildings. You need air in these buildings, and we're the ones that move the air around in these buildings! So, we thought that was a good project and we kicked it over with the instructors and everybody thought it was a great idea. The apprentices loved the idea. . . . They have creative minds. I'll show you some of the fittings that they do make; some of the simple fittings that we use in our work are very creative.[11]

In addition to the float, the apprentices had also created a tin man. This immediately caught our attention as folklorists because it is very ancient tradition for apprentice tinsmiths to make a tin man under the guidance of their masters to test or demonstrate their skills.[12] Perhaps because Local 28 members are accustomed to working on large projects, even their tin man was large: "Yeah, we scaled it up and made one six foot tall! We made different hats for him, we can change the hats. Now that we have a lot of sisters in our Local, we'd like to make a woman, you know, a lady, a tin lady."[13]

We asked Maldarelli if he thought apprentices knew much about the history of the trade. Yes, he did. In fact, he felt it was vital to the health of his profession that novice tin workers have a sense of belonging to an occupational community with a long history and common goals. And he was sure most of them did because historical information was imbedded in the apprenticeship program:

> The first thing, when they become a pre-apprentice, we have a six-week program that [teaches] the history of sheet metal working, when it started, going as far back as 3000 B.C. . . . [with] bronze. The silversmiths became the tin knockers. It goes back so far back in time, so we teach them that history.[14]

Talking to Maldarelli and other union members, we found that they stressed not only solidarity with their union, but also a sense of accomplishment in the union's ability to diversify its membership in recent years. Like many other construction unions, until fairly recently the ethnic and racial makeup of union membership did not reflect the city's population. About thirty years ago, with outside pressure from politicians and the courts, this began to change.[15] African Americans, members of other minority communities, and women were brought on as apprentices and became full-fledged members. In recent years there has been an influx of Caribbean and Latino tin workers. We were repeatedly told that in addition to participating in the annual Labor Day Parade, there were a "bunch of [ethnic] clubs in our union," and they borrow the float for events such as the Hispanic Day Parade, Brooklyn's Caribbean Parade, and the Puerto Rican Day Parade. Maldarelli took this issue seriously:

> I think our trade has made enormous moves in this. . . . Everybody gets together. I'm proud of this union—It's a coalition of everybody and we're all one. We're all brothers and sisters, and in the true meaning of brothers and sisters. The way I feel is the way this union runs. So, when they have parades, we have everybody. When I go to that Caribbean Parade, I love it. They just had the parade up in Harlem; we had a big contingent of Local 28 people that went up there. Puerto Rican Day, they used our float. . . . Yes, we do get involved in all the parades, because our union is made up of all ethnic, you know, different types of people that are just beautiful.[16]

There was so much else that Maldarelli wanted us to know about the Sheet Metal Workers. After all, he and his colleagues were the people who capped the New York skyline—he repeatedly pointed out that nobody went higher than they did. He hoped that the average New Yorker would pay more attention to the work of his fellow tinkers. But his most important message seemed to be that the young apprentices he was training to carry on his trade, his father's trade, and his grandfather's trade, should take pride in their work:

> The thing I like to tell them . . . You know, when you work with your hands you're kind of just like a laborer. If you work with your hands and your mind, then you're pretty much a craftsman. But, if you work with your hands, and your mind, and your heart—like the sheet metal worker does—then you're an artist![17]

THE SIXTH BOROUGH

New York and the Subway

M ASS TRANSIT is New York City's sixth borough. It is one of the most important factors that shape and unite the metropolis. Each day it fulfills the needs of more than 5 million area residents. And at the heart of the New York transit system is the subway. The greater part of the subway, which celebrated its one hundredth birthday on October 27, 2004, was built over the course of three decades by several competing private companies, but because of its importance to the economic viability and social structure of New York, the lines were eventually acquired by the city. Today, the system, which operates 24/7 every day of the year, is run by the Metropolitan Transit Authority (MTA) and is supplemented by an extensive network of MTA buses, ferries, and one charmingly toy-like aerial tram. Approximately 70 percent of Americans who ride mass transit each day do so in New York City. Unlike other U.S. cities in which members of the upper and middle classes commute in the isolated splendor of their own cars, most New Yorkers use "the trains," the buses, and the ferries at least twice a day.

There are any number of facts available about the New York subway: It is the world's largest system with 714 miles of track along 244 miles of routes.

There are twenty separate lines and 468 stations—of which only 277 are below ground. The deepest lines run some 180 feet below the streets of Manhattan; the highest station on the elevated portion of the F & G lines at Smith and 9th Street soars 120 feet above the Gowanus section of Brooklyn and offers stunning views of the Manhattan skyline. Every day, six hundred trains transport approximately 4.5 million people to jobs, schools, entertainment, and errands. Individual train lines are designated either by numbers (1, 2, 3, 4, 5, 6, 7, or 9) or letters (A, B, C, D, E, F, G, J, K, L, M, N, Q, R, S, V, or Z).[1] To avoid confusion, especially on transit workers' radios, which in the old days often had less than clear reception, nicknames developed for the different lines. As train operator Sandra Lane recalled:

> I remember we used to do that. The Rock & Roll for the RR—[now simplified to the single 'R']. C for 'Charlie'—we still do that. The J is Johnny, the M is Mary, N for Nancy. Boy train is the B; A is Apple; E is Echo. Most of the names that would be hard to distinguish on the radio. . . . N and M would be difficult . . . Nancy, Mary . . . so that's why they do that. A lot over the radio would be very difficult. . . . And then the number trains are no problem.[2]

The city's longest subway line is the A train, the one celebrated in Duke Ellington's 1941 recording. It's possible to board the A at its terminus at 208th Street in northern Manhattan's Inwood neighborhood and ride it for thirty-two miles to Far Rockaway, Queens. Riders who "Take the A Train" from end to end start their journey in the dark underground tunnels of Manhattan, are whisked under the East River and through the "open cut" tracks of central Brooklyn, and eventually find themselves on the elevated sunlit tracks of Queens. Beyond Ozone Park in deepest, darkest Queens, the A train turns south and crosses decidedly nonurban marshes and through the undeveloped reedy wilderness of the Jamaica Bay Wildlife Refuge. It barrels through the fishing villages and hamlets on Broad Channel island, treating riders to a landscape that would not look out of place on the Jersey Shore. Finally, accompanied by sea gulls and herons, it crosses a series of low bridges spanning the open water of Jamaica Bay and ends its run on the off-shore island of Far Rockaway. From the elevated stations that are the A's last stops, you can see sandy beaches and the endless waters of the Atlantic Ocean. It's quite a ride. Locals sometimes pack a lunch.

But the subway is more than trains, stations, and tracks. Like all other aspects of city life, the subway could not operate without the skills and knowledge of thousands of transit workers. More than thirty thousand people work for the MTA and it was their stories that the Smithsonian documentation project set out to capture. Listening to them talk about their jobs and their experiences gave us a better sense of how the city itself works. Among the many people we spoke with, we were lucky to find a number of particularly eloquent guides who shared their stories about working in the legendary system.[3]

One of our key informants was Torin Reid, a Bronx-born New Yorker who has had a lifelong fascination with trains. As a child, he "had model trains and stuff like that."[4] After spending some time in the military, he went to work for Amtrak, but in 1988 he traded in the long-distance allure of the Amtrak trains for a job with New York's MTA. Today, after years of hard work, he has been promoted from a conductor—the person whose primary responsibility is to open and close the doors at each stop and make announcements—to "train operator" or "motorman"—the person responsible for driving subway trains.[5] A thoughtful man, who is also a talented photographer and published author, with an impressive resume of great subway photos and stories about the trains, Reid clearly loves his work:

> I enjoy driving the trains. When you have model trains, you end up wanting more. The subway to me was the biggest, baddest set of electric trains you could possible have. The ultimate in electric trains. So, I thought at the time working for the subway would be a good choice for myself, personally.[6]

Reid has given a lot of thought to what makes the New York City subway unique:

> I've worked all the lines, all the different lines. So, I've had a chance to see a good cross-section of New York. In the twelve years I've worked on the subway, I've come to realize [there is] a symbiosis between New Yorkers and the subway. . . . I've traveled to some other cities in Europe and the States—it's not the same somehow. There's a little bit of it in Paris and there's a little bit of it in Boston . . . [but] many of the other cities, the subway systems are simply too new—too new as in thirty or forty years. . . . Cities like Washington and even San Francisco, the subways there empty out at night. Once the rush hour is gone, the hallways are empty, devoid of life. People seem to leave and gravitate to something on the surface. But, New York [subways] . . . have a life, not just people traveling around.[7]

Queens resident Lane, another train operator and key informant, spoke to us at length about what it was like to work in the subway. She was enthusiastic

Elevated subway lines, like this one in Queens, sometimes give passengers and subway workers a magnificent view of the urban skyline. Motorman Reid took this photo in the late 1990s. PHOTO BY TORIN REID. REPRODUCED WITH PERMISSION.

that she had recently been transferred from the underground F line to the J, which began its run near her home in Flushing, Queens, and looped through Brooklyn and into southern Manhattan. For most of its run, the J is an outdoor, elevated line:

> It is a high seniority line. I'm older now and I'm spoiled. I don't want to be far from my front door. And the line, being that it goes outside in the summer, most [motormen] want it. And in the winter, they probably go to an indoor line, like the E line or the R line. Something indoors—away from the elements. I stay with the J year round.[8]

We asked if it was better to drive an underground line, or if she preferred an elevated route?

> Well, [elevated] feels less hazardous to your health, actually, because of the steel dust and other factors like that. Lack of daylight—you have no concept of time when you're underground constantly. And it's somewhat

depressing, actually. The only light you see is when you come into the stations. You don't know what the weather is. Most people prefer to be outside.[9]

When he was initially interviewed by the Smithsonian in 2000, before the World Trade Center disaster, Reid seconded Lane's love of working the elevated lines. He was especially taken by the views and the fresh air:

> You get a look at the neighborhoods and stuff like that. Brooklyn has the best views; the F, B, and D lines have the best views. Springtime—old MacDonald Avenue is probably the best 'cause you open a window up and you can get the air, you can get a cross-breeze going. You just drive the train and there is a high degree of satisfaction with the job. When you are on the F line going towards Manhattan, on the F, the B, and the D lines— exclude the N because the N is in the cut—you have the World Trade Center on your left and the Empire State Buildings on your right and the train is going to go right between them. . . . On a good day, where there's not a lot of smog, you see Manhattan from the elevated structure.[10]

Some subway workers, especially those whose assigned lines or daily responsibilities did not take them to the elevated portions of the lines, sometimes concentrate so closely on schedules and duties that they lose track of time. It's easy to do because,

> All you see is stations, station lights, darkness. You don't know if it's night or day—other than you basically know, because you know what shift you're working. . . . But you don't know when the sun's come up or gone down.[11]

Even when working on the underground lines, Reid said:

> You are keeping track of your time 'cause you're looking for your breaks [at the end of each run]. A lot of times you lose out on your break time because there are track workers on the tracks . . . who want to repair something.[12]

Despite being occasionally confused about the time and out of touch with the weather, most subway employees agreed that they generally knew exactly where they were because all the stations look different:

After a while you become accustomed to knowing what station it is by the way the light comes in, by the way it's curved—certain factors about that station. You have to know a lot of the physical aspects of it. And then, we have to know where to stop.[13]

We asked if the stopping place was different at each platform.

Yes, because they're made differently. You would assume that you always just go to the end, but that's not true. It depends on the length of your train, the length of the station, and [whether] you have a full train or a cut train. Sometimes you carry less cars than in normal service. They tend to do that late at night and mid-day—non-rush hours, non "hours of commission."[14]

Some lines have a reputation for being rather boring to drive. To Reid, the F line was one of these:

On the F line, a station's a station. On the F, I make like thirty-eight stops on one trip—that's an hour and forty minutes and you're concentrating for an hour and forty minutes. [The stations] almost sometimes blur together. The only really memorable station is West 4th Street, where there's 2 four-track trunk lines from the original IND. They converge at the southern end of West 4th Street and there's trains on three or four levels at the same time and you see trains going every which way.[15]

As Reid had previously told us:

Sure, I know every station. Yet, if I am driving the train and you knock on my door and say 'how many stops is Houston Street?' or 'how many stops is Second Avenue?' I couldn't tell you. [When] you drive the train, you get into a zone, you just see the stations. You don't even look at the names—you just know where to stop. You look for the 'ten-car marker' or the 'eight-car marker,' or whatever sized train you have. You just look and make the station stop. You're just driving this train to the end of the line. . . . Most of the night jobs are hard jobs. Many of the trains make local stops at night. So, it is just stop, after stop, after stop. You get into a zone—so, you don't know where you are, but you know you are getting there.[16]

Ceramic mosaic tiles on wall of 51st Street subway station on Manhattan's East Side guide riders through busy transfer point. PHOTO BY COMSTOCK/ COMSTOCK IMAGES COLLECTION/ GETTY IMAGES.

Knowing exactly where you are is helped by the fact that many stations, especially on the older lines, are decorated by elaborate ceramic tiles. Street numbers or avenue names are often spelled out amid ceramic dingbats and attractive arrangements of floral tiles. Some of the most beloved tiles make colorful pictorial references to historical events that took place at or near that specific stop. For example, the beaver tiles at the Astor Place stop on the number 6 train remind New Yorkers that nineteenth-century millionaire John Jacob Astor, after whom the square above was named, made his fortune in the North West Coast fur trade. A ferry boat tile in the Fulton Street stop commemorates inventor Robert Fulton and the first successful steamboat line in the United States. Recently, the MTA has commissioned elaborate new art installations throughout the subway system. Perhaps most impressive is the West 81st Street

C and E station, located beneath the American Museum of Natural History on Central Park West. Here, the walls and floors of the station's two levels are playfully inlaid with two-dimensional casts of dinosaur bones and colorful mosaic images of their modern descendants. Completed by a team of artists in 1999, the station's evolutionary-inspired theme reflects the treasures awaiting visitors in the museum above. At the West 68th Street station on the number 1 line, mosaics of characters from famous operas echo the existence of the Metropolitan and City opera houses overhead at Lincoln Center for the Performing Arts. Further downtown, at the 14th Street stop on the Eight Avenue Line, a metal alligator by the renowned sculpture Tom Otterness peaks out of a manhole cover, menacing an array of small, sinister creatures that peer out at riders from corners and crevices throughout the station.[17]

CITY THROUGH THE WINDSHIELD

The transit system is the great equalizer for all New Yorkers, and perhaps because of the varied ridership, most subway workers believe they have seen it all. Even if they haven't, most of them have at least a few great stories. According to one motorman, "It's like a safe looking glass into the people, into the grittiness of New York. Through the subway, the people get a concentrated taste of what New York is like."[18] Transit engineer Bruce Alexander had an interesting take on the subway:

> I do ride [the trains] everyday, and yes, it is a museum. It's a living, rolling, active museum—we carry 4 million people a day. . . . Below 42nd Street the city grows by one or 1.5 million a day; we bring 2 million people to work in the morning, and those same 2 million people, well, we've got to bring them home at night. We're not allowed to lose too many of them.[19]

"I've worked all the shifts," Reid told us:

> At 3:00 or 4:00 in the morning the trains are a balance of those going home after a long night of partying and those going to work to open up the city for the new day: Yeah, the party people. There's the party people that go out. . . . There's those who just want to be out, or kids who are out without permission. Sometimes, the sad part is those that are out and nobody cares that they are out. Yes, there are those who are out catting or doing what they aren't supposed to do. And then there are those who just work at night, just night workers, night shift people.[20]

Subway workers agree that 99 percent of their riders are just well-behaved unremarkable people, focused on getting to work or to school or visiting friends and relatives. But they're not the ones that inspire the most memorable stories. If there are "8 million stories in the naked city," transit workers probably know a lot of them. "Sometimes we get numb," engineer Alexander told us, "but every once in a while you'll see something that will bring the child back in some of us."[21]

Stations often reflect the composition and attractions of the neighborhoods they serve. For example, during the day in mid-town Manhattan: "We have people going to work in suits and ties and dresses and almost formal wear."[22] But then:

> At night on the West Side, on Broadway going towards Lincoln Center, you'll see people going to the opera in tuxedos—you can also see them going to the opera in short pants, too.[23]

Some neighborhoods seem to have a higher degree of characters than others. Lane had two favorite stops: "I remember 14th Street because I might get to see spiked hair. . . . I have seen more colors of the rainbow in people's hair at 14th Street."[24] But it was West 4th Street, a large hub station in the heart of Greenwich Village serviced by numerous lines, which was the subject of one of her favorite stories:

> I like West 4th because that's where all the characters are. When I pull into West 4th Street, I can see someone six-foot tall with thirteen-size shoes—in a dress. . . . I can't wait to stop so I can see whatever I'm going to see. And every time I think I've seen it all, someone shows me this is definitely not true![25]

For example, she was pulling into West 4th Street one Halloween eve when:

> I saw Bat Man walking across the tracks. Someone just walking the tracks in a Batman costume! OK. I have a radio. My rule book says I'm supposed to call in anything unusual. I'm going to call control center and say 'Batman just walked across West 4th Street, across three tracks?' I know if I call in Bat Man running back and forth in front of my train, I'm going in for a blood alcohol test immediately. And then they'll put me somewhere. So as long as the train was in the station, this man just went across four tracks, flinging his cape back and forth 'til he got tired of it and then he went upstairs, I

guess, to partake in the [Halloween] parade. . . . I'm standing there thinking 'I know I saw Bat Man, but I'm not calling Bat Man in.'[26]

Because so few New Yorkers own their cars or trucks, the objects that people transport around the city on mass transit are impressive and occasionally surprising. It's not unusual to enter a car and see a wedding dress hanging from the hand straps, bicycles, a window washer going to or from work surround by his buckets and poles, or a double bass. Small pieces of furniture are a given—end tables, lamps, chairs, and especially "street finds"—objects left on the curbside by one New Yorker for garbage pickup that another New Yorker believes is the perfect treasure to enhance their home. Street finds, including healthy-sized pieces of heavy furniture—are frequently discovered late at night, especially by New Yorkers on their way home after the bars close. (Admire a cabinet, chair, or desk in a New York apartment, and you might be proudly informed that "I found it on the street!") All this and more finds its way into the subway. It could be worse: narrow subway stairs filter out at least some items. "I have a friend who's a bus driver," Tony Palombella told us, "who stopped this guy trying to carry a *mattress* onto his bus. The guy was going to move his apartment!"[27]

Crime does occur on the trains, but the underground crime rate is actually lower than the city's surface crime, and both have fallen tremendously since the early 1990s. Disturbances are more common than actual crimes. On weekdays, the noise and chaos level rises precipitously for about half an hour each afternoon around 3:00 when elementary and high schools throughout the city release tens of thousands of students with a day's worth of pent-up energy. Wise New Yorkers often delay their journeys by a few minutes to miss "The Children's Hour."

Conductors, who are responsible for keeping an eye on the passengers, as well as making announcements and opening car doors on the appropriate side at each station, occasionally have to intervene if they spot trouble. Most of them have a proven technique to break up the occasional disagreement or scuffles. "First, you tell them to stop," said Reid:

> Then, if they refuse, you threaten to stop the train and call the police. This gets the other passengers involved in the process. You wait for somebody—there'll always be one soul—who will shout 'Cut it out!' or 'We gotta go to work!' or 'I want to go home.' . . . Once that happens, that usually takes care of whatever problems there are in the subway.[28]

On such occasions, Lane also gave New Yorkers high marks for being helpful:

I have a very appreciative public. And I'm very surprised. Because you hear so much about New Yorkers. . . . The reputation that New Yorkers have does not match the true New Yorker. They're very helpful. There's been situations where people have been ill, and they've been very helpful. There's been trouble on the train, and my passengers have come to my assistance. I've had teenagers—they're sometimes rowdy—and people have put them off the train where I can't do it. I've had it happen quite a few times, because they want to get to work. I will make an announcement that, 'OK, this train is being delayed by some youths.' And people will come and get them off the train before the police even get there—just throw them off.[29]

Transit engineer Alexander vividly recalled a disturbance that took place many years ago when he was working late one night, checking to see if a door system he and his colleagues had redesigned was functioning properly. They were testing it at midnight on an F train leaving Times Square, and as they pulled out of the station:

Everything was working great. Picked up a full load of passengers—by this time, it's midnight or maybe even later . . . and the train is packed. An eleven-car, 550-foot subway car pulling out of Times Square and we have what is called a 'swinging load'—that means they're packed cheek to jowl and everyone has their hand on a strap. We had a full train. Well, the next stop is Fifth Avenue. And this fellow gets on—twenty, twenty-five years old—fit and trim as a marine. In fact, he was in a marine fatigue uniform—except the hat that he had on, he had a pacifier hanging down, and a feather in the back. I got a look and I'm saying, 'this is one of our NY characters.' (Remember when Bill Cosby was a lot younger, one of his skits was 'There's One in Every Car?' Well, this was one of those fellows.)

As we were moving out of Fifth Avenue . . . he took off his jacket, rolled it up very tightly. And then proceeded to get down on the floor of the subway car with this tightly rolled jacket between his elbows, and he starts doing a belly crawl along the floor! You'd think there were live bullets going across—he literally slithered across the floor. And he would go and he would look at people, just like a snake. And, of course, New Yorkers, you learn not to make eye contact. And here it is: it's after 12:00 at night, and people are getting scared.

The conductor was ready to take the train out of service, and I said, no, let's see what we can do. I moved through car and told people to leave.

They started to clear out. I locked the door at the [one] end. . . . He was so focused on what he was doing he didn't realize that there's nobody left on the car. I came back and I locked the other door. Now he's stuck. We stopped at Lexington Avenue and because I'd flipped the circuit breakers on that car, that car didn't open up its doors. Now he realizes 'something's gone wrong!' People came in on the other cars. Now he went bananas! He actually started swinging holding on the straps, kicking the windows in the doors. I have never seen an athlete like this! He was, like, in the Olympics.

Well, the conductor called his motorman, the motorman radioed ahead. We had a whole contingent of police at the next big station, Queensborough Plaza. By this time, he realized what was going on. [A policeman] went into the car, he got out—and took off like a gazelle down Queensborough Plaza station. (Well, as one of the advertisements says, for New Yorkers 'wait is a four letter word.') Now here's a man who delayed maybe a thousand people going home late at night. Well, what happened? They say New Yorkers are not going to help you. Well, I learned something that night. Half a car load of people took off after this guy. The cop that showed up that was in charge was kind of short, and kind of dumpy, and a little too old—in no way, shape, or form is he going to take this guy. Well, half a car load of men and women took after him, they tackled him, they dragged him back. Two people grabbed one arm, two people grabbed another arm, one on each leg and we literally carried him. . . . The cop took off his handcuffs, cuffed him onto the station banister. And at that point, a smile crossed this man's face. He accomplished what he wanted. He was now in custody. Although they were going to arrest him and put him in a cell for a while, they had to feed him. He had gotten his meal ticket—his dinner was taken care of that night. We left him, people got back on the train, train went back into service, and the test continued.[30]

Some of the 8 million stories in the naked city actually involve naked people, and a few of these take place on the subway: "I was a conductor on a [number] 4 train a couple of years ago," one motorman recalled,

We were coming into Jay Street/Borough Hall (Brooklyn) real late at night. It was summer and it was really hot. And there's this naked guy standing on the platform—just standing there waiting to get on my train! I'm thinking what should I do? So I lean my head out of the car window, and I yell down to him: 'Hey, you, you can't get on this train!' And he says, 'Yeah, why?' And I says, 'You didn't pay your fare!' And he shouts back, 'How do you know?' So I told him: 'You ain't got no pockets.' And he just nods, steps off, and goes up the stairs.[31]

"I had one on the F train," Lane told us,

> She took off her clothes at 4:00 in the afternoon in the doorway of the F train at Rockefeller Center at rush hour. She got completely nude. And she was so *nasty* looking. It's like—no offense to Rosie O'Donnell—but if Rosie O'Donnell was to strip and she was a little taller, she would have been this woman. If Rosie had been about 5'11" before she went on Weight Watchers, this is our woman. And I would give Rosie O'Donnell her clothes back. . . . So, she's standing there greeting people as the doors open. She had gotten uncomfortable because the car did not have air conditioning, so she just decided to take her clothes off. Now she's cool. She just took them off and she stood in the doorway of the F train. Police came and removed her.[32]

Reid also had a problem on his train several years ago, one that involved a couple of women who wanted to make a political statement.

> Several women decided to protest because in the summer time men were able to take off their shirts. And so they protested that 'we should be able to take of our tops and ride topless.' And they had, like, a demonstration. Two women rode the subway topless for a while. New York subway riders are famously able to ignore everything that you see in the subway car. So unfortunately, they were older women and they needed their bras, shall we say. . . . They took their tops off on the Lexington Avenue subway at rush hour and got absolutely no reaction.[33]

Many stories told by subway workers involved technical aspects of their jobs. For example, soon after she started her job as a train operator, Lane was crossing the Williamsburg Bridge, a magnificent structure that soars high above the East River between Manhattan and Brooklyn. The subway rails lie on open ties, which cross the bridge without a roadway below. Through the ties, you can look down hundreds of feet to the turbulent waters of the East River. Not a place for someone with acrophobia, like Lane:

> I was crossing the Williamsburg Bridge and my train went into emergency [stop]. After getting off and investigating, I didn't find [anything].

Someone had tossed a frozen pumpkin onto the tracks. We have a device underneath the train that puts it in emergency. And I had to get off the train, because this pumpkin put the train in emergency, walk the length of the train. I never saw pumpkin because, Lord knows, I wasn't looking for it. I get on the train, I take it out [of emergency]; and it puts it into emergency a second time.

At that time I had a definite fear of heights. And the Williamsburg Bridge is the greatest place to overcome this fear. I stepped out. According to rules, once you don't find anything, you have to walk another train length [behind] to try and find the object that tripped your train. I broke the rules. I stood behind the train and I thought—'Oh Lord, how long would it take me to walk back there?' I counted and walked back in, and I told command that I didn't find it.

The person behind me—his train came up to a pumpkin. It had a stripe mark—there's a piece underneath the train that places it into emergency when it comes upon something. And the stripe mark was there on the pumpkin. It was a frozen pumpkin! He brought it in and I reported it into command center. *They* thought it was hilarious! They wanted to know if I was planning to make a pumpkin pie. Whereas, I had a fear of heights and being on the Williamsburg Bridge, in the cold, the comment wasn't funny. It wasn't funny at all. Nowadays, it would be considered politically incorrect—because they would be indicating because I was female I wanted to cook. . . . They didn't have a lot of women then. If they did it now, I could press charges![34]

PUBLIC SAFETY: ACCIDENTS, DELAYS, AND GETTING THERE ON TIME

Public safety is a paramount concern for all MTA employees. As MTA engineer Alexander told an audience at the 2001 Smithsonian Festival:

I don't mean to get too serious with this, but we operate 625 trains at any one time in rush hour; we operate over twenty thousand train trips a day; we carry 4 million people, and we do it safely and we're proud of it. But every once in a while, we have some interesting experiences—we have derailments, we have collisions, [years ago] we had a car actually crack in half like an egg when you go to fry it on a Sunday morning for breakfast! One train hit another train because as it was coming around a bend, the other train was sitting there—the motorman had neglected to follow procedures. Luckily, there was nobody on board. The first train was actually moved one entire car length! We have scary stories like this, but they don't happen very often. But when they do, they are spectacular, in a very negative aspect.[35]

Sometimes, problems come not from the old equipment, but from newer untested systems, like a now-resolved problem with subway doors that occurred some years ago.

The job I was working on had to do with doors. And you've all heard the phrase, 'Power corrupts, absolute power corrupts absolutely?' Well, we added a third piece to that: 'Automatic features lead to automatic failures, automatically.' Yes, we had a door problem. They opened when we wanted them to, and sometimes they opened when we didn't want them to. . . . They had made it too streamlined, too automatic. . . . Did it happen very often? No. But it happened often enough that it embarrassed upper management.

And the story is that they opened on the F train at Bergen Street—all the doors opened up on one side of the train. Well, luckily, they were only going at about five miles an hour. And one woman actually started to fall out, and thank god, there was a fellow standing right nearby and he reached out and he grabbed her, and he pulled her back in, so she wasn't hurt. But not five minutes before, that train was coming off the Smith and 9th Street station on the viaduct over the Gowanus Canal. And it's about 120 feet in the air! Well, you can imagine what would have happened. We would have been in trouble. Needless to say what would have happened or could have happened to one of our passengers. I mean, the Coast Guard really would have been upset at us for dropping people into a navigable waterway![36]

Although accidents are rare, delays are not unknown.

It's one thing when we have a train delay in the morning, they only have to explain to their bosses—but at the end of the day when we get what we call a 'swinging load' and they're packed in cheek to jowl—there can be 250 people on board that car, it's really bad. And it wasn't all that long ago [the system] wasn't air conditioned: And you can imagine a June evening at about 5:00, and it's a Friday. [Riders are] getting out of work, and they get into one of these [subway cars], and they get about half way home— and they're in the Steinway Tunnel [under the East River] and the lights go out. Needless to say, they're not very happy. *Our freight goes sour real fast.*

The reality is there is no room for failure because we're carrying people and people have special needs. Our job is to take care of their needs.[37]

In fact, although train reliability has improved greatly in recent years, New Yorkers often allow each other ten minutes "I got caught on the trains" leeway at the start of appointments. Nowadays, although delays do occur, it's equally likely that the trains are used as an excuse by someone who has just misjudged their time. Commuters caught on a delayed train can note down the number of their subway car and give that number to their employers, who, in turn, are able to call a special MTA phone number to confirm their employees' "why-I'm-so-late" story.

SUICIDES AND FATALITIES

Subway work is dangerous and perhaps because of its iconic status, the New York subway system does attract a fair number of suicides, suicide attempts, and near misses. Thirty to forty people die on New York subway tracks each year. In the past, most of them were track workers whose responsibilities demanded that they work in the dangerously narrow confines of subway tunnels and bridges. Although the safety record for track workers has improved considerably in recent years, one MTA employee reminded us that for many years, there were more fatalities among track workers than New York City police officers. (Each year, another handful of accidents are also a result of a particularly stupid New York form of entertainment known as "subway surfing." Practiced primarily by teenager boys with more machismo than common sense, subway surfing involves clambering onto and riding on top of the subway trains that run on the elevated or "open cut" lines through Brooklyn, Queens, and the Bronx. The frequency of tunnels, low hanging equipment, and wires tends to severely limit the life spans of subway surfers. Many locals think the astonishing lack of judgment displayed by subway surfers makes them excellent candidates for the Darwin Awards, anyway.

It is a bit reassuring that some of the goriest and best known tales about people meeting terrible fates on the New York City subway seem to be "urban legends"—tales that sound as if they ought to be true, but probably are not. Not a few of these urban legends began as works of fiction before repeated retellings gave them the patina of truth. For example, there is the frequently repeated tale of the man who jumps or is pushed from a subway platform into the path of an on-coming train and winds up wedged in the few inches of space between the train and the platform. Fully conscious, he requests a beer and a cigarette and bystanders rush to fulfill his request since everyone at the scene knows that he will die immediately as soon as the train is moved.

Reid told us another story that might be true, but seems apocryphal because of its pre-holiday timing and neat symmetry:

> This person jumped in front of the train the day before Christmas a few years ago at 63rd Drive [Rego Park, Queens]. And the person got run over, but wasn't injured—he was between the rails. The person got out from under the train, jumped up, and was hit by the express train that came by [on the adjoining track]. A week after, I think it was, the person's spouse did the same thing, but was run over by the local.[38]

Unfortunately, a number of transit employees know that at least some of these tales are true because they were personally involved in such an "incident." Lane, one of the key Smithsonian informants, was a lovely, intelligent woman who did an exceptional job as a presenter at the 2001 Festival before her untimely death a few months later. Originally from Pennsylvania, she had a background in special education and school teaching before she became a subway motorman. During her years as an MTA train operator, she had the misfortune of being involved in two fatal incidents. The first involved an apparently homeless man who had been drinking and may or may not have known he was putting himself in danger by being on the tracks. The second, several years later, involved a young man in his twenties and was much more upsetting.

> I was leaving Euclid Avenue, northbound on the A train—going towards Manhattan. It's a very fast track coming into Broadway/East New York. As soon as you hit this light, there's a staircase there. Young man, twenty-six years old, jumped just as the train came into the station. August of '92; decided he had had enough. He gives me eye contact, smiles, and he goes in the air. No chance, no chance. Indoctrinated as much as I am by the Transit Authority, when he hits the air, I put it in emergency. I go to the PA system, and I say: 'Due to a passenger injury'—the guy hadn't been hit yet—'This train will be going out of service when it comes to a stop.' I place the train in emergency, he hits, his body rides outside of the train for about half a platform, drops off. And at the middle of the station, the train comes to a complete stop—because when you put it in emergency, the weight and the speed does not let it stop [immediately]. . . . I could see his body right underneath my windshield. I'm no longer in control; the train's going to slide because of the speed. So I'm making my announcement

that when it stops, everybody has to get off. The young man that I hit, he didn't die immediately, but he died later [in the hospital] from internal injuries.[39]

Sometimes the train operator can stop the train in time, but as subway engineer Alexander explained, the laws of physics are against them:

One of these cars weighs about seventy-five thousand pounds—like thirty-seven tons. It can carry another fourteen or fifteen tons of people. So each car is about fifty tons; and each train is about ten cars—so you're talking about five hundred thousand pounds of mass. It's going to slow down at a 'three rate'—three miles per hour per second. . . . These cars can do thirty-five, forty, fifty miles an hour. Now at forty-five miles an hour, slowing down at three miles per hour per second, it's going to take fifteen seconds to stop the train after the motorman puts it into emergency. . . . So imagine barreling into a station—because normally they come in full speed and about half way into the station and then they'll take a full service brake. As soon as they see something go wrong, they're going to dump the train into emergency. And at that point, there is *nothing* that the motorman can do except wait those ten or fifteen seconds . . . and just hope that those brakes will stop that train before he gets to that person. . . .[40]

Lane was eloquent about how difficult the suicide of the young man that morning at Euclid Avenue had been for her. Speaking eight years after the event, she admitted:

I've had nightmares since around the anniversary date. And his eyes will live forever—[his] giving me the eye contact . . . I don't know—people just think it's a quick way to die. They usually get maimed more than they get killed. It's something that the public doesn't think about when they do these things. They don't realize they're having an impact on a human being. It's not a machine or a system; it's an individual operating this vehicle. It does have a lasting effect.[41]

Today, when such accidents happen, the authorities have come to understand that the train operators and conductors involved also may have been traumatized. After a routine test—to make sure they have no drugs or alcohol in their systems—they are usually given several days of leave. Years ago, the person hit actually had to die at the scene for the motorman to be given leave. After

Lane's accident, she "had to take the train from the scene" back to the yard. Then "they took me for a blood/alcohol test and found out that I was clean." That evening she was called back in to work an evening shift: "They didn't realize, I guess, that it does have an impact. . . . Just hitting someone and watching it is traumatic."[42]

Unlike Lane, motorman Reid has never hit anybody with his train, but he did have a close call:

> I'll tell you a good story. I had a guy—in fact, the day before Thanksgiving—there was a guy. I had the F train and I was coming into Jay Street station [in Brooklyn]—Now this is a crowded station, it's a well used station. And when you enter the station there's a slight curve; and then it goes downhill a little bit. I was coming in pretty fast and this cat was on the track! He's on the tracks, his arms are on the platform—the platform's about four feet high when you stand on the tracks. I saw him and I blew the horn and I put the train into emergency. . . . You place the train in emergency just by habit. You don't even look at it. You just wrap [the handle] around the opposite way; it actually goes *past* emergency to handle off. And the train seemed to jump—like lunge at the person. . . . And the guy looks at me, looks at train, and he takes his last, best jump—and he made it! Thank god, I missed him! Turns out the guy had *one* leg and—I don't know—maybe his crutch fell to the subway track, but I don't know why he was down there. And he made his last best jump to try to get out of the way of the train, and he got up to the platform, with his crutch, and rolled over![43]

Perhaps it happened too fast for fellow passengers to react—Reid never heard the full story—but what upset him was the lack of action by the bystanders:

> The thing that struck me was, there were at least one hundred people there and nobody tried to help him. It's just people with their briefcases and pocketbooks, and they all look down—they are all watching it happen! I thought you might see an arm or something try to grab him or something. But they just looked, man, it was like Rome—had the fist extended whether the finger goes up or down. I was like wow![44]

Like Lane, Reid was still shaken by the incident years later. It may or may not have been a suicide attempt, but:

I consider myself a secondary victim because it scared the shit out of me. You know, your heart stops and jumps, and you stop and consider for a second and wipe your brow and say, 'Oh shoot!' . . . Even then, suicides are hard to talk about, because you are devastated when that happens. . . . You become an unwilling part of this thing that's happening to you, because if you see the person on the tracks, you react: You put the train into emergency and basically that's all you can do. The rest becomes a matter of physics and momentum. The train is still moving, the train is going to hit this guy and you have done all you can do. . . . And you are watching this. This is not a movie, it is going to happen. You are supposed to remember to call command, and call the ambulances, but your mouth is dry. . . . You lose a few seconds thinking what should I do now? What do you do? For a minute you lose your training because of the horror of the moment. It's something that makes you nervous. That makes you far more cautious, that makes you run late, basically, when you have that on your mind.[45]

But, as Alexander noted: "You can't lock out the danger. People talk about building enclosures over the trains, like they have done in certain cities, [but] there are just too many different types of subway cars, too many variables. . . . But look at this in light of the million and millions and millions of passengers who ride and get home safely each day."[46]

ANIMALS ON THE SUBWAYS

Not all the stories told by transit workers are as grim or serious of the ones involving accidents. Animals are a favorite topic. Setting aside the legendry albino alligators said to be happily residing throughout the New York sewer system, transit workers have surprisingly frequent encounters with urban pets, as well as urban wildlife.

With the exception of seeing-eye dogs and a seeing-eye miniature pony reported on the West Side lines, riders are not supposed to bring animals into the subway system, but this rule is often ignored, especially by owners of small dogs, who secrete them through the turnstiles in carry-on cases and backpacks. And then there are the numerous cat owners, transporting their pets to and from vet appointments. Larger dogs are brought on from time to time because riders "don't understand that if they're not aiding a handicapped person, they're not supposed to be on a train."[47] However, very few create the amount of difficulty encountered late one night by Lane:

I had a guy go drunk. It was a Saturday night, he had had a few too many. He passed out. Fell asleep. He brought in a pit bull . . . nice sized pit bull, very well trained to protect his master. He had it strapped to his arm! . . . When we got to the end of the line at Broad Street, we had to go beyond station limits with an empty train—so you can change direction and come back out. I couldn't get this man off. I couldn't get near him! I couldn't wake the guy to save my life. And if I go near him, the pit bull is going to go into attack mode! I called the police [and] they couldn't approach the man. . . . We eventually had to just leave him on there, lock him in that car. I had to descend to the roadbed, go around [the locked car], and go back up to the next car to be able to do it. This man made three trips with a pit bull on his wrist—gave him his own car for the last two.[48]

Like the pit bull, most animals venture into the subway with their owners, but not all. There is a one-legged chicken that lives beside the subway tracks outside Prospect Park "that bops around, doesn't bother anyone," and never gets hit.[49] On the J line at Canal Street there's a resident cat. "We see it every-day, people leave it food. It's smart enough not to get caught. And it's well fed, *very* well fed."[50] Occasionally, riders like to use the subway to show off their bird or reptile collections: "We have people who like to wear their snakes in . . . I had a guy wear one as a tie and a belt. . . . On my line, they really love to wear snakes."[51] Wrap around boa-type snakes seem to be the most popular, and although all seem to be non-poisonous, the unexpected appearance of a snake will often send quite a few riders in search of other cars. Birds, such as parrots and cockatoos, are also seen riding on the shoulders of their owners from time to time. Like the snakes, they are great conversation starters and bring not only a hint of color, but a great deal of what their owners are looking for—attention.

Amazingly, there are wild birds that have woven the trains into their daily routines, especially at the ends of the lines in the outer boroughs. Reid reported that he often sees them:

Animals, especially birds, have grown used to the subway system. There's a line out in the Rockaways, the A train, that runs south of Howard Beach over to Far Rockaway—it runs through the Jamaica Bay Wildlife Refuge. And most of the birds there, eagles and whatnots, they actually stand on the tracks and wait for the trains to come and then fly up. They wait for the wave of air from the approaching train and it's an easy ride for them— they fly up in the sky. And the pigeons at Far Rockaway will actually *ride* the train one stop. They'll allow the doors to close, they'll ride the train one stop and they'll fly out and fly back to Far Rockaway![52]

Reid, an enthusiastic photographer, has occasionally snapped photos of animals on the subways. At the Festival, he proudly showed us a photo he took of one particularly hardy pigeon:

> This pigeon rode the entire J line from about . . . 121st Street in Queens all the way to the end of Broad Street [in Manhattan] standing under this bench. He would move to dodge people's legs and feet, but the pigeon stayed there and stayed there on the way back. He was able to fly, so I don't know why he stayed.[53]

And, displaying another of his photos, he added: "Now this is a possum that was in the seat. I think it is a possum? I can't identify it."[54]

People leave all sorts of unusual objects on the subway. Objects that show up in Transit's Lost and Found regularly include such items as dentures, artificial legs, wigs, and cameras. Even with that in mind, subway engineer Alexander contributed one of the more bizarre subway stories involving animals. The story bears a resemblance to certain urban legends—especially, the one about the person who gift wraps their dead pet and leaves it in a public space hoping that a stranger will steal it, thus helping them to dispose of the corpse. However, Alexander insists that this story is true and actually happened some years ago. We include it for the record:

> There was a body found on a subway train one night, except it was naked, it was decapitated, and it didn't have any skin on it either. And, of course, it was kind of gruesome! And the police were called. They came and took it away, brought it to the morgue. And some pathologist started to do work on it, and they realized that while it looked almost human—wait a second, the bone structure isn't right, the hands aren't right. . . . It turns out that it wasn't human! It had been a gorilla! Someone had *skinned* a dead gorilla and left it out there for us. Just another one of those things that happen not quite every day on NYC subways, but often enough to keep us on our toes.[55]

Like any underground enterprise, and despite determined efforts to get rid of them, the New York City subway system is blessed with rats. Subway workers had lots of stories about rats. They're particularly numerous at the ends of the lines:

> They're in our crew room, they're along our walks. They try to come into the offices. They're not afraid of people. Where we have to get our lay-ups beyond station limits—like at Parsons Archer [Queens], where you're beyond, behind the station—It happens to be where they store the refuse. Plenty of rats! We have to report to a dispatcher's office going past the garbage. So you go past the rats. There's plenty of them.[56]

Not all subway employees are so nonplussed about the rats:

> I saw a conductor on the E line. A rat was in his cab and he was screaming like he was being [attacked] or something! I never saw a man scream that high pitched before. Oh, man, it was funny![57]

Many customers are equally upset on the rare occasions when adventurous rodents leave the tracks and venture onto the platform or, on even rarer occasions, into a subway car. "I saw them empty a car," Lane told us:

> I was working the A train once and we made a stop—we were going local and we made a stop at 110th Street and people came out the car because the rat came in. The rat came in and it emptied the train real fast.[58]

In another A train incident:

> Last Saturday, when I came into Euclid Avenue, I had a rat waiting for my train. I heard this woman in the car behind me screaming—honestly, I thought she was being attacked. . . . She was screaming because the rat was waiting for the train. She upset the rat so badly, the rat said, 'I can not put up with this.' It went over to the local tracks, and waited for the local train. . . . Honestly, the rat was not fazed.[59]

"We have rats pulling Burger King and McDonald's bags down the tracks," Reid added. "You can't get them to eat the poison, because they know they can eat fast food. Rats only want fresh food. . . . they're far too smart. Whenever the tunnels flood, they find a way to get away. They never die. They're too used to people and they're too used to trains."[60]

Sometimes, an animal gets trapped on the tracks in front of an approaching train. "I've chased a cat on the subway from Northern Boulevard to 45th Street," Reid continued, and "I've chased a squirrel across the tunnel at 36th Street on the M line." Lane's favorite animal-on-the-tracks story involved a dog:

> A few years ago, there was [a dog] named Token—most people had seen it in the paper because it got run over. So we had a directive that we were no longer allowed to hit dogs. (We were *never* allowed.) Two weeks behind Token, a dog happened to wander onto the system at 125th Street; got on my tracks. At one and half miles per hour I got to follow the dog from 125th Street to 207th Street. One mile per hour behind this dog, in rush hour, full load, to 207th Street! I blew the horn a couple of times to hurry the dog up, and passengers told me to stop, I was upsetting the dog! We were thirty-five to forty minutes late and no one complained about being late for work. Well, one person out of that entire crowd—one!—out of a rush hour crowd. Everyone else was a dog lover. The dog was rescued. The ASPCA took him, and I understand he was adopted. The dog was tired, I was tired.[61]

BUSKERS AND ENTERTAINERS

> The subway is such an entrenched part of New York City culture that all sorts of people try to make a living on or around it.—Torin Reid

New York subway tunnels are anything but quiet, but adding to the aural fray—usually in a positive way—are street musicians and entertainers. In recent years, the old English term "busker" has been revived to describe an artist who makes or supplements income by performing on the streets or in the subway for tips from passersby. (In recent years, a fair number of New York buskers have taken advantage of advances in home recording technology and now also offer their own CDs for sales.)

The variety of New York buskers reflects the diverse ethnic and geographic origins of the city's population. African drummers, Dominican accordionists, Caribbean steel piano ensembles, Bluegrass bands, and Chinese *erhu* players abound. Jazz trios, Andean string and wind ensembles, and old-time string duets are common. Some operate with the approval of the MTA sanctioned program "Music Under New York," many do not.[62] Sometimes more than one ensemble will share the aural space of a single station creating a polytonal environment that would impress even the most avant-garde classical composer.

Pre-recorded electronic "backing tracks" (accompaniments) that range from single piano to full symphony orchestras make it possible for solo jazz trumpeters, opera singers, country fiddlers, and classical flutists to sound their best. Unusual pan-ethnic combinations can occasionally be spotted. For several years, there was a duo that consisted of a Colombian accordionist and a talented *erhu* player.[63] They spent a great deal of time accusing each other of being out of tune and arguing about intonation. In the last few years, subway riders have been treated to a wave of small "hit and run mariachi" ensembles. These consist of two or three Mexican singers with guitars that rush onto a subway car, sing a few verses of a Mexican folk song, collect donations, and move onto another car at the next stop. There have always been the occasional itinerant solo singers or do-wop ensembles strolling from car to car, but organized instrumental groups are a new and improved Mexican version of an older tradition. And the quality of the Mexican musicians tends to be excellent![64]

Although nothing is supposed to be sold on the trains, it's not usual to encounter people walking from car to car hawking toys, batteries, or candy bars for a dollar or two. Reid told us that "Begging was in vogue for several years in the late 1980s, but the riding public is all begged out. So, those who wish to make money off the subways . . . realize that they have to perform." And some of the entertainers are unusual, or at least unexpected in a mass transit setting. "I'm not talking about your run-of-the-mill derelict or bum or nothing like that," he continued, "or somebody who's out of money and out of time. I'm talking about guys who are almost semi-professionals."

> Now there's one guy, he was a magician [who] works the L line and [number] 2 line. He actually is good at what he does. . . . He kept a bird and he could exchange the bird for a rabbit inside a small box that he wheeled in and out of the trains. The magician makes a lot of money, but he doesn't like to work the trains. He hopes one day to catch the surface and make the big time.[65]

Reid, who kept an eye out for aspiring subway talents, told us about a few more of his favorites:

> Once I worked the J train, and there was a guy, we called him 'the horseman'—The horseman has a kind of a cloth horse that's in front of him and in back of him; [he had] false legs. And he goes through the train moving his hips and the horse actually moves up and down. That's how he collects. And he makes this little noise . . . as he makes the horse go, the

horse actually hops up and down. He's one of the most memorable of the people that come through the train. . . . He was one of the best performers. He is probably the best performer I have ever seen.[66]

Other notable buskers included balloon artists; sketch artists; painters; Mexican cotton candy sellers; a preacher on the E line, who "preached down the whole car for five stops" and "made everybody either sick or inspired"; and "this guy, I think he was a thief, who was selling some clothes on the subway. He hung them up on a line—and he actually made a couple of sales on the A line!"[67]

Today, graffiti, which formed such a prominent part of the subway's landscape in the 1970s and 1980s, has passed its prime—in no small part because many of its most prominent practitioners discovered they could make a much better living creating the distinctive lettering and compelling visual style developed in urban streets and subways for ad agencies and internationally respected art galleries. "Now they're professional," Reid told us, "they charge for what they do now, after having learned their trade in the [subway] tunnels." The MTA's vigorous campaign to eliminate graffiti from trains and stations was largely successful; however "Actually, it's not all gone. Mostly, graffiti is now in the tunnels and [scratched] on the windows." Recently, he had seen new work in one of the "more inaccessible" tunnels, where some graffiti writer boasted he was "Bombing trains in New York and Chicago." Another of his recent mid-tunnel favorites thoughtfully included a legend he thought was intended for train operators; it read "Something to look at while your train is delayed."[68]

STREET PEOPLE: MAKING THE SUBWAY HOME

Although the problem of people living in the subway system is less pronounced than it was at the height of the homeless epidemic that swept the United States during the 1980s, there are still some people who prefer to live in the squalid splendor of the New York City subways. (Often, their choice is based on an unfortunate combination of mental health problems and substance abuse.) Actually, in some cases, their living conditions are not all that squalid. Subway employers reported watching in astonishment as rugs, refrigerators, mattresses, TV sets, cooking stoves, and furniture were periodically cleared out of particularly large, well-heated manholes and forgotten back rooms throughout the subway system.[69] "They know how to raid and steal power," a motorman told us, "I've seen them watch television" in the tunnels." And, another added,

They know how to use the track clips that they use to light the tunnels when they have track work. So they steal the clips—one piece clips onto the third rail and the other clips onto the return running rail. And that will actually power a hot plate, or whatever you need. People have been able to live down under the subways for months at a time. They come up only for food.[70]

A number of homeless people remain in the system. One of the most colorful characters interviewed for the Smithsonian project was "Mayor Tony," a well-known subway denizen. At the time he spoke with folklorist Steve Zeitlin, Mayor Tony had established himself at the Broadway/Lafayette stop on the number 6 line. As Zeitlin pointed out:

There's something almost larger than life about the NYC subways because they're so massive and they go everywhere. It attracts people who are just fascinated with the subway, and Tony is one of those people. He knows all sorts of things. And he considers himself a 'volunteer transit associate' at the Broadway/Lafayette station. Like whenever a train is late, he's cupping his hands and making announcements; telling people the Broadway/Lafayette is not the same as East Broadway . . . and things like that.[71]

Tony is well known and liked by the MTA workers, who nicknamed him "The Mayor." It was Tony who introduced Zeitlin to one of our key Transit informants, Reid. During the Festival, Reid recalled how he knew Tony:

The Mayor? Tony the Mayor has been down there at least as long as I have been down there. I worked the F train five days a week and at Broadway/Lafayette station there's a guy—I don't want to call him a bum—how about an alternative lifestyle person? He doesn't want to work, you know, he lives off of the goodness of others.

I first met Tony the Mayor [when] I used to work midnights on the F at 179th Street. [The Queens end of the line.] Now at the time, in the middle of the night, 2:00 a.m., 3:00 a.m., the trains run on a twenty-minute headway [i.e., space of time between trains]. You have time to get in a chess game. Instead of going on the breaks, guys would go down to the station platform where Mayor Tony would be along with some of the other homeless. He would play chess with some of the midnight crews . . . and I would watch. Later on, I would see him at Stillwell Avenue, Coney Island [at the end of the line in Brooklyn], where there's a crew room.

There's a TV there and it had the football games on or the baseball games on. He would go outside the crew room and look in through the window and see the baseball games there, football games. . . . So, one day I handed him some of the materials that I had [written] on the subway.[72]

When folklorist Zeitlin told The Mayor that the Smithsonian was looking for subway workers who were knowledgeable and who would be good talkers, Tony recommended Reid. How the Smithsonian got in touch with Reid is a great New York tale in its own right:

The best story, to me, is how I got here [the Smithsonian Festival]. I did some writing on the subway years ago. Now Mayor Tony always likes to read. . . . So, one day I dropped off some photocopies of my articles to Mayor Tony. And about two months later, he comes to the train—because he knows the times when I come by—he comes to the train [window] and says: 'So, look man, I know somebody, man. You have to have your best—well, stuff—together. I'm going to introduce you to somebody.' So I thought, 'Who does he know?'

A couple of weeks later, I come to the station. He has all his bags out—basically everything he owns in these shopping bags. And he says, 'wait, wait right here.' And he goes searching through these bags. And I'm holding up the train; people wondering what's going on. . . . You just give them the regular, 'We'll be moving shortly,' but people realize that I'm actually waiting for this guy to search through his bags to give me something. . . . He comes up with a business card—dirty, of course—and the business card belongs to Steve Zeitlin. So, if he is going to go through all this, maybe there's something to it. In a couple of weeks, I called Steve and we had an interview . . . so this is how I got here. This guy, this alternative lifestyle person, was basically my agent. . . . Now, since this guy is my agent, I had to pay him—you have to pay your agent if you expect any work again. So, I gave him fifty dollars in an envelope. So, he's alright. He should be set for a while.[73]

In addition to people like Mayor Tony who actually make their homes in the subway, there are a huge number of buffs, who are fascinated by all aspects of the subway systems. Today, the MTA refers to these people as "aficionados." Lane told us about one on her line:

We have aficionados—we're not allowed to call them buffs anymore. We have a lot of people who are train aficionados. The M and the J line has one, Joey, that's his name—he knows the equipment better than we do, the scheduling. . . . He comes occasionally and visits. He's usually escorted by someone. . . . He comes and he just says 'hi' to everybody because he knows everybody from the old days. He's probably been an aficionado all his life. When small, he probably used to ride trains back and forth.[74]

A few years ago, the MTA was embarrassed by a teenager aficionado who was so fascinated by the trains that he "borrowed" a subway train for a joy ride. According to Reid,

> He was a kid who befriended a motorman on the Franklin [Avenue] Shuttle and thought that he had learned how to drive the train—but he didn't learn everything. He used the motorman's pass number and called up . . . the crew office and got a job. He went and signed in . . . installs himself as a motorman, and drove the train. Somehow he got the tools and everything! He drove the train successfully to the end of the line, Lefferts Boulevard. . . . Made all of the stops—the conductor didn't know. . . . Apparently, he may have gotten practice. We don't know that. Whatever he knew, it was enough to get him to the end of the line. On the way back, three stops away from the beginning of the line where he started out, he hit a red signal. That tripped the train breaks in emergency; he didn't know what to do. So, he didn't answer the radio. . . . The trailer noticed that the trains were backing up [so] they sent the supervisor. . . . Still thinking that he was a motorman, they took him down to Jay Street [MTA Headquarters in downtown Brooklyn] to take a urine test. When they got down to Jay Street he broke away from them and ran home.[75]

Within a short time, the MTA had tracked down the teenager through the motorman whose number had been appropriated and authorities made sure the escapade would not be repeated. Although New Yorkers were disturbed by the story, many understood the boy's obsession with the trains—and a few probably wished that they had had the nerve to try such a stunt themselves.

RUNNING THE TRAINS

There are usually two MTA employees on any subway train: the train operator—also called the motorman—and the conductor. It is the train operator's job to drive the train from stop to stop and take care of minor mechanical issues along the way. Every motorman carries two small wrench-like pieces of equipment:

their own "break handle" and their own "reverser"—the first allows them to set the train in motion, the other sets the direction of the train. New York subway cars are designed with a "dead man's switch," which means that the train operator has to maintain pressure on the speed control lever for the train to move. If the motorman releases his grip on the speed control, the train will come to a halt. (This safety feature ensures that should the motorman lose consciousness or leave the cab the train will not continue to move.) In addition, every motorman carries a vest, a flashlight, a radio, and a working time piece:

> That's standard equipment—the equipment that I definitely use to operate . . . And we have our own portable radios now, walkie-talkies. They're not as efficient as I would like them to be, but they're there. We have our own—so this way, when we get off the train to make repairs, control center's in total contact with us at all time—to interrupt us while we're doing something.—Bad, very bad, because they have no concept of time. No concept whatsoever of how long it takes to make a repair. I had this recently. My train went into emergency and I was on the elevated structure. And I had a repair. And they're calling you every three or four seconds. You get very little accomplished. You really want to turn the radio off, but you know better.[76]

Although it is the conductor's responsibility to make public announcements, in an emergency situation train operators will also make announcements. In an unusual situation "I always make announcements," Lane told us. "I've put people through fires; I evacuated trains; and I've found out that as long as you keep them informed there's no problem. And I always smile when I say it."[77]

Before he retired several years ago, the number 1 line enjoyed the presence of Harry Nugent, a conductor who treated riders to a fully narrated trip up and down Broadway several times a day. "Fifty-Ninth Street," he would cheerfully announce, "just a little bit to right of Carnegie Hall." The fact that for 95 percent of its run only dark tunnel walls could be seen out of the number 1 train's windows did little to dampen Mr. Nugent's enthusiasm as a tour guide. And he had fans—regular riders who would wait for his train each morning![78]

Today, more and more trains have automated taped voices making routine announcements. "They're trying to do that more," Lane thought, "because you're getting a new population of transit workers and their English isn't always the best. And sometimes, it's hard to determine what is being said."[79]

The train operator and conductors as well as the token booth attendant are the public face of the MTA. "They're our ambassadors, if you will," subway engineer Alexander explained:

I'm an engineer, by definition, I'm boring. I get to solve problems; I *love* to solve problems. Whereas *they* have to deal with people and people problems. The problems I get to deal with are about subway cars—much more straightforward; much more simple. People problems are far more difficult. . . . They're the ones who have to deal with all of the people who get angry if people on *my side* in car equipment don't do our job. We try, but we may not succeed all the time.[80]

So, are there any joys of driving a train? Despite their stories and gripes, most MTA employees were enormously proud of what they do. As Alexander explained:

At a certain level MTA workers see themselves as family. And I'm not the only one, there's a great fraternity out there—not a fraternity anymore, because we have women employees too. So it's both a fraternity and a sorority—and that's called a family. There are fifty thousand employees in one of the most contentious families that's ever been created on the face of this earth. And that's what it takes to move 4 or 5 million New Yorkers a day through the tunnels of New York, under the streets and over the streets to get them to work in the mornings—not because they want to, but because they have to. And then turn them around at the end of the day and get them home.[81]

And according to Lane, some lines seem to enjoy a good deal of camaraderie:

On the J line especially. We're very happy. It's like a family. We know when people are ill; we are concerned with each other. The E train is above us, a level above us, so most of us go back and forth between the two lines.[82]

Workers on individual lines meet each other in crew rooms located at the ends of their runs. If a train runs late, breaks down, or is delayed, a train operator's breaks are sometimes briefer that they are scheduled to be. "I've had breaks as few as sixteen minutes, and as much as thirty-five to forty minutes. Lunch is actually the longest break, usually in the middle of the job. That is usually between forty [and] fifty minutes," and

We have crew rooms, but most of us on my line . . . tend to stay in the dispatcher's office more than we're supposed to. . . . Everybody has stories. Always. Everybody has stories and they're trying to top yours. Everybody just has their own experiences. And there's enough of them.[83]

Many of the MTA employees we interviewed expressed concern that their workplace was changing: Some felt that there was less socializing at work in recent years, "Because the whole face of transit has changed from a small company type of atmosphere to one of a corporation. So, yes, we had occasional parties. We may have had a little more happiness and joy in the past, whereas now it's more of a job."[84]

During a public discussion between several train operators and New York City bus driver Tony Palombella at the 2001 Smithsonian Folklife Festival, the bus driver made the mistake of stating that, in addition to numerous other factors, buses were superior because he got to meet and know his passengers. Train operator Lane took immediate exception to his statement:

> Oh, no! Not on my train! I have regulars who look for me. . . . I'd greet them everyday. I'd go in before I start [my scheduled run]—My passengers look for me. They're upset with these two weeks [i.e., because she took leave to attend the Smithsonian Festival]. My 12:30 batch knows that they'll *never* make their bus because I'm not there. I have people who go on vacation and let me know they're going on vacation. No, we have a one-on-one—I'm sorry![85]

So, do subway workers find themselves as captivated by the trains as the people who ride them? Like most other New Yorkers, many MTA employees rely on the subway system themselves. For example, when Lane was asked to come to a Smithsonian interview at City Lore's office near the Second Avenue subway stop, she admitted:

> I very seldom see what's upstairs. Like this is my first time upstairs at Second Avenue. I've never come upstairs. I just know it underground. And when people give me directions, I have to ask what train stop are you by? That's what I use for my geography, the subway system. Even if I'm driving, I know where the stops are. So they have to tell me what train they're by, and I can get there by that.[86]

We asked Lane if she would say that she loved trains. She gave it some though. "No, not really," she said. "I love a paycheck. I love the security. I'm very happy with my current placement because we have supervisors and co-workers who have worked with each other for a while."[87] Nevertheless, watching her guide visitors through a subway car that had been transported to the

National Mall for the 2001 Folklife Festival, and listening to her enthusiastically explain the extensive body of knowledge a motorman needs to drive the trains, it was obvious that being a train operator was more than just a job.

When we asked the same question of our other key informant Reid, he admitted the trains still fascinated him. In fact, despite being "more of a job" these days, during his off-hours Reid still finds pleasure spending time with his sons working on a set of model trains in the basement of his Queens home:

> I have the plastic ones you put together, as well as the handmade brass ones imported from Korea—they're plated silver and they are handmade. They cost a pretty penny. They run on eighth-inch scale tracks. They're up forever in the basement of my house . . . [but] I haven't tried to recreate the subway system. That is a little too close to work.[88]

URBAN PROFILE: THE 86TH STREET CROSSTOWN BUS

Please Take a Seat, the Show Is Starting

A LTHOUGH THE majority of Metropolitan Transit Authority (MTA) workers interviewed during the Smithsonian's New York City documentation project worked for the city's legendary subway system, we did record the experiences of several MTA bus drivers. Most colorful of these was Tony Palombella, an Italian-American New Yorker who had spent almost two decades driving buses—first in the Bronx, and more recently, in Manhattan. At the time we spoke with him, he was assigned to drive the 86th Street crosstown route, which took him from the shores of the East River on the Upper East Side's Yorkville neighborhood to the edge of the Hudson River on the Upper West Side.[1]

As Palombella explained: "After 18 years, bus driving is very boring." So he developed a "sit-down" comedy and trivia routine—a patter for his riders that gained him both media attention and a following amongst uptown riders.

> I pull up my bus and before I cross Central Park, I make sure that I tell them, 'OK, this is your friendly bus driver speaking. I know you've paid

$2 for this club, which seats 40 people and we serve no drinks—although some people carry their own. While many bus drivers have the personality of crash dummies, I turn my job into a lively and rewarding profession. I turn my bus ride into a house party! Now would you like to hear some jokes, or NYC trivia?'[2]

People rarely object—the regulars look out for Tony's bus; those from elsewhere in the city are probably just astonished. As he pulls away from the curb, the monologue begins:

Well, not only do I do it to entertain people, but to entertain myself, because it's a monotonous job, and I turn into a robot. So seven or eight years ago, I perfected my trivia and comedy by going to Barnes & Nobles on the weekends. I started taking out books—and anything [that] caught my fancy. And I started getting interesting stuff [about New York]. Like the bagel: the first bagel, for example, was born in New York in 1896 on Clinton Street. The first pastrami? 88 Delancey Street in 1888; the first martini?—1781 at Number 1, Broadway; and toilet paper was invented in New York in 1857 by Joseph C. Gayette—he used to live on 33rd Street. He put his name on every sheet and every roll was being sold for fifty cents. He called it Gayette's Medicated Paper—it was made of manila paper.

So I only take interesting stuff: Like the first transvestite governor of NYC? His name was Edward Hyde—better known in England as Lord Cornbury. He used to parade Broadway wearing his wife's clothes. The army came by, arrested him, and threw him back into his mansion. He also used to take taxpayers' money and use it for his own behalf. And in his last year, he was arrested and had to spend a year in jail in order to pay up all his debts. He was married, he had seven kids. They used to love to go to parties in New York and they used to love to steal silverware. Lord Cornbury—1702 to 1708! I do the street origins: Why did they name it Lexington Avenue; why did they name Madison Avenue, Park Avenue? . . . I do the history of Central Park. Where is the longest cross street in Manhattan? Why do they call it the Big Apple?

I do, like, a thirty-five-minute show. Too bad the crosstown bus is only going for like fifteen, twenty minutes—I can't finish my shtick. Anyhow, I do it to entertain the people; I do it to entertain myself. That's about it.[3]

An 86th Street bus approaches Broadway near the end of its crosstown run. PHOTO BY NANCY GROCE, COURTESY SMITHSONIAN INSTITUTION.

On a more serious note, Tony sincerely believes that buses are vastly superior to subways. He contends that "Most people use the subway only if they have to . . . [they] try to avoid the subway. We call it a badge of social status to say you don't have to use the subway." He pointed out that "elderly people can't go down subway steps"; "people are afraid of standing on platforms; afraid of pickpockets on the subway." Additionally, there is a "higher ratio of employees to riders" on city buses; the bus driver is "dealing one-on-one with people; they're out with their customers and not locked away in a cabinet." Moreover, there is "no one to greet you as you go through the [subway] turnstiles," there is "no view in the subway," while on buses, "people like to stare out the windows and dream a little bit."[4] And last, but not least:

> Every time you come on the bus, who's the first person you see? We handle the fare box, open and close doors, [help] handicapped people. So we do four to five jobs all at once! . . . I have to change my lines every two or three months because I get too friendly with the regulars.[5]

Not into trivia? Tony alternates his New York trivia shows with a half-hour barrage of bad jokes. The routine begins with such gems as "Where do you find a dog with no legs? (Right where you left him.)"; and "What do you call a boomerang that doesn't work? (A stick.)"; and continues in the same vein.[6]

Sure, there are occasional complaints and requests for silence—with which Tony always complies, but "When the temperature is 90 degrees, and I've got a standing load, I think a little trivia and a little comedy relaxes the people."[7]

URBAN PROFILE: ROSENWACH

The Water Towers Builders

Paris has the Eiffel Tower, and Pisa has the Leaning Tower; we have the water tower. —Andrew Rosenwach, Rosenwach Water Tanks

NEW YORK'S water towers: once someone points them out to you, you can't believe how many of them there are. Thousands upon thousands of huge wooden barrels are perched like alien spaceships on rooftops throughout the city. It's impossible to imagine the cityscape without them, but it's also possible that you've never noticed them. Because they are such an integral part of the city's infrastructure, the Smithsonian New York City Project put water towers near the top of its agenda of things to be researched. Because more than half of the ten thousand water tanks presently standing in New York City were manufactured by the Rosenwach Company of Greenpoint and Long Island City, we approached the 150-year-old firm to learn why New York has water tanks, and what it is like to work high above the rooftops of the City.[1]

Water towers began to appear in New York in the nineteenth century, when laws mandated that every building over six stories tall must have two sources of water or 3,500 gallons of water on the premises to assist firefighters. Building wooden tanks on rooftops of buildings seemed like an excellent solution. Water tanks work on the "artesian well" principal.[2] The hydrostatic pressure, created by the level of the Croton reservoir system in upstate New York where the city's water originates, is equivalent to a six-story building. Tanks maintain water pressure throughout a building, and the city's high water pressure (forty to sixty pounds per square inch) means that the water can be easily pumped to the roof and gravity fed throughout the building.

Water tanks do not sit directly on the roof; instead, because the city requires that the standpipe system begin no less than twenty-five feet below the bottom of the tank, the tanks are erected on iron scaffolds built on top of the buildings. Water from the bottom part of tank, "standpipe water," is dedicated strictly for use in case of a fire. Drinking and domestic water comes out of the middle of the tank. Usually, domestic water supply will not drain a tank below the half-way mark, but when the water falls below a certain point in the tank, (say three-quarters or so), a floating level mechanism similar to the sort used in toilets signals the pump to begin refilling the tank. Because all water for drinking, plumbing, and fire prevention in a building is dependent on having a working tank, it is essential that when a tank needs to be replaced, the work is done in as short a time as possible, usually within a day.

Once installed, tanks need to be cleaned and inspected every year. Wood is excellent insulation from weather: "In the winter, three inches of lumber will be equivalent to two feet of concrete."[3] This keeps the water from freezing in the winter and keeps it relatively cool in the summer.

A primary "reason the tanks are still here today is, more than anything else, one of economics."[4] A wooden tank costs approximately twenty-five thousand dollars, which compares nicely with the sixty-five thousand dollars that a steel one might cost. Although wooden tanks last only about thirty-five years—shorter than the seventy-five- to one hundred-year life span for steel tanks—they are less expensive to maintain because they don't need to be painted and are easier to clean. And, one of the water tank builders added, "If someone shoots a hole in water tank, we just plug them with a wooden dowel!"[5] In taller buildings there will sometimes be lower zone mid-floor tanks or pressure-reducing stations, but more often, buildings will have a single water tank on their roof.

Historically, wooden water tanks were used for a much wider variety of industrial purposes, including for wineries and breweries, but nowadays, most

Dozens of water towers, new and old, perch on rooftops throughout Manhattan's Garment District in this 2001 photograph. PHOTO BY NANCY GROCE, COURTESY SMITHSONIAN INSTITUTION.

of the wooden water tanks built in the United States are made in New York City. Water tanks might not be cutting-edge technology, but company owner Andrew Rosenwach sees them as an economical "gift to the city."

BUILDING AND INSTALLING THE TANKS

Putting tanks into new buildings before the tenants arrive is not usually a problem. However, when an old tank needs to be replaced, the entire process must be completed within ten hours because the residents are dependent on water from the tank for drinking, plumbing, and fire protection. Rosenwach walked us through how tank replacement is done in a "standard pre-War" (i.e., World War II) building: First, the Rosenwach crew starts dismantling the old water tank around 6:30 in the morning. The old tank is drained, a hole is chopped near the bottom to let out any residual water, and then it is completely dismantled and taken off the structure by about 10:00 A.M. Meanwhile, workers start laying out the wood for the new tank, as well as the necessary pipe fittings and hoops. Barring unforeseen problems, it usually takes three hours to install a new tank.

Pieces for the tank have been pre-cut and assembled in the firm's small factory in the Greenpoint section of north Brooklyn. Knot-free Canadian cedar and redwood are the woods of choice. After carefully assembling the tank in the factory to make sure all the pieces fit together snuggly, the entire tank is then *disassembled* for transportation to the building site. We asked if it wouldn't be easier to send an assembled tank. Well, yes, they said, but how would they get it onto the roof? To our astonishment, we learned that in almost all cases, replacement water towers are constructed, disassembled, and brought to the building in pieces so that they can be transported to the roof via the elevator, which in the case of residential buildings is sometimes quite small. The trick, it seems, is that many of those elevators are constructed with a removable panel in their ceilings to allow longer objects to be brought up.

The disassembled tank pieces are brought to the site by one of Rosenwach's small trucks, which are adorned with the company's name and charmingly folk-like paintings of water tanks on their doors. "The bottom goes together similar to your standard dining room table," Andy Rosenwach explained; the "leaves" are typically eight-foot long, twelve-inch wide boards, which are then doweled together. A twelve-foot diameter, ten-foot high tank—the standard size used on many of the city's smaller apartment buildings—requires about fifteen boards. Such a tank will hold 7,500 gallons of water, of which 3,500 gallons is reserved for the "fire supply" and the balance is earmarked for domestic supply.

Once the new tank parts have been brought up in the elevator and the old tank has been brought down, it usually takes about three hours to install a new tank and make the plumbing connections. The sides of the tank, which are called "staves," have been notched so that they snap together with their neighboring staves. The horizontal staves fit into another pre-cut notch around the bottom of the tank. At first, the tank is loosely assembled—temporarily held together with ropes and internal support bracing. The crew then begins closing the six- to seven-inch gaps between the wooden boards. Folklorist Kathy Condon and photographer Martha Cooper interviewed Rosenwach on a West Side roof top, where his crew was installing a medium-sized tank on a pre-war apartment house. As they arrived, Rosenwach explained what was going on:

> We're about thirty feet off a building that's about twelve stories high; at the 'edge of the world.' And everyone has to concentrate and focus and know what they're doing. In a few minutes, we'll be handing up the rings, which are called hoops, that circle the tank. They're normally in three pieces because this is a twelve-foot diameter [tank]. They'll be putting it

together and then tightening with a hoop gun . . . then we use hand tools to tighten the rest of the way for adjustment—which is a tremendous feat in itself. . . . Construction of this type, in the position, and the piping that's needed to connect to it, a group of men can restore the building to a 'water condition,' ready for water, by about seven o'clock at night. In my mind, that's a tremendous organizational capability; it takes a tremendous amount of skill and dedication that you only learn on the job. And the men you see here today, the majority of them are with us for many years. And that's because we do something right.[6]

Rosenwach is tremendously proud of his workers and skills they bring to their jobs, skills that he himself claims not to have. In fact, they seem to not run in his family, he said, launching into a story about his father, Wallace:

Once old-timers asked him to throw up the hammer, and when he threw it, it didn't get that far, which the old-timers thought was pretty funny, because he wasn't that good at it. Normally the momentum is to toss it up, and it's quite a feat to be able to have that confidence to do that, but it saves a good few minutes, which add up to hours, and things get done.[7]

You have to be "very careful about not having things go over the edge," he cautioned. "To stand here now . . . we can appreciate the craft and the skill of what each man can do in terms of the balance. To imagine the tank being put up any other way would probably triple the price." Fortunately, there have been "no accidents I can recall. And I've been here for about twenty-five years." There is a strong motivation, he thought, on the individual level to do the job right, perhaps because "it's sink or swim."[8]

The Rosenwach family has been making New York water tanks since 1896 when Andy's great-grandfather Harris, an immigrant carpenter from Poland, bought the firm from William Dalton for fifty-five dollars. (Dalton, in turn, seems to have established the firm in 1866.) The firm was then passed down to Harris's son, Julius, who in turn brought in and trained Wallace. The family story is that Wallace was dead set against going into the business, but an extended stay on a South Pacific island during World War II, courtesy of the U.S. military, made him reevaluate his feelings about both his city and the family business. To let his father Julius know he had reconsidered, he made a humidor out of tropical woods in the shape of a water tank while waiting for demobilization in the South Pacific, and sent it to his father, complete with a sign that read "Rosenwach & Son."

BUILDING TANKS ABOVE THE SKYLINE

"Takes a long time to get a crew like we have," carpenter Charlie Zimmerman told us, "we have a unique crew. We have a crew that can do almost anything. Just the way the guys are. A lot of skill."[9] Most of Rosenwach's workers have been with the firm for many years; a few of them followed their fathers into the trade. We spoke with them about their craft a number of times over the course of several months: first during visits to their Greenpoint factory and Long Island City shop, then during a rooftop job on West 75th Street, and finally at the 2001 Smithsonian Folklife Festival in Washington, where Rosenwach workers constructed a twelve-foot diameter tank, (complete with specially cut walk-through entrances on either side), in the middle of the National Mall. During the two-week exhibition, the water tower builders explained their craft to hundreds of thousands of fascinated museum visitors, including a lot of surprised New Yorkers who tended to approach the display shouting: "Hey, come here! Look! No kidding! It's a water tank!"

A recurring motif in the Rosenwach workers' stories was the sense of pride and accomplishment they took in the work: "I love this job very much because of the excitement," said Adoinis "CJ" Cegisman, a Guyanese immigrant who had been working for Rosenwach for about seven years. "I realize to myself that this job is really and truly a difficult job, and not a lot of people can do it, because of the heights, the towers, and it's a very good job. I love this job."[10]

Part of it is skill, and a work force that gets along well together, but another major factor is trust. This was brought home to us as we watched one of the men working on the side of the tank perched on the scaffold positioned over the side of the building. In his two hands, he held a hoop gun, and he was being held securely around the waist by another man, who was holding onto the tank ladder. "Yeah, you have to trust who you work with here, and we look out for each other, we take care of each other," the workers told us, "we do that all the time."[11]

"The company will go through a lot of people to get people who will stay around," shop foreman Kenny Lewis remarked. "A lot of guys will show up on the roof, and that's their last day, if you know what I mean. If they see what kind of work it is, if they don't like heights, they're not gonna be here."[12]

Tank builder Tony Aviles told us, "It's not just putting up the tank. It's also bonding between each other. Because it's dangerous what we do out there, so we look out for each other. You have to trust the person you're working with. It's something that grows as you go along." "Someone who just started, you won't have them up there," Roger Martinez added. "You know, you'll have who you trust up there. The others, you'll have 'em where they won't get into no trouble or hurt anybody else. [They learn] little by little. We start trusting 'em, they go back up—little by little, and after a while."[13]

Wilson Felix had only been building tanks for six months when we interviewed him, "but Roger [Martinez] is my cousin," he told us, "and John DeGeorge I've known for some time, and Tony and CJ, so when I started working here, I know that I could trust them 'cause those are guys I know. And you know, they tried to break me in quickly—'Go up there and do this'—and it's scary. I'm not afraid of heights; I'm afraid of *falling*. It's scary. You do things real slow. Sometimes when you're up there and you're scared, you lose your strength. I've gone up there to help them do stuff and I'm like, 'Oh, my god, let's do this quickly!'"[14] David Bonilla agreed:

> It's like Roger said. You do form some bonds here. You have to trust one another. But one thing I really like is the communications part. Everyone is talking at each other. And there's always someone who's on the 'bad spot.' And I like that they give him the courtesy of taking his time. Whoever's on a really bad spot where there's nothing but sidewalk—you know, the 'express stop.'[15]

The *express stop*? "Yeah, we call it the bad side." In other words, where there's nothing below you but the sidewalk! "The guy who's on the bad side gets all the courtesy: 'Take your time, put your hoop together.' It's all about safety."[16]

Kathy Condon asked during a group interview at the Greenpoint shop if the heights ever bothered any of the men while they were installing a tower. This sparked an interesting exchange between Martinez, Bonilla, and Felix:

MARTINEZ: "I respect the height, you get used to it."

BONILLA: "It's a healthy fear."

FELIX: "I guess you always have to have a little bit of fear, so that you're careful."

MARTINEZ: "You do it so often that sometimes you don't even think about it."

BONILLA: "That's what scares me—when you're too comfortable."[17]

Many of Rosenwach's present crew "started about five years ago, after a generation of old-timers retired." Old-timers are still remembered with respect and sometimes awe, like Dave Miles a "lifetime carpenter" and concentration camp survivor, who trained shop foreman Lewis. Lewis still remembers stories he told him about Europe. The crew also told us about "characters" like Arthur Gibson, Jimmy Walker, and Mike O'Neill, who "used to walk around the top of the tanks, just on the width of the staves, two and three-eighth inches! When he was a younger man, Miles used to walk the top of the staves *and* bang them in from either side to straighten them up."[18]

Not everybody is cut out for working heights. "I remember my first day," said Robert Olecki, "When I was walking around the scaffold, I wasn't used to the heights, and my butt was [flat] against the tank." When you do difficult tasks, they said, "You gotta be fast, and at the same time you have to watch yourself. The first thing you gotta think about how safe it is—before anything else."[19] The Rosenwach crew had numerous tales about those who didn't make the grade. Like the brother of one of the workers: "He came in, he saw the tower, and he quit the next day." "My brother-in-law," another added:

> One time [he] came to work with us, and he was passing the lumber [up]. He was at the bottom and another guy told him that the next day he was going to be working with me in the tower—and it was like a thirty-foot tower. So he didn't show up the next day. That was his last day.[20]

That reminded the group of another novice employee:

> He climbed up the tower and he [got] stuck on the ladder. He said, 'Oh, gosh, I can't—I'm staying right up here!' And he started screaming: 'I ain't goin' down!' And he's holding the ladder, you know. And we're screaming, telling him: 'OK, all right, take your time, take your time. . . . Come down slowly, take your time.' And he comes down and he said, 'I'm not going back up on that height!'[21]

"That's the reason why I know that I have a secure job," Cegisman said, summing up the discussion, "because there are not a lot of people could go up there and do that, you know?"[22]

"UP ON THE ROOF"

As in many other jobs, a fair amount of hazing of new employees and joking seems to go on among water tower builders. Even those who make it past the initial tests sometimes find themselves the butt of practical jokes. Sometimes this is done for fun, but it is also done to test people's mettle and make a point about what to do and not do on the job. Like the time, for example, that a novice workman left a hammer on edge of a roof and "somebody hid it and said it went over the side."[23] It scared the daylights out of him, but it also taught him not to leave tools on edges where they might plummet to the sidewalk.

Other devilment directed at novices includes such standards as: "A lot of time they ask for false things, like 'a cut out to the center' (there's no such thing as cut outs!)" or "a bucket of steam!" "Sometimes they turn the pump on, in the winter, when you're inside the tank and give you a nice shower." "Three or four men sitting around and they're putting on their shoes, getting ready for work, and one guy is putting on his shoe, and he starts standing up, but he can't walk away 'cause the shoe is actually nailed to the floor." And, Zimmerman added, we "fill the guy's bag up with rocks, bricks. Oh, yeah, we do it all the time." Condon asked if this was what Felix, who was still new to the company, had to look forward to. "I stopped bringing a bag," Felix shot back.[24]

And then there is the common bane of all New York rooftops: the pigeons: "We put a pigeon in a guy's bag so he finds it when he's going home." A pigeon? "Yeah, we found it on the roof, stuck in the tar. So we got it out of the tar, put it in a guy's bag. A living pigeon, in a guy's bag." Even better for the pranksters, the worker involved didn't find it until he got on the subway train and opened his bag to look something. "He found it on the train!" Bonilla then proudly told the group that "I busted Roger for putting a dead [pigeon] in my bag. That was funny, 'cause I just stood there, and he's being real careful, and he looks back and sees me, he goes, 'Agghhh!'"[25]

Fortunately, no one could recall any serious accidents, although Bonilla said he had once fallen fifteen feet while working on top of Studio 54. And "I went about eighteen, twenty feet once," added Zimmerman. "I got hit with a two thousand pound piece of steel and got hit down to a lower roof. And another time a ladder went out on the side of a steel tank and I hit the bottom—with the ladder—I held on for dear life! Rode it all the way down to the ground!"[26]

No matter how safety conscious everyone is, accidents will happen. Cegisman and Martinez told us of the time they fell into the tank together. It was partially filled with water and then, Felix continued, "a drop light apparently fell in, and they thought they were about to be electrocuted. They were fighting each other to see who would get out of the tank first."

> MARTINEZ: Because I was telling him not to touch the metal, and so the first thing, he jumps to grab the door, and it's *all* metal—and so I try to pull him down.

CEGISMAN : You were pulling me down because you wanted to get up!
So we're both inside the tank, holding each other, jumping. 'Shut
the power, shut the power!'

To Bonilla, who had been outside the tank watching this drama unfold:

It looked like Moe and Larry. The cord was all the way at the end. I had
to run down a little narrow path to go and get it out. I think they both
freaked out because each one of 'em thought the other one was getting
shocked.[27]

Even if they joke about it, the sense of danger is real. When we asked what
other professions were comparable to theirs in terms of skill, danger, and need
for mutual trust, they responded police, fire fighters, and the military: "Guys
who depend on each other for their safety." "If somebody makes a mistake on a
typewriter," one added, "no one gets hurt."[28]

WATER FOR THE CITY: RAIN OR SHINE

Condon asked the men if there were any particular towers they had built and
installed of which they were especially proud, thinking that they would rattle off
a number of famous addresses and large buildings. Instead, the installers agreed
that they were proud of all of them: "Every time you go up there, it's something
special, something different. It's like a mission."

Each tank presents a unique challenge they said. Rosenwach agreed and
told us about recently putting up a tank on Chambers Street that is "designed to
be seen"; and then there were those high winds they had to contend with during a recent installation near Battery Park. Weather is sometimes a major factor,
he said, and told us stories of servicing tanks with frozen pipes or trying to fix
electrical malfunctions in the middle of snowstorms. On new buildings, tanks
must go in whenever the building is ready for it to maintain the construction
schedule. "We work whether it's ninety degrees or five degrees outside. Whatever it is, we're like the postmen":

We're a conglomeration of talent, from carpentry to plumbing, to just
knowing how to think rationally and logically and be able to determine
what to do when. If you ever want to go through an experience, come
up to our roof when it's five degrees outside. You would just be amazed
at the strength of an individual up there to solve a problem, because it's

bitter, bitter cold. You put a glass of water up there, and within a second, it'll freeze.[29]

The men recalled with admiration a legendary old-timer named Jimmy Walker, who had a reputation for wanting to do the job no matter what the weather. Jobs start with taking down the old tank, and once you've cut the hole in the wood tank to fully drain it, you're committed. No matter what, you had to finish the installation:

> 'You can do it, lads,' Jimmy would say . . . and would chop a hole in the tank so the crew would *have* to do the job regardless. Oh, yeah, you'd have to watch him. I remember on Park Avenue there was dogs and cats coming, all day, and we have to work because he made the hole. I mean, rain—we're talking about *nickles*. He was very well known for that. You gotta keep an eye on him because otherwise before you know it he's [chopped a hole], and you gotta do it. This guy at lunch time, he used to have sandwich in one hand and be working—one of those guys.[30]

"And don't forget, it's all teamwork," Cegisman reminded us, "You have to work as a team to get it done. And everybody has to come together as a team and say, 'Well, yes, we have to finish this.'"[31] Sometimes, after they finish a job in the winter, they have snowball fights. Years ago, on hot days, building supers would sometimes let the men go for a swim in the water used to test the tank.

BEING ON TOP OF THE WORLD

But it's not always just about the work. At one point during our group interview at the Greenpoint shop, Martinez said something interesting:

> I don't know if you noticed when you went up there, [but] it's like a freedom, also. I don't know how to explain, but it's like you see the city, you're like up in the air—it's like flying. You're way up there, and you look up, you see the whole city, and the feeling—I don't know how to explain it.[32]

A number of the builders agreed with Martinez, and then, they added, there were other perks: Sometimes in ritzy neighborhoods you could look down and see the penthouses of celebrities—in fact, they had all been privy to the preparations for a recent celebrity wedding on the roof of a West Side museum while working on the roof of a neighboring building. They liked that the job kept them in shape;

liked to be kept moving and the hard work. And, one said that when they got a call to work on a tank near "where friends are working. . . . I call them and tell them to check it out." Perhaps foreman Lewis summed it up best:

> Me personally, I like it because it's a unique job. There's not a lot of jobs where you can walk around the city and see what you do. And people who I meet that know what I do, they never noticed a water tank. They live in the city fifty years, and they never even notice that they're there. But once they talk to me, the next time I see them, they say, 'I couldn't believe it, I was up in the office building, I looked down, those tanks are all over the place!' And I say, 'Well, thank God they are or I wouldn't have a job!'. . . Most people can't believe that they're even still in use. They think that they're just old, waiting to come down. I go through the city and I show my kids 'That's what I do,' and they can see what I do. To me, there's a certain amount of pride involved in being able to actually *see* what you do.[33]

Many years ago, to make sure people knew which tanks were theirs and because they were proud of their work, Rosenwach designed a "floret," a four-sided "R," to grace the apex of the roof on each of their tanks. Today, the company's distinctive florets can be seen silhouetted on thousands of rooftop tanks throughout the city.

HOW TO MAKE A WATER TANK

At the heart of the craft is the ability to make a huge, water-tight tank. Water tank building is "like barrel-making," shop foreman Lewis explained, "It would be like being a cooper a hundred years ago. It's the same principle, pretty much."[34]

Lewis's job consists of milling wood for the staves, floors, and roofs of each tank. With two other woodworkers, he fits them together in the Greenpoint shop, and then disassembling for transportation to the installation site. Lewis makes the bottoms, the other two carpenters make the sides. When they're not busy, they make smaller parts, such as the rosettes, but "There's never nothing to do." Wood is usually milled specifically for each job. They could make the bottoms and staves ahead of time, but they try not to because they would weather sitting outside, so it's "better to make them when you need them."

Newcomers have to learn how to "run the lumber" through the milling machines because a piece of lumber can't just be taken and put in the machine. "You have to watch which way the knots are, 'cause the knots have to be on the inside of the tank, the heart has to be on the outside." Rosenwach buys as much clear, knotless wood as he can. Any open knots have to go on the inside, so the wood touches the water and swells the knots closed. Troublesome knots are treated with a watertight seal to cut down on leakage, which might occur before the wood swells. A little seepage through the knots in a brand new water tower doesn't particularly concern the tank makers, but they try to do away with all of it, "Mostly it's just because the customers; hey, they want to see the tank right away holding water."[35]

We asked if Lewis's job could be mechanized:

> I guess somebody could come up with something to do that. But you still have the human factor. A machine is not going to look at a piece of wood and know whether to turn it up or flip it. It has to be looked at. And every piece is bowed and different. You have to look at it, and lay it out the way it's supposed to be. And once you drill it and put it together, every piece is not 100 percent straight, so you have to plane it and make it uniform and drill the holes, and then use the router on it to put the angle on it.[36]

Water tank making is such a specialized craft that we wondered how they learned their trade. Lewis was trained as a carpenter by his father; they worked together in a Manhattan shop that did finish carpentry. He started at the bottom at Rosenwach: "Started sweeping floors, worked my way up, and then I became the foreman here." To Lewis,

> [Tank making] is more of a rough carpentry, it's not like finish carpentry, like cabinet making or frame making. This is more like barrel making, or ship making, almost. At first, well, I was twenty-two years younger, and I didn't know. It was a job, and I just started it. And as I started to learn, I liked it. And I kept moving up, so I stayed here. David Miles was foreman when I came. He was a concentration camp survivor, then was in the Israeli army, then came here. Carpentry had been his family business in Poland.[37]

Rosenwach told us Lewis was being overly modest: "The installation staff really counts on Kenny, whose work is luckily 99.9 percent accurate. The easier it is in putting up the tank, the less chance there is of someone getting hurt."

Lewis prefers "keeping his feet on the ground." To do installation work, he said, "You have to have it in your blood. . . . It's gotta be something that you're very comfortable with, because if you're not comfortable with it, it's a dangerous place to be." Although he might not accompany his creations to their final rooftop homes, he is proud of what he does:

> There's a lot of jobs where you don't see your product out there. You know, you don't see what you're doing. And it's part of the history of New York. They've always been here. As soon as the buildings went up over six stories, since then, they've had water tanks. And that's nice, you can walk down the street and you can see what you did. I remember all the addresses that I have done, so if I'm on 59th Street, I know that I have a tank somewhere on 59th Street, and I can see it.[38]

It's like boat building, he concluded: "We're putting together something that has to be watertight, but we have to have the water on the *inside*, where the ship wants it on the *outside*. We're doing the same thing, but we're keeping the water in different places."[39]

"IT'S NEW YORK'S GREATEST SECRET"

"You have to be a New Yorker to know what a water tank is," Rosenwach told us when we first spoke with him. Today, Rosenwach's company is one of the last wooden tank companies in New York. He doesn't known what the future holds, but he speculates that there might be new, high-tech alternatives to wooden tanks in the next twenty or thirty years. And then there are other issues that might change his profession: increasingly heavy expenses for labor, raw materials, environmental and safety issues, insurance issues, and maybe even, he conjectured, a declining need for people to come together in large buildings:

> It's hard to imagine tanks going out without an alternative in sight—but who would say the Berlin Wall would come down, or Gimbels would close? How can we know these things? I hope you don't think I'm being negative here. I actually love being in a business that can contribute something, produce something, give something to the city.
>
> Once I was in traffic in one of the vans with the company name on it, and the guy passing us put up his hand and says, "Rosenwach Tanks, keep on going!" That made me feel pretty good. It's the service part. We look at the skyline and see that *we* did that. Last week, that was me![40]

URBAN PROFILE:
RUSS & DAUGHTERS

Lower East Side Appetizing Dynasty

NEW YORK CITY has contributed several distinctive foods to the American diet, but perhaps none are more closely identified with the city than that mainstay of the Jewish community: bagels and lox. New Yorkers are very particular about both, and it seemed like an excellent idea to interview some of the key people in the New York food world who were maintaining these great local gastronomic traditions. We asked Dr. Annie Hauck-Lawson, a noted food historian and nutritionist from Brooklyn College, to head our research on the "forklore" of New York. She identified and interviewed numerous chiefs, food shop owners, and bakers from ethnic communities throughout the city.

Among those she spoke with about Jewish food was lox-expert Mark Federman, owner of the legendary appetizing shop Russ & Daughters. He was proud to talk about his business and his attempts to maintain the legendary Jewish food traditions of New York. More than just the food, however, the story of his family and the challenges and struggles faced by his family business over the past century mirrors the history of many other Eastern European Jews who came to New York. So, from the city that contributed "brunch" to American culture, here is the tale of Russ & Daughters.

RUSS & DAUGHTERS: AN APPETIZING MECCA

Russ & Daughters is a New York institution. Located at 179 East Houston Street in Manhattan, just east of First Avenue, in what was once the heart of the Lower East Side Jewish neighborhood, it is a small, beautifully maintained old-fashioned shop filled with Jewish appetizing products. On one side of the shop, in tall, glass-fronted cases, there is a stunning display of smoked salmon, lox, white fish, cream cheeses, and a kaleidoscope of colorful salads. Attractively arranged on the other side of the narrow store are barrels, counters, cases, and shelves filled with dried fruit, coffee, nuts, candies, and pastry. Behind the counters, a small band of dedicated employees are hard at work filling customers' orders. Most are experts in that highly specialized skill identified almost exclusively with New York: lox slicing. It is a walk-in retail shop; there are no seats and no tables. However, there is a constant stream of loyal customers: some from the neighborhood, some from across the city, and others from even more distant points.

Russ & Daughters' neon sign on Houston Street has been a beacon for generations of New York City food mavens. PHOTO BY NANCY GROCE, COURTESY SMITHSONIAN INSTITUTION.

THE FISH BUSINESS AND THE FAMILY BUSINESS

In the middle of Russ & Daughters, you can often find Mark Russ Federman, the third-generation owner of the shop, appetizing maven par excellence, and a great raconteur. Hauck-Lawson stopped by with a tape recorder one autumn day and asked Federman to tell us about his family business, the appetizing trade, and life in general.[1] He seemed genuinely pleased that the Smithsonian would be interested in his small family business, which began with his grandfather:

Russ & Daughters was started officially in 1914 by my grandfather, Joe Russ. He was an Eastern European immigrant with a typical story of fleeing the poverty and pogroms and general despair of *shtetl* and small-town life. He came from the area known as Galicia, which at various times belonged to Austria, Poland, Russia. (I think probably nobody wanted it.) And he had a sister here, who was in the herring business on the Lower East Side, where most of the Jews settled. You know, the typical route was through Ellis Island, Lower East Side—Lower East Side had enormous old tenements, low-cost housing.

So he started with a horse and wagon, and then a pushcart, and eventually had his own store, which was officially established in 1914. The original site was on Ludlow Street. And at that point, it was called Russ's Cut-Rate Appetizers. *Appetizers* or *appetizing* was a term used then, and we continue now, to distinguish it from *delicatessen*. "Delicatessen" connoted meat, and appetizers connoted dairy and fish. It had to do with the *kashrut*, the Kosher laws, because meat and dairy [had to be] separated. So he started his store and began eking out a living on Orchard Street.

In those days, there were probably two or three of this kind of place on each street providing the staple foods for the Eastern European, particularly Jewish immigrants. The taste that they brought over in terms of fish was [for] preserved or salted fish—particularly herring. Herrings [were sold] in big barrels, and they were sold at probably three for a quarter. And salmon was plentiful in those days, and was sold salted. There was really no smoking going on [in New York] until the teens and early twenties. What's known as "lox" comes from the Germanic words *lachs*—meaning salmon, salt-cured salmon.

My grandfather was a typical Eastern European immigrant. No formal education, very smart in terms of being self-taught. Very hard working. It was six days a week and fourteen, fifteen hours a day. But he also

Mark Federman, third-generation owner of Russ & Daughters, presides over his famed appetizing empire. PHOTO BY NANCY GROCE, COURTESY SMITHSONIAN INSTITUTION.

had no patience. You know, you didn't learn patience or finesse. So a customer would come in and say "I want it from here or there," and he'd throw them out. He couldn't be bothered. That's not necessarily good for retailing.

He had three daughters and no sons. He brought them in when they were young to help out in the business. And they grew to be kind of the focus of the business—because he had three pretty women fishing herring out of barrels and cutting lox. It wasn't as sinful as you think. First of all, the conditions were very bad. There was no real refrigeration; everything had to be iced. [It meant] moving ice and herring and barrels. . . . And no self-respecting herring buyer would ever buy a herring off the *top* of the barrel. Barrels were constantly being "turned over." . . . You'd always have to reach way down.

So there was cold herring juice, reaching down, grabbing herrings. You had these three charming young ladies, pretty and charming, doing this, and it freed my grandfather up to go to concentrate on buying quality and price. And that's kind of how it developed. There's no issue of them, meaning the daughters, going to college. It was an issue of survival. They were children of immigrants. They were born here, but they were children of immigrants. Their duty, responsibility, whatever, was to help out in the business.

They started to come in the 1920s . . . while they were in high school, I guess. And they stayed with it, and ultimately, through the business, they met their husbands. In the case of my parents—my mother is the youngest of the daughters—my paternal grandmother would come from Brooklyn once a week to shop in the store, 'cause Russ became known as the quality shop. There were twenty in this neighborhood, but Russ was known as the quality shop. And my mother would wait on my to-be grandmother. And she must've said something like, "Have I got a boy for you! He's the sheik of Brooklyn—you've got to meet him." They met, they fell in love, they married.

And I guess my grandfather approved of all of the sons-in-law, based upon whether they'd be good working stock. Looking at them, sizing them up: can they do it, can they cut lox, can they lug, tote, pull, sell, count? So their husbands came into the business. At one point, there was my grandfather (my grandmother never really worked the business), and his three daughters, and their three husbands. As they had children, my generation, they were allowed to raise their children at home. Their husbands were here to work, but they would also come in on the weekends, because it was the busiest retail period. The store was open from 7:00 A.M. until 2:00, 3:00 in the morning on a Saturday morning. So that's the long history.

Around the 1950s, the middle daughter (Ida) and her husband, I guess, were having trouble with my grandfather—he's not the easiest person in the world—and they decided to strike out on their own and open their own business out on Long Island. . . . And then it became the two daughters and their husbands. That's my eldest aunt, Hattie, and my mother, Ann. So it was Hattie and her husband, Murray, and my mother, Ann, and my father, Herb, who ran the business over the years. And the business grew and flourished.

But the neighborhood changed. This neighborhood, which was the Jewish barrio, the Jewish ghetto, changed particularly after World War II when the veterans came home. The Jewish boys came home, and they had some money in their pocket, and they started moving their families out to Long Island, to Westchester, various parts of the country. . . . The area went into a slow decline in terms of retail, but it started to become more precipitous in the late sixties. It sort of lost its Jewish flavor, except for some pockets and some old businesses that remained—like Russ & Daughters. . . . There's a few others: Katz's and Yona Schiemel's and Ratner's—some on Orchard Street. But by and large, Jewish life in the neighborhood started to recede. Other waves of immigrants—Hispanic and Asian—continued up until recently. I was born a block away from here on Ludlow Street, so I consider myself a real Lower East Sider.

So we have . . . my aunt and uncle [and] my mother and father, and around the mid- to late-1960s, early seventies . . . they want to retire and they leave the business. And at this point, I'm doing something else. I'm practicing law. And, you know, a fancy firm uptown, and I decide . . . it's not all it's cracked up to be. My father has a heart condition and he's finding it increasingly difficult to run the business, and I decide that I can come in here and help him so Russ & Daughters should not leave the town. And I thought that I could practice law at the same time—which was totally fanciful because the first day I came in here, almost twenty-three years ago, was the last day I've ever practiced law. Just caught up in the nature of the business. It's still kind of overwhelming that it requires such focus and concentration and obsessiveness that it excludes anything else. . . . The business becomes your life. Fortunately, I kind of love the business. As it turns out, it's fish that's in my blood and not law.

And insofar as I'm a people person. . . . I'm able to enjoy that aspect of life. . . . And the various people who come in here! You get the throwbacks, the little old Jewish ladies come in for a "half a quarter," a "halve a *gertle*," it'll make ya crazy! . . . And then you have some of the most important people in the world coming in here. So I really enjoy that aspect of it.

The question I'm often asked is what happens after me? You know, I'm the third generation and . . . and I'll tell you what happens—the short answer is I don't know. . . . I was quoted in *The Times* as saying I'm a disappointed Jewish father, the only one disappointed his son is in medical school; he wants to be a doctor. I'd rather have him in here. My daughter?

It's not clear yet which way she's going to go, but she does get her historic and genetic roots with this place.[2]

What is kind of ironic about this whole situation is that, historically, all right, my grandfather did this; he started this kind of business because he didn't know what else to do. And his sister, who was somehow dealing with herring, was a natural leader. My parents' generation, my mother and my aunts, father, uncles, did this because they also had no options. They came out of the Depression, they came out of the war—this is what they did. And everybody worked very hard. They worked long hours, terrible conditions, and they did it [so] they were going to have children who would *not* have to do this. They were going to work hard, make enough money, give their kids a good education, and their kids can go and be doctors and lawyers and whatever else Jewish kids are supposed to do. There was no romance in this business at all. There is now, but there was not then. So it's changed an awful lot.

I was kind of the brainy one . . . and I did well, and I went to law school, and I practiced law for ten years. I was a big shot, you know, a serious-looking resume. I come in here, and I'm running this business, and I'm able to have more of a philosophical look at it. The food business, in general, has become very romantic, very exciting. And I look at this and I think, I want my kids in here. You can't be doing anything more important. There's some work that I call real work, important work. And lots of work that's "make work"—that's moving papers from this part of the desk to that part of the desk and sometimes when you move them, a billion dollars is moved with it. But I don't consider it real work. That may be arrogant for me to say, but that's the way I look at it.

Here, I think that we're providing a real service. . . . I think we're making the world a little better place just by being here and continuing to provide quality and service to the customers and this continuity of food tradition. Now clearly, there are some changes. . . . What is this, wasabi-flavored fish? My grandfather is probably rolling over in his grave! I have tofu cream cheese. I have a whole cheese section with manchego and rosinante and bries. . . . But that's just an issue of adding and moving with the times and with people's taste. He had lox, salt-cured salmon. That was it! I have ten different kinds of smoked salmon; some with pastrami spices and dill! You couldn't have imagined any of this.

"What is your typical day like?" Hauck-Lawson asked Federman. "Has it changed much in the two decades that you've been here?" To which he replied:

When I came into the business—remember I practiced law for almost ten years: fancy schools, fancy firm, hot shot!—I came in all puffed up. And I said to my father, "Okay I'm here, I'm here to help you out"—putting emphasis on "helping *you* out." Now, teach me what a good fish is from a bad fish. He said: "No problem. Here's what we do. We go to the smokehouse, four, five, six in the morning, whenever it's appropriate. We looked at the fish, we picked the fish, we cut the back of the fish, we tasted fish, we bring the fish in here, we weigh off the fish again, we put away the fish, we weigh it, we rotate it, we take the fish out, we taste the fish, we slice it for customers, we taste it again." And, he says, "if we do all of this, then, maybe in ten years, you'll know the difference between good fish and bad fish." And I thought he was kidding—but he wasn't!

Surprisingly, smoked salmon wasn't always a staple on the Lower East Side. Hauck-Lawson asked Federman how and when the delicacy became popular. And she asked, what about the huge number of smoke houses that used to exist along the Brooklyn waterfront? Were they still there, and was smoking still being done in New York City? Federman explained that:

Smoking [fish] has always happened, particularly in Europe, in Russia, in Germany I think they were smoking, Scandinavian smoking. Probably the American Indians over here were smoking fish. There was no refrigeration to preserve food, particularly fish. There were two ways to do smoking: either you salted it or you smoked it; or you salted it *and* smoked it. But it wasn't the palate of the general population here; it didn't become readily available until maybe the 1930s. The people who were selling the herring and the raw salmon got into smoking. And then the Jews got into the business, probably some old Germans originally.

Then you had salmon both from the Atlantic, which was known as "Nova Scotia" because most of the salmon came from the Nova Scotia area of Canada, and you had salmon from the Pacific, which we [called] "Nova." They're two different species; they kind of look alike and they taste somewhat the same. Today, most of the wild stock of salmon has been fished out. Virtually all of Atlantic salmons have been commercially fished out—99 percent of what you eat in salmon is farmed salmon. That came initially from Norway. They developed aqua-culture and fish-farming and they produce the big, fat, salmon. But it now happens all over the world, [salmon farming] has become a major business.

We deal with the Atlantic salmons, and it depends on where the best salmons are growing, and that could be any place in the world. We rely on the smokers to buy the better salmons and we buy from the smokers. Now, the smokers? When I first came into the business, they were mostly second and third generation, like I was. And the people that I was dealing with, their grandfathers had started the smoking businesses. This all made for very nice kinds of relationships. They knew what I wanted. . . . We could buy from lots of different people and keep them happy. (We pay our bills. My grandfather's rule was you pay your bills right away so everybody's happy.) But the smoking industry has gone into lots of consolidation. There's still some old-line smokers that I deal very closely with, third generation. And there are new guys on the block, and then there are little boutique smokers, and there's fish coming in from Scotland, or Ireland, or Norway. . . . so we have to deal with a lot more people now.

But I have major suppliers who are [New Yorkers]. Particularly in the items like dilled herring, Jewish items are local. Whitefish, chubs, sturgeon, sable—all done by the local smokehouses. They're really the only ones who know how to do that stuff. The water is different here in New York. You can buy smoked fish in Florida, in California, in Chicago—it's not going to taste the same. If you've been raised on New York smoked fish, it's got a particular taste. I think it's better and most people do. . . . New York likes fat and rich fish. And they're right. It's better. It's kind of like steak—fatter steak is a better steak—the difference is that fish is better for you than fat meat.

Several years ago, Federman was asked by some food editors to give a speech at a prestigious food conference on the history, health benefits, and "other aspects of eating smoked fish." The topic of his panel was "Is Deli Dying in New York?" So,

I asked a friend of mine, Abe Lebewold, who owned a place called the Second Avenue Deli, this famous deli in New York [to talk] about his field: meats, you know, pastrami, salami. . . . And I got up there and I went on and on and all about fish and it's healthy, and omega 3 fatty acids, blah, blah, blah. They finally had to take me off with a hook. And Abby got up there, and he looked them in the eye and he realized who he was dealing with, and he couldn't b.s. it, and he said: "What am I going to tell you? My food is going to *kill* ya!" We gave our speeches . . . and then we put up a line-up of our foods, arranged on platters. It was just like your dream Bar Mitzvah there. And all these supposedly sophisticated, educated, food-wise editors and writers tore into it like a bunch of kids at a Bar Mitzvah.

Hauck-Lawson asked if that didn't say something about the "happiness factor" associated with your product:

Oh, god, yes! What is food? Food is the ultimate comfort when everything else fails us. . . . It's to reward us when we feel happy and successful. It's everything: it's our roots, our traditions; it's a throw-back. Food is what it's all about. Food and probably sex. But I'm not sure what the correct order is . . . I'd say have sex first, get that out of the way, now let's eat!

So this place, Russ & Daughters—it's not until recently that all of this kind of sank in. . . . So you ask me, what did I do when I came here twenty-three years ago, what do I do today? The same thing. You know, I buy fish, I weigh fish, I take care of customers, I handle the phones, I run the personnel aspect of it. We're busier than ever, so it's a little more overwhelming than ever.

I do pretty much supervise the whole operation. I've gotta schmooze the customers, too. We've become some kind of food celebrity. I mean, that's kind of interesting. I go to a party or a Bar Mitzvah or a wedding where they sit you at a table, right? They put you at a table; ten, twelve people at a table. At some point, you go around the table and always, "what you do?" It's like in school: "Stand up and tell us what your name is, where you're from, what your parents did, blah, blah." This always happens. So you go around. The guy says he's a CPA, and a woman gets up and she's a major investment advisor, and a guy's a CEO, and the other guy's a brain surgeon. And they get to me, and "What do you do?" "I sell fish." And that, like, stops them. What's he doing at our table, right? "I sell fish." "What kind of fish do you sell?" "I sell smoked fish." "Oh yeah? Where?" "Lower East Side?" "What kind of place?" I say "Russ & Daughters." "Russ & Daughters?!" Then the entire conversation for the evening—which disgusts my wife, because she's tired of talking about the business—"is, tell us about this fish, and that fish," and they're happy as clams. "And my grandfather shopped there, and my grandmother took me there, and I still go there." So, it's like, you know, nobody anymore wants to hear about a tax case, or that you did brain surgery. They don't want to hear. They want to hear what's good in caviar and smoked fish, and who was in the store recently.

It may be wrong for me to say, but it's a major ego trip. And I get off on that. It's a living, clearly, but I love it! You're looking at a guy who likes what he does; *loves* what he does. As I get older and the business gets bigger . . . we become more famous and more people want us. And now we're into the mail order business and we're on the Internet. It's tough keeping up with the business. During holiday periods, I virtually turn away business. I turn it away. My grandfather would be *very* upset. This is not just Jewish food anymore. The whole world wants smoked salmon. Right?

Chapter
Nine

URBAN PROFILE:
CONEY ISLAND BAGELS
AND BIALYS

STEVE ROSS is a third-generation baker and the owner of Coney Island Bagels and Bialys. The shop, which was founded by Ross's grandfather Morris Rosenzweig around 1900, sits behind a modest storefront on an otherwise unremarkable block on Coney Island Avenue near Avenue U between Brooklyn's Coney Island and Gravesend neighborhoods. In fact, the shop is really a modest-sized bakery fronted by a walk-in retail area. It's the sort of place that tourists—what few there are in this modest, middle-class residential neighborhood—might pass by without a second glace. But New Yorkers know better. For behind the small-windowed brick storefront sits not only a wonderful bagel bakery, but also an epicenter for that even rarer and highly sought after local delicacy: the bialy.

As a complement to our interview with Russ & Daughters' Mark Federman, we thought it was essential to interview an artisan who was keeping alive the traditions connected with the bagel half of New York's bagel-and-lox equation. So Dr. Annie Hauck-Lawson took the subway out to 2359 Coney Island Avenue to interview Ross about his family, his craft, and the traditions surrounding bagel and bialy making in New York City.[1]

Workers at Coney Island Bagels and Bialys follow time-tested methods of hand-rolling and baking bagels in their Brooklyn shop. PHOTO BY ANNIE HAUCK-LAWSON, COURTESY SMITHSONIAN INSTITUTION.

In recent years, bagels have gone from being a specialty food rarely found outside New York, to a popular staple widely available in malls and chain stores throughout the United States—well, sort of. In fact, most New Yorkers are united in the opinion that bagels found outside of New York don't taste quite right. Some Gothamites go as far as referring to them as "bagel shaped objects" (BSOs), insisting that real bagels can only be made with the magic qualities inherent in New York City tap water. Third-generation baker Ross agrees.

BAGELS AND BIALYS: A HISTORY

There are any number of stories about where and when bagels were invented. Ross believes that bagels first appeared in 1683 as a special bread created by Austrian bakers to honor the Polish King John II Sobieski, who had recently defeated the Turks and saved the city of Vienna. King John was an enthusiastic equestrian and, it is said, the bakers created a special bread in the shape of a riding stirrup to thank him. The German word for stirrup, *beugel*, Ross told us, later morphed into "bagel." Whatever their origins, they proved to be extremely popular with New York's early-twentieth-century Eastern European Jewish community. In fact, they became indelibly associated with American Jewish culture, where they were traditionally served with cream cheese and smoked salmon—which was locally known as "lox"—for breakfast.

Bialys are also a favorite New York Jewish bread product, but otherwise have little in common with bagels. They originated in Poland as *Bialystocker kuchens*, onion-topped rolls with a distinctive taste reminiscent of sourdough and toothsome consistency that is considerably different from bagels. Bialystok's Jewish population was decimated during World War II, which has frustrated Ross's lifelong interest in tracing the roll's European history: "I did a report back in junior high school on bialys and there was nothing. There are no pictures. There is nothing left of the history of the bialy in Bialystok." Like bagels, they were traditionally served with butter and sometimes cream cheese. A New York specialty, they have not gained the same nationwide popularity as have bagels—at least not yet. But Ross is doing his best to change that.

Hauck-Lawson began her interview with Ross by asking him about how he got into the baking trade. It started, he began, in the early 1900s when his grandfather, Rosenzweig and his brothers came to New York from Poland. She asked him if he knew from where in Poland his grandfather came.

Bialystok. That's where bialys originated. They knew about bialys from Poland. It was something that they had picked up out there. They opened up [a bakery] in East New York, Brooklyn. The initial store they were doing strictly wholesale, there was no such thing as retail. The two brothers left the business. One moved up to Connecticut; the other one, I think he gave up the business altogether. And basically, my grandfather stayed in the industry. Later on, he moved into Coney Island on Mermaid Avenue and West 31st Street. He opened up there.

It had to have been late forties, early fifties. [The shop] was there for a number of years. And again, it was strictly wholesale. At the time, they didn't even have a van or any type of automobile. It was horse and buggy, horse and carriage. I remember stories of the driver finishing up with the route, unhooking the horse . . . and the horse went right to the stable. Just one wagon.

He purchased this building back in the late fifties. . . . My grandfather passed away in 1959, 1960. Again, when this store was opened, it was strictly wholesale. There weren't even windows here. The door—they used to keep it open to get air in. People kept walking in all the time, asking if they can buy. And eventually, my father knocked through the wall, put in a window, and started a retail business. That would be around 1960, early sixties.

"Was you father baking at that time?" Hauck Lawson asked.

Everybody in the family baked. It was a family bakery. My father and his two sisters were involved in the business. When my grandfather passed away, it was split amongst the three of them. The sisters didn't want the business, they sold their shares to my father, and he took it over. I was eight years old when I first started working here.

I swept, I packed bialys, and like most normal kids, I climbed flour sacks. But, you know, it was a family business. My brothers and sisters would come in and help also. I'm the oldest, so as we all grew up, we all knew the business. And we all started from the bottom and we worked our way up. I'm the only one left in the business.

"Going back to your grandfather's product," Hauck-Lawson asked, "can you describe [his] bialy?"

The bialys, we were making it back in the early 1900s . . . again, to get the actual date's hard. At the time it was strictly bialys. That's all that we made.

Bialys were made with a hand press. The dough was mixed in a mixer and then it was scaled out into what we call a "press ball." Each press made approximately three dozen. Then it was put in a manual machine that would cut that press ball into thirty-six smaller squares—what we call *tegel*, it means "a piece." And then, each one of those squares was rolled out into a round ball by hand. They're allowed to "proof up," and then they're baked. The proofing process takes anywhere from fifteen minutes to forty minutes, depending on how much yeast is put in the dough. And then they were topped with raw onions and baked. We use fresh onions. Wash, peel, and then grind—we use a commercial meat grinder because they don't make an onion grinder, per se. We use about 200 pounds of onions a week.

"So really," Hauck-Lawson continued, "The whole process except for the automatic press"

has stayed the same. And we're known nationwide. I started about 1996 shipping over the Internet. And all I hear from people is that "We can't get a bialy," and "I remember your product from New York," and "Thank god you're shipping," and "'Let me order!" And it's word of mouth. We do no real advertising.

There's only three bialy stores in New York. . . . New York is the only place you can really get a true bialy. A lot of bagel stores that do wholesale out in New Jersey, a lot of bagel stores out there make their own "bialys," but they make it out of bagel dough! And unfortunately, out of sight, out of mind: if you haven't seen it in so long, or haven't tasted it, you end up getting used to it [tasting like a bagel].

Hauck-Lawson asked if Ross made different doughs for bialys and bagels.

It's two different doughs. Well, first it's the water. Award-winning New York water—you can't beat it. It's a softer dough. The ingredients otherwise are basically the same. You can get them anywhere: flour, salt, yeast. But it's the water; the water's the main ingredient. . . . I don't use any artificial additives or preservatives.

And then it's the process of how it's made: There's only a handful of people that know how to actually make bialys. There are very few people now, back in the early sixties there were a lot of people. They formed a [bialy bakers'] union. Now, there's maybe fifteen people in the bialy end of the [bagel] union; years ago there were hundreds. Years ago, we used to have shifts with two or three guys working. Now I've only got one guy left in the union. And that's here in the store.

"What do you do when [the union member] is sick or goes on vacation?" Hauck-Lawson asked.

All my guys are cross-trained. One guy is retired so he comes in. He works one day a week 'cause he is so busy. Plus, I know how, and if, you know, push comes to shove, I've been known to throw on my whites and go in the back. And usually you'll see me baking during holidays, with extra orders going out. Or we'll be busy in the front [shop], I would be pushing the bialys out for the customers. We didn't start making bagels until around the late seventies, middle to late seventies. We saw a trend of bagels coming into the States.

Hauck-Lawson asked if they were exclusively a bialys bakery before the late seventies.

Exclusively bialys. We started baking bagels, it must have been around 1970 is when we started. My father saw . . . I don't remember where—at a convention or a show—but he saw bagels being made. And the difference between them, although you're talking two totally different breads, the process isn't really that different. My father sent my uncle out to learn. And they taught him how to make the dough and roll the bagels by hand and we started to produce bagels wholesale.

The middle seventies—seventy-five, seventy-six?—they came out with a machine. . . . They were nothing like the machines we have nowadays. It would cut the dough into small pieces. It would sit in what we would call a "hopper" or a "little cup," and then that cup would travel almost around the entire store so that [the dough] would proof a little. Then we'd pull it down into a shaper and shape it into a bagel. And then, they would pick it up and put it onto the [baking] boards.

My father did not like the machines. They kept breaking, jamming. Again, we were one of the first ones to have it because of the amount of wholesale we were doing. So we called the company up and told them to pick it up, take it away. And we went back to handmade. And we've been with handmade since.

At any given time, we would have as many as six guys rolling bagels within a twenty-four-hour period. This is going back, I guess, by this time it was late seventies, early eighties. Nowadays, everybody's gone into the bagel *industry*; bagels have become very popular. Lenders is the [company] basically that made it that popular, he commercialized it. And then the fast-food restaurants started picking up on it. I've known a lot of people going into the business, [but] as fast as they went in, they went out. . . . Everything looks nicer on the other side of the counter! Everything looks a lot easier until you realize you've got to be up at 3:00 in the morning, and you don't get home until, if you're lucky, 3:00, 4:00 in the afternoon. And then again, the headaches start. My father used to leave phone numbers with where he would be. Nowadays, because of how hi-tech we've become, I've got a cell phone or I've got a beeper, which I call my electronic leashes. So I'm never that far away from the store. They can get me, and they have, twenty-four hours a day!

"What kind of problems?" Hauck-Lawson wanted to know. What would constitute a bagel or bialys emergency?

It can range anywhere from someone not showing up [for work], to one of the ovens not starting. Once, I was at an awards dinner in a tuxedo and I got beeped, the oven went down! My wife in a gown and myself in a tuxedo came down here and had to fix the oven. . . . I've slept on flour sacks, I've slept in the car. These are all part of owning a business.

The business has done very well for myself and my family, but it's a hard business. During the summer it can get as high as 110 degrees in the store. During the winter it's very comfortable in here. I enjoy the business, I've grown to love the business. My family, you know, the same thing. I mean there are times!—Because of the hours, I'm up at 2:30 in the morning. I live in New Jersey. It takes me forty-five minutes to an hour to get here. So I'm out of the house between 3:00 and 3:15 A.M. I'm in the store between 4:00 and 4:30. And I'm home anywhere between 1:00 and 3:00, depending on the day. I take Sundays off, which is unheard of in this industry. When I initially started doing it, everyone says you can't do it, but my father used to [work] on Sundays. . . . I remember he didn't get home until 12:00, 1:00 in the afternoon and he was tired, he wanted to eat, he wanted to take a shower. Then at that point, there wasn't much to do. And I didn't want to do that with my kids. So Sundays I take off. Emergencies, I come in. One of my guys goes on vacation, I'll come in; I'll cover for them. So it's really I've got one day off a week.

As we interviewed Ross in his shop, there was a steady parade of customers: neighborhood kids buying a still warm bagel on their way home from school, housewives picking up half-a-dozen bagels for tonight's snack or tomorrow's breakfast, suburbanites sprinting from double-parked cars to buy a dozen bialys to take out to Long Island for the weekend. Hauck-Lawson noted that Ross's retail operation was steady and asked if he had any plans to expand. He gave it some thought, and said:

> Like any other business, with the economy I've had bad times and I've had good times. . . .We do deliver into New Jersey. That has improved slightly over the years, mainly because your baby boomers are moving out [of the city] now. And those are the ones that grew up on bialys. Their parents used to bring them home Saturday night, Sunday. The weekends we'd have lines out the door! Those days, unfortunately, are long gone. At any given time I can have two or three people behind the counter not because there's a line, but because times have changed. People are in a rush. And people don't like to wait. And I don't like for my customers to wait. They come in; they're double parking. . . . If I got two or three, four people in the store we try and get them out. I'll have one of my bakers come up [to work the register]. They're cross-trained, and they know how—they know better than I do.
>
> And it has become a family. One of my bialy bakers started with my grandfather. One of my bagel bakers started with my father—he's baking with me for years. I've got guys who have only been with me for a couple of months, and I've had guys who have been with me for as long as eight, ten years. As a boss, I think I'm a fair boss. I pay way over minimum—everybody has to make a living. They have a life to maintain, families to take care of. So I try and be as decent as possible.

Hauck-Lawson asked if Ross would walk her through how he made bagels.

> Nowadays, there are two types of bagels. There's a *water bagel* and a *rack oven bagel*. Water bagel is your traditional bagel. The process for a bagel is how the dough is made. It takes about twenty, twenty-five minutes to mix the dough. It's taken out as one big [lump of] dough, cut into strips, and then rolled into the shape of bagels. Again, we bake strictly by hand. Those [shops] that have machines will take the dough out of the mixer, cut it into slabs of dough, and then feed that into the machine, and the

machine will process the bagel into its round form. Everything here is shaped by hand. Bagels are then allowed to proof up, which will again take anywhere, just like a bialy, from fifteen minutes to as long as—it could take even as long as two hours, depending on the type of dough. A regular plain dough, or white dough, can take anywhere from fifteen minutes to forty-five minutes. A raisin dough can take as long as two hours, because of the acid in the raisins.

Ross now makes almost two dozen different kinds of bagels, expanding past the traditional plain, poppy seed, and onion into flavors that would have amazed his grandfather, including apple cinnamon, sun-dried tomato basil, pumpkin (in the fall), and for the indecisive, the everything bagel.

Once the dough is ready, once it's become proofed, it is then put into a *walk-in box* refrigerator. And that keeps it from rising. Our doughs will stay in there no more than three days; anything longer than that the dough becomes old. Usually, with the amount of baking that we do, it doesn't reach that point. Very, very rarely reaches it.

That's a bagel. With the bialy, the day you make it is the day you bake it. With the bagel, now I've got over thirty-five varieties of bagels. They're all boiled. With the *rack oven* bagel, what they do is they take the bagel out and they wet it down. They *don't* boil it. They wet it down, then they put it onto a tray. And that tray is put into a rack oven, and it's basically baked by steam.

But *water bagels*: What a water bagel does is it pulls the starch out. Makes it softer. And it stays softer for a lot longer. A rack oven is not doing that. It's basically baking it and, you know, what's good about a rack oven is you can make your bagels anytime during the day—as many or as little as you want. With a water bagel you've got to have the kettle on and the oven on [ready] to bake it. And you've got to wait for the water to boil. Again, you're paying for water, you're paying for gas.

"How long do you have to boil bagels?" Hauck-Lawson asked.

You boil it anywhere from ten seconds to as long as forty seconds. Then it's put onto the wooden burlap-covered boards, then placed in the oven. They're baked in a rotating oven, or what they call a *pan oven*. They go around and they're baked for about two and a half to three minutes. At which point, the bagels are flipped. Now, if you put a wet bagel onto the shelf it's going to stick. What we do is we bake it until the bottom is dry, or in this case, the top is dry. Then we flip the bagel and the full baking process begins. That will take about seven minutes, six to seven minutes. Bialys, the process takes, once it's in the oven, about the same thing, six to eight minutes.

Bagels have gained a nationwide following in the last decade or so. Even in the smallest of American towns, it is possible to find at least one fancy food emporium or even standard grocery store that sells fresh or frozen "New York style" bagels. (Not that there are any other styles!) Hauck-Lawson asked Ross if he thought bialys would be the next food fad.

You were asking me before what I see as the future. The Internet has been very good to us. In the past five years more and more people are using it. Last year we did phenomenal; this year, business has increased. People have asked me to open up [a shop] in New Jersey, open up in Arizona, open up in Las Vegas, open up all over the country. I don't foresee that, at least for now. An operation like this, it's not automated enough. Bagels you can open up anywhere. Machine-made bagels and rack oven bagels— you really don't need a skill to make the dough; you don't need the skill to bake the dough. A lot of chain bagel stores deal strictly with frozen doughs—they make the doughs and they ship it out to the individual chain stores.

Bialys, unfortunately, are not like a bagel. Bagels you can make out of a fifty-pound bag of flour. You can get about twenty dozen bagels, fifteen dozen bagels, depending on how big you're making it. Put it into your [oven] and you bake it off as you need it. Minimum amount of bialys is about, to make a good tasting bialy, a good dough, minimum is about thirty dozen. Anything less than that, you start to lose taste; you don't get a good mix. So unless you're prepared to throw dough out or wholesale it, you really aren't getting a true tasting bialy.

The other thing that tends to happen with a lot of stores is absentee management. Businesses aren't run that way. One thing with this business, my grandfather, my father, myself—people came in, they knew me. And they still do. They come in, they see me behind the counter. They can pick up a phone and call if there's a problem; if there's anything in particular they want. We try and cater to our customers. They know, just ask. . . . No one walks out mad. If someone walks out mad, they can tell everybody. Very few people will say how great it is, but everybody will always say how bad it is.

HAND ROLLING: KEEPING ARTISAN TRADITIONS ALIVE

To Ross, keeping the traditional baking methods alive is vital because he firmly believed that it results in a better product. We found it interesting that in a competitive food world where newly minted up-scale food shops do not hesitate to advertise themselves as purveyors of "artisan breads," "handmade" or "bespoken food," Ross is rather self-effacing about the quality of his product and the amount of skill and training that goes into producing it. Hauck-Lawson asked Ross how long it took to learn the basics.

> It can take as short as one week to learn to roll bagels by hand, to get the basics down. To get the speed, that comes with time. Bialys? I saw someone learn it within three weeks. It usually takes about a month-and-a-half to two months to learn it. And then again, the speed comes with time. People don't have that commitment. They want that [skill], you know, right now.
>
> I remember growing up, we had a crew, and we still do. We're baking or we have someone here twenty-four hours a day. We used to have bakers from midnight until 6:00 in the morning. We had one baker from 6:00 in the morning until 12:00 noon. We had another baker from 12:00 until 6:00, and another one from 6:00 until midnight. Then came the weekends—each shift basically had two people on it. My father used to make two or three deliveries a day. He had two or three trucks going out at different times. They used to produce hundreds of dozens, if not a thousand dozen a day. Now, maybe a couple of hundred dozen a day we'll produce on bialys. And that's with additional special orders and what not.

"During your dad's time, how many bialys were you making a day?" Hauck-Lawson asked.

> I'd say we were going through a thousand dozen. That would be actually closer to the weekend [totals]. But then those days, you were getting anywhere from five cents to fifteen, twenty cents. We're now up to forty-five—and unfortunately, it's going to be going up to fifty. The flour that you use goes up; the weather conditions are a big factor. Con Ed has not been too kind to us, gas companies, utilities which are usually gas, water. My water bill—I used to pay one thousand dollars a year, we pay now almost ten thousand dollars a year for water.

IS THE BIALY AN ENDANGERED SPECIES?

So will bialys survive in twenty-first century America? We asked Ross to talk about what the future might hold and whether he thought Coney Island Bagels and Bialys might continue as a family business. His thought for a minute and said:

> With any type of business there's always a question mark. I've been offered in the past to sell the business. I've had legitimate people who have come in and offered me good money for the business. The problem is, what am I going to do? My work is, literally, nineteen hours a day. I'm up at 2:30 in the morning; I go to bed around 8:00, 9:00 at night six days a week. My kids tuck *me* into bed at night. . . . I'm up eighteen, nineteen hours a day. My wife hates going on vacation with me because even on my days off, I'm up at 5:00 in the morning. . . . So it's not easy. Would I sell? The temptation could always be there, but what would I do? . . . For me to sit around and do nothing—I'd go stir crazy!

Hauck-Lawson closed her interview by asking Ross what he thought the future might hold for his family's iconic New York business.

> My father, Donald Ross, was very well liked. Unfortunately, my grandfather died and he had to support the family, so he fell into the business. . . . He was nineteen, twenty years old when he came into it. . . . He did have help from friends that were in the industry. They looked out for him, they liked him. I've got a lot of old customers, wholesale customers, retail customers that come in and are constantly: "Tell your father I say hello, there is no one like your father, he was a true *mensch*, a true gentleman." I strive to be like that. I go out there, I talk to my customers. If there's a problem, it's me that they're dealing with.
>
> My [teenage] children, I got a boy and a girl. They both have come into the store to work. They work the counter, the register. They want to work it. They haven't really learned how to pull bialys or roll bagels. They pack bialys, they sweep—things I used to do. I was thirteen years old, I was pulling bialys. . . . [They're] still young. Will they get into the business? As much as I'd like to see it continue, I'd like to see them get into something easier. It's a hard business. We live comfortably, but it's hard. But if they decide this is what they want, I'll back them up. I did the same.

THE CULTURES
OF WALL STREET

Y OU CAN'T HELP but notice them, especially on the subway: the smartly
dressed men and women of Wall Street. Sporting a briefcase in one hand
and a neatly folded *Wall Street Journal* in the other, somberly attired waves
of them emerge from the subway stops along Wall Street and disappear into
the fortress-like buildings that loom above the narrow streets of Manhattan's
Financial District. Most New Yorkers have little or no idea what they actually
do at their jobs, although many envision circling sharks, multi-generational
wealth, and lavish lunches in hushed, dark-paneled rooms. As our interviews
reflect, these assumptions are astonishingly inaccurate. In fact, the workers of
Wall Street proved to be one of the most fascinating and unexpectedly tra-
dition-bound occupational communities documented in the course of the
Smithsonian's New York City Project.[1]

Although some of the individuals quoted in this chapter were a bit reluctant to be publicly identified by name because of the sensitive nature of their
positions, we found that they were all delighted to speak with us about their
work culture, an occupational community of which they were extremely
proud. Most people, they said, came to ask them for prognostications about
the markets, not to talk about the history of their profession, which dates

Statue marking the site of Washington's first presidential inauguration looks across Wall Street in the shadow of the historic Trinity Church. PHOTO BY GEROGE MARKS/RETROFILE RF COLLECTION/GETTY IMAGES.

back to the eighteenth century. Journalists, often on short deadlines, simply wanted to know if the market was going up or down, but had little interest in the complex skills they had to master, how they acquired their occupational knowledge or practiced their trade, or the colorful individuals who trained and mentored them.[2]

Once asked, we found they were not only delighted to talk about "The Street," but that they also often shared eloquent insights into both the financial world and the people who are involved in that occupational community. The first thing that they wanted us to know was that there is no single Wall Street community: rather, The Street consists of a series of smaller occupational communities. Although Wall Street workers do share some common folklore and customs, the traders on the floor of the New York Stock Exchange (NYSE) have different stories and traditions from members of the New York

Mercantile Exchange ("The Merc"), and members of the New York Board of Trade (NYBOT) sometimes use expressions and hand signals unknown to traders a few blocks away at the American Stock Exchange (AMEX). The distinctive traditions and histories of these trading organizations give each its own sense of identity, history, and culture. Nearby these large exchanges, but also within the Financial District, are other related but discrete communities of bond traders, bankers, insurance brokers, and a myriad of other sub-specialties that make New York the financial capital of the world.

Listening to Wall Street workers describe their jobs challenges stereotypes. Instead of forebodingly abstract strings of numbers and analytical pronouncements, The Street quickly breaks down into real people doing real jobs. After all, both Dow and Jones of the Dow Jones Industrial Average were real New Yorkers with first names (Charles and Edward), careers, and private lives.[3] Like other traditional occupational communities, Wall Street workers use orally transmitted stories, narratives, jokes, hazing, cautionary tales, and generations of accumulated knowledge to do their work efficiently and effectively. In an industry where custom, tradition, personal relationships, and trust are highly valued, the impersonality of Internet trading is more than an economic challenge, it is a threat to a centuries-old occupational culture.

EARLY HISTORY OF THE STREET

In the course of our interviews, we found it interesting that many of our Wall Street informants began their narratives chronologically by telling us stories about the early history of the Financial District. Today's Wall Street follows the path of an actual stockade wall built by the Dutch in 1653 to mark the northernmost end of their New Amsterdam settlement. Legend has it that the Dutch felt they needed a wall not so much because they feared the Indians, with whom they were on reasonably good terms, but to guard them from their rivals, the English in colonial New England. They were proved right in 1664 when, in the aftermath of the Second Anglo-Dutch War, New Amsterdam was transferred to Britain in exchange for Curaçao and the Spice Islands.[4] The victorious British promptly renamed the forty-year-old settlement New York after King Charles II's brother William, Duke of York, but otherwise, the mercantile character of the rapidly growing settlement remained basically unchanged. Many local merchants were actually "brokers," which is a term derived from the fourteenth-century French word *brocour,* which referred to a person who broaches a wine cask and sells its contents by the glass or bottle. During the colonial period, these intermediaries brought buyers and sellers together and took a commission on any resulting deals. Many years later, when Wall Street brokers began to specialize in the buying and selling of securities, their places of business came to be called "brokerage houses" or "brokerages."

In the spring of 1789, George Washington stood on a balcony overlooking the intersection of Broad and Wall Streets—directly across the street from the present day NYSE—and was sworn in as the first president of the United States. Beginning in 1785, under the Articles of Confederation, and continuing under the newly ratified Constitution, New York served as the capital of the young republic for five years. The economy was a pressing matter of concern, and under the brilliant guidance of the first Secretary of the Treasury, New Yorker Alexander Hamilton, the United States issued bonds and "publick stock" in an attempt to retire debts incurred during the Revolutionary War.[5] New York merchants were soon congregating along Wall Street, near the newly established Treasury Department, to trade government stocks, bonds, and securities. William Duer, a signer of the Articles of Confederation, member of the Continental Congress, former Treasury employee, and personal friend of Washington, was heavily involved in the manipulation of these financial instruments. When his considerable empire collapsed in March 1792, amidst allegations of impropriety, it led to a virtual collapse of the nascent New York bond market.[6]

In an attempt to reestablish trust and revive a New York economy badly shaken by the scandal surrounding Duer, as well as to address some other financial problems that existed at that time, twenty-four of New York's most prominent merchants gathered in the shade of a huge buttonwood (sycamore) tree outside a coffee house at what is now 68 Wall Street and drew up a set of rules and regulations to guide the trading of stocks and bonds (the terms were used interchangeably in the late-eighteenth century). Signed on May 17, 1792, this compact, known the Buttonwood Agreement, marked the founding of an organization that after a complicated history and several changes of name would later gain international prominence as the NYSE. (The buttonwood tree itself became part of Wall Street's folklore, and it was widely mourned when it was eventually felled by a storm in 1865.[7])

In 1794, signers of the Buttonwood Agreement began meeting indoors at Wall Street's famed Tontine Coffee House on the corner of Wall and Water Streets. Although activity during the first decades was slow, their trading interests gradually expanded to include shares of bonds issued by other nations, and stock in private companies, especially those involved in enormous projects such as the construction of canals, turnpikes, and railroads that needed to raise large amounts of capital. "That's the thing that people don't realize about Wall Street," one trader told us:

Setting up a way that private people could underwrite invention and innovation has given America this edge on the rest of the world. Rather than waiting around for stuffy government bureaucrats, anyone with a good idea—and sometimes with not such good ideas—could go directly to other Americans and try to raise enough money to give it a try.[8]

From the start, only NYSE members or brokers could trade at the exchange, which was reorganized in 1817 and rented a space of its own for two hundred dollars a month at 40 Wall Street.[9] However, in nearby streets, alleys, and offices non-members, who were dismissively called "curbside traders," also tried to make their fortunes in "financial paper." The number of shares traded in the surrounding neighborhood often outstripped the volume traded at the NYSE and many stocks were introduced by the curb traders before being officially "listed" on the blackboards inside the NYSE.[10] These outdoor activities laid the foundations for the New York Curb Exchange, which literally took place on the street curbs surrounding the NYSE until 1921, when it moved indoors to its present home a few blocks away on Greenwich Street. The Curb Market or Exchange did not change its name to the more formal American Stock Exchange or AMEX until 1953. Outdoor trading also gave rise to the commodities exchanges described in this chapter which, together with the NYSE, firmly established the Wall Street area as the epicenter of American finance.

In the decades that followed the Buttonwood Agreement, the NYSE developed a distinctive culture of its own. In 1817, the group reorganized itself and formalized its hours of operation. Chairs were provided for each exchange member, and members would rise from their assigned "seats" when a stock they were interested in was "called" to be traded. Although actual chairs are a thing of the past, today traders must still "buy a seat" to do business on the NYSE's trading floor. Initially, the name of a specific stock was called or traded twice a day—once in the morning and again in the afternoon. In the 1870s, this custom was replaced by the "continuous call system" that is still in use.

While some New York brokers were busy buying and selling stocks, others began to specialize in buying, selling, and speculating in commodities. Gold and silver, as well as sugar, corn, and cotton were among the products traded on early New York exchanges. (Gold was originally traded on the NYSE, too, but during the Civil War profiteering in gold came to be seen as unpatriotic and trading of the metal was discontinued by the NYSE. Always ready to take advantage of a money-making opportunity, curb brokers organized their own gold exchange.[11]) Later, commodities exchanges were established for everything from orange juice to heating oil and platinum to palladium.

Commodity exchanges came and went, often sharing quarters with one another for a few years, splitting off to establish their own trading spaces, and reuniting, but always remaining within a few blocks of Wall Street in what came to be called the Financial District. Today, there are two major commodities exchanges in New York: The Mercantile Exchange (Merc), which merged with the Commodities Exchange (COMEX) in 1994 and moved into a specially commissioned building of its own about six blocks northwest of Wall Street; and the New York Board of Trade (NYBOT), which is better known on The Street as "Coffee, Sugar and Cocoa."[12] During the 1990s, NYBOT was located in the lower levels of the World Trade Center's South Tower. After the destruction of 4 World Trade in September 2001, the NYBOT temporarily relocated to Queens before resettling in rented space in The Merc's riverfront building in 2003.

LIFE ON THE TRADING FLOORS

Although each facet of the financial world has its own stories and traditions, we decided to concentrate on documenting the most fabled and colorful aspect of Wall Street's financial world: the traders and the trading floors of the stock and commodity exchanges. Traders are the men and women who spend their days on the trading floors and in the trading pits negotiating transactions with their colleagues to fulfill buy and sell orders sent in by customers throughout the world. Despite their differences, what unites New York's major exchanges is that they all have a central physical space where financial paper is bought and sold by brokers through "open outcry." In the open outcry system, a buyer and a seller meet each other on the "trading floor"—or, in the case of the commodity exchanges, in the "trading pit" or "ring"—and verbally negotiate a buy or sell deal. The agreed-upon deal is then duly noted and later formally documented away from the floor. The traders sincerely believe it is the most forthright and beneficial system for all involved. As Merc trader Scott Hess explained:

> Open outcry gives you the transparency. You know who is bidding and offering [what] and, for the most part, you can usually tell the volume [i.e., number of shares]. They don't always have to tell their volume or state their volume, but most of the time they do. . . . It's the transparency, and it just gives you a forum for negotiating a transaction.[13]

Joseph Cicchetti, another Merc trader, offered his rationale for the survival of open outcry. Like many of the traders we interviewed, he admitted the possibility that the present system might soon be replaced by online electronic trading over the Internet, however:

> A lot of times, true price disclosure cannot be achieved unless it's done between people. . . . There may not always be a forum for that type of trading. It may not always be as prominent as it is now; it may stay as prominent or get more prominent. If electronic [trading] is done properly to facilitate the execution of full price disclosure, one can complement the other. . . . I can sit at home and watch a baseball game—the best coverage you could imagine. . . . I can watch the stitching come in on the ball while the guy pitches! Yet, fifty-thousand people will shell out major money to go see a game *at* the game and it will be sold out. So there may always be a place like a gladiator's forum—a place where people can yell and scream, if for nothing else, just because it's *the* place.[14]

TRADING FLOORS, RINGS, AND PITS

So what is it like to work on the trading floors? Popular impressions of the trading floors come from the nightly news during which a well-dressed reporter looks directly into the camera and intones: "And today on Wall Street. . . . " In the background, viewers hear a dull roar of voices and the clanging bell that marks the opening and closing of the NYSE's trading day. To the uninitiated, the trading floors of Wall Street's stock and commodity markets seem like unmitigated chaos. But like much occupational madness, there is an underlying structure involved. In the case of the exchanges, workers' jobs involve performing an intricate ballet of actions, practices, and behaviors, many of them choreographed by generations of tradition and governed by internal and external rules and regulations. The organization of trading areas and the customs and specialized terms ("jargon") used to negotiate and finalize trades at each of the major exchanges are somewhat different. Each is worth a visit, and because it is the oldest and best known, our ethnographic tour begins with the culture of the NYSE.[15]

THE NEW YORK STOCK EXCHANGE

If the world of capitalism had to be represented by a single iconic image, it would probably be the trading floor of the NYSE. To the visitor, it is an astonishingly hectic, confusing, noisy, and thoroughly intimidating work space. To the traders, clerks, pages, and other employees of the NYSE who spend their lives there, it is just "the floor." Like any other work environment, it is a place filled with friends, colleagues, competitors, managers, assistants, and bosses; the place where workers confront the daily challenge of making a living.

The complex work culture of the NYSE trading floor has evolved over the past two hundred years. The NYSE moved several times during the nineteenth century before finally establishing itself in its present home at the intersection of Wall and Broad Streets. Since 1903, the NYSE has been located in an impressive Greek temple-inspired building. The massive columned edifice is intended to convey solidarity and bolster investor confidence. The heart of the NYSE is the original trading floor, "The Main Room." The Main Room, the one usually pictured in the media, is still the center of action, but over the years, because of the huge increase in the number of seats on the NYSE, the number of stocks traded, and the daily trading volume, the trading floor has been expanded several times. Since the 1950s, ancillary trading floor areas have been carved into adjoining spaces in the original building, as well as several neighboring buildings. At the time of our interviews, in addition to The Main Room, trading at the prestigious NYSE took place in what employees refer to as the "Blue Room," the "Expanded Blue Room" (EBR), and "The Garage."[16]

Although the trading floors are usually closed to visitors and our interviews were conducted elsewhere, the NYSE was kind enough to take us on several tours of the floor. With information provided by our knowledgeable guides, what at first seemed to be utter chaos began to have a sort of logic to it. They started by giving us the fundamentals: First, to trade on the NYSE, one must have a seat on the floor. Today, there are 1,366 seats or members on the NYSE. Because the number of seats was frozen in 1953, on those infrequent occasions when seats are put up for sale, they fetch healthy prices. (The current record of $4 million for a seat was set in 2005.) Many of the traders do not own a seat; rather they work for a firm that does, or they lease a seat from an individual who is not actively using theirs. Some of the member firms are small, but others such as Merrill Lynch or Smith Barney are huge concerns. Members work out of their own booths located around the perimeters of the trading floor, which they or their firms rent from the NYSE. Today's booths are a far cry from the original chairs or simple desks of the past. They bristle with telephones, recording and reporting devices, computers, TVs, and myriad state-of-the-art electronic gadgets. A firm's booth accommodates not only the seat's traders, but also an entourage of supporting clerks and pages who assist the traders to receive and fulfill ("fill") the orders that arrive via phone, fax, and computer lines. The booths themselves are tiny workspaces. Some firms have remodeled their areas and combined several of the NYSE's 1,400 booths to create "superbooths." A

Historic photo of the Main Room of the New York Stock Exchange before the introduction of modern technology.   PHOTO BY SUPERSTOCK, INC./SUPERSTOCK COLLECTION/GETTY IMAGES.

relatively new phenomenon, superbooths are looked upon with envy by less fortunate traders. NYSE's engineer and facilities manger Joe Gabriel described them to us as:

> A conglomeration of six, eight, or ten booths that one member firm has rented and redesigned to be more functional for them. Smith Barney, Prudential, J.P. Morgan Chase, Solomon Brothers—all the big guys [have superbooths]. They're expensive to build. A little two-dollar guy isn't going to have a superbooth.[17]

During the Civil War, a short-lived rival exchange, the Open Board of Brokers, arose to challenge the NYSE. The Open Board introduced several innovations that were later adopted by the NYSE when the two organizations merged in 1869 and that helped shape the NYSE's contemporary workspace. First, members no longer sedately sat waiting for twice-a-day calls to trade a particular stock. Instead, a "continuous auction" took place throughout the day and members interested in specific stocks would gather at designated spots or "posts" on the trading floor. (The term *post* apparently was borrowed from the curb traders outside, who gathered at specific lampposts for the same purpose.) A number of informants told us the possibly apocryphal story that posts for specific stocks began when one of the early traders broke his leg and, unable to move around, stood in one spot and waited for other traders interested in his stock to come to him. Because almost 2,800 stocks are traded on today's NYSE, space constraints dictate that numerous stocks are traded at each post.

WATERED STOCK

According to Wall Street legend, the term "watered stock" can be traced back to the mid-nineteenth century robber baron "Uncle Daniel" Drew. Early in his career, Drew worked as a cattle drover in Westchester County and devised a scheme whereby cattle headed for city meat markets would be fed salt at Brewster, about 40 miles north of the city, and not permitted to drink until they reached northern Manhattan—at which point, the thirsty animals would fill up on Harlem River water. Because cattle were sold by the pound, these temporarily heavier animals brought higher prices from New York butchers. On Wall Street, watered stock came to mean issuing more shares than warranted, making it possible for the unwary public to own more than 100 percent of a company.

We were lucky to have as one of our key informants the respected trader, Wall Street historian, ex-NYSE governor, and senior trading-floor representative Arthur D. Cashin, Jr., who, in his own inimitable fashion, explained why the posts are so important:

> At some point, competing exchanges and others suggested to [the Exchange] why don't we do continuous trading? Gee, what a wonderful idea! How will we do that? Suppose nobody's got anything new? How many times am I going to call this list? Guys are going to start throwing spit ball at each other; people are going to be upset. Yeah, you're right. Well, why don't we kind of separate it out, and let people who have business in Erie Canal go to Erie Canal? Where would that be? Well, why don't we give each stock a spot? And it was the most marvelous and inge-

nious thing! I can't believe they were smart enough to understand what they were doing. By doing that, they centralized the best bids and the best offers—all have to go to one spot.

If you're down on the floor and I met you coming through the door at 11 Wall Street and you said, "I have 100 AT&T to buy," and I said, "Well, let's save our shoe leather and just see where it is" . . . the rules say you can't do that. You've got to go to that one spot where the auction's taking place. And the good part of that is if you were the seller, there might be more buyers there than you knew. And you might get a better price than you would from me by just looking at that [ticker] tape. The other thing that this did—and this is one of the more remarkable accidental pieces of genius—is that it allowed for a "real time tape." Now, not only could you get the best bids and offers coming together in that auction, but I know *when*: you traded one hundred, and then two seconds later, I traded one hundred—that's the way they print. They print [trades] exactly as they occur. Now, I know to most lay people that doesn't sound like much, but it is. It's a disciplinary tool. It's a client protection tool—because if you gave me an order—and if I were a far more venal character—I [could have] walked over to a friend of mine and said, "I just got this order to buy by telephone. Why don't you buy it first, and then I'll buy it from you, and then you'll make some money on it."[18]

Today's trading posts are anything but simple. NYSE facilities manager Joe Gabriel told us: "My job over the years has been to marry current technology with a hundred-year old building. Making sure the building can accept it. It's a good career—it's rewarding [and] you get to see it everyday on television." And he continued, the recently updated trading posts are carefully designed and follow a "standard footprint," so

> From a functional/architectural standpoint it's very good. Because [it is] a segmented circle, it allows everybody a piece of space that's their own. No overlap between one trading crowd and another.[19]

In designing the current trading posts, the designers paid lots of attention to ergonomics, arranging things in the best, most efficient way, while at the same time they were "careful not to slow process down." For example, the new posts have specially designed "hospital" or "cantilevered arms" to display screens, so "each person gets their best shot" at seeing current prices and information. Modern posts have all been fitted with "the bonnet"—an overhead metal ring suspended from the ceiling by cables. The bonnet contains "all the technology that drives the post." There are also numerous electronic screens carrying specialized information such as the Display Book, and an electronic Super DOT workstation that keeps track of all orders.[20] It's impossible to look in any direction on the NYSE floor without being confronted with enough electronic display screens to remind you of Times Square.

In addition to the traders, another key element essential to the inner workings of the NYSE is the "specialist." Specialists are specific firms that are appointed by the Board of the NYSE to act as buffers; sort of brokers' brokers who moderate the price of a stock by buying and selling it at strategic points. In recent years, the existence of specialists has been questioned, and there are some who contend that this aspect of the NYSE has outlived its usefulness. Whether or not specialist firms survive in the new millennium, their continued existence reflects a much older stratum of the NYSE's history. Many of the specialists are members of family firms that have handled the same stocks for several generations. As financial journalist Jason Zweig explained:

> Specialists' business is as close to a pure hereditary trade as you could find— almost like blacksmithing in New England in the nineteenth century. In the old days, the specialist per stock ratio was much higher because there were so many fewer stocks, but the number of specialists was not that much smaller. Today, it's typical for specialists to handle a 'book' of several dozen stocks. But it used to be just a handful, and they knew the source of every trade [and] the temperament of people behind the order. . . . It is interesting how hereditary that business is.[21]

THE TRADING DAY

So what actually happens on the trading floor? A trading day begins promptly at 9:30 A.M. with the ceremonial ringing of the Opening Bell. Celebrities, politicians, or directors of firms being honored or making an "Initial Public Offering" (IPO) of its shares on that day are often invited to "open the market" by ringing the bell. Publicity stunts, including handing out free products or food on the floor or people dressed in costumes, sometimes accompany introduction of a new stock.

As a buy or sell order arrives at the trader's booth via phone, e-mail, text, or fax, it is noted down by a clerk, who passes the order along to a trader. The booths themselves are quite small, and even for those working at firms with superbooths, space is at premium. There is no room for desks; clerks work at counters and perch on stools as they weave around their colleagues trying to accomplish their tasks and hold telephone conversations with clients and "back offices." Many floor employees spend their entire workday standing up.

Upon receiving an order, a trader walks to the appropriate trading post to see if he can "make a market"—find a buyer or seller willing to fulfill his client's request at the amount the client wants to pay. Trades are negotiated and confirmed on the trading floors. In years past, when a trade was completed the broker would note it down on a small piece of paper and give the information to a Floor Reporter, a NYSE employee who was responsible for collecting transaction data and entering it into the computer system so that it would be reflected on "the tape." This is changing rapidly. The recent introduction of handheld devices may allow most floor employees to update information themselves. After completing the transaction, the dealer traditionally tore up the order slip into small pieces and threw the scraps on the floor.

The formal paperwork surrounding the trade—such as issuing certificates confirming the change of stock ownership, and confirmation of sales and purchases, is done not on the floor but in the firm's "back rooms" located away from the trading floor. Depending on the market's volume, cleaning up the paperwork may continue long past the 4:00 P.M. closing bell. (On August 16, 2007, the NYSE set a record volume of 5,799,792,281 transactions in a single day. The record for the NYSE's slowest day remains March 16, 1830, when a meager 31 trades took place.[22]) Especially before the introduction of electronic recording devices, on busy days the NYSE's ticker tape often "ran behind." There is a complex system of checks and double checks to make sure everything balances:

> What should happen, it should all go into the computer and both sides should match. But if it's a same side trade—we both thought we were buyers and no one sold—that information should instantaneously start red flashes [on the handhelds]. "Listen, we have a problem!" When disputes arise, a floor monitor is called in to resolve the matter.[23]

Throughout the day, the traders will continuously check the tape recording the latest sale price of individual stocks both on the NYSE and on other exchanges throughout the world. This information is transmitted to the floor via electronic "wrappers," continually scrolling electronic tickers tapes which replaced the older giant chalk boards and mechanical tickers tape machines. Many years ago, the trading floors used to employ "board boys," whose task it was to constantly revise figures as stock prices went up and down. Being a board

Invented in 1867 by Edward A. Calahan of the American Telegraph Company and now obsolete, ticker tape machines were named after the noise they made printing stock prices on long rolls of thin paper tapes. PHOTO BY ARTHUR SCHATZ/TIME & LIE PICTURES COLLECTION/GETTY IMAGES.

boy was a high-pressure job, with little room for mistakes. Speed was essential and a few people told us stories of young men who were hired as a board boys because they was ambidextrous, which allowed them to change the figures more rapidly. The main board at the NYSE came to be known as "The Big Board," and the NYSE itself is sometimes still referred by this nickname.[24] To save space, stocks are listed by their "stock symbol" followed by an up or down arrow indicating direction of change, numbers giving the amount of change, and the current price. Currently, almost 2,800 stocks are traded on the NYSE and each stock has its own symbol—a series of letters, usually based on the name of that stock. Traders know most, if not all of the symbols, and are always on the lookout for those stocks in which they have an interest. Some stocks have developed nicknames: for example, "KO" is the symbol for Coca Cola, and "GLO" is the symbol for Corning Glass, but:

> On the floor of the Exchange they call that "glowworm"—they don't even call it Corning—McDonalds is called "hamburger"—not even close to what their symbols are. So that's a whole other language outside of the symbols.[25]

In the fast-paced world of the trading floor, communication is critical, and inattention or mistakes can be costly. If a trader is away from his booth, he will keep in close contact with his colleagues by stopping to call in from one of the many "hitching posts"—a simple 6″ x 6″ wooden post with six to eight phones attached—that are scattered throughout the NYSE floor. These are still used, even though almost everyone now has a cell phone.

The need for precise communication is also reflected in the agreed-upon language, the "verbal codes" that are used on the floor. "I'll tell you a real quick story about language," said Cashin:

> You get all these new, young [traders] come in, and everybody wants to put [on] their own little spin. This is the way I do it: "Buy" does not sound like "Sell." But we will have people come in and they want to do something almost Damon Runyon-esque, and they'll say: "I can *use* a lot of shares." And some other idiot on the other side will say something like: "If he wants to sell, I could *lose* them right here." Well, "use" and "lose" sound exactly alike. And we had a $150,000 error here ten years ago for that simple reason. . . . They were both on the *same* side of the trade and *there was no trade*. So it becomes very dangerous . . . with the high speed going on. If it's all verbal trades . . . you can't afford too much confusion about what we just did: I bought, you sold. I've got to know that; you've got to know that.
>
> Another example is at times you'll get people trying to help other people out. You're on the phone over there talking to your person, and I know you're bidding and I'm bidding, and I mis-hear [something like] "You did this with him." Did? Did what? Did I sell or did I buy? And you assume, well, he knows you're a buyer, so that must mean you bought it. The other guy didn't hear buy or sell—he heard "did," too. And he's a buyer, also. So what happened here? So the preciseness of the language is important to save time and for accuracy. Very important![26]

The floor itself is very hot, and most floor employees stop at downstairs locker rooms to change their shoes and put on a lightweight cotton jacket, which is usually imprinted with their company's name. To help everyone sort out who works for which firm, traders, clerks, and other floor employees from each firm all wear the same colored jackets. "I mean, you can get away with a suit," said one trader, "but you'll feel strange. There's just no place for a suit jacket. And very few people wear, you know, street shoes. [They wear] leather-soled shoes or leather-heeled shoes. Your feet just couldn't take it if you're going to be on the floor all day."[27] In addition, everyone is required to wear a badge with their official badge number on it. As NYSE's Todd Bertsch explained to us, that's so:

> When you trade in a crowd—say, I'm Smith Barney—I give you my badge number and you'll give me that you're Merrill Lynch and your badge number. So I write down your badge number, the contract information, and the time of the trade. That all gets typed in.[28]

Working conditions on the floor are, in the words of one trader, "brutal . . . you're standing up all day long. . . . You're eating your lunch in probably twelve seconds. It's a brutal environment."[29] The noise of the trading floor, the constant din of voices, buzzers, bells, phones, shouting, and televisions, is the first thing that strikes a visitor. However, to the traders, noise is both a comfort and an important tool in helping them assess what is going on in the market. One trader told us a wonderful story about the importance of noise:

> For a long time I worked in what is known as "The Garage" area. Each [area] has a name: there's "The Main Room"; The Garage, which is a small area; then a number of years ago, when the trade expanded, they opened up an entirely new room, which they painted blue. So that, of course, was named the "Blue Room." (It was very creative.) The specialist units and brokers who went into the Blue Room, after a few days they were complaining about the lack of noise. There are a lot of people on the floor who feel, rightly or wrongly, that they can judge the market by the noise. . . . When the level goes up or down it usually indicates that activity's going up or down. And some of us old fogies think that the pitch would tell you whether to buy or sell. . . . You know, there's a power of projection: "Buy them!" It sounds almost like a Russian quote. You hear the rumble. When you sell them, it's almost like a fire: "Sold! Sold!" The pitch would be higher to sell it. And these folks went into the Blue Room [and] they were in a *quiet* room. They circulated a petition! The Exchange had to *pipe in* the noise.[30]

Traders and booth workers usually stay on the floor from the Opening Bell at 9:30 A.M. to the Closing Bell at 4:00 P.M. Lunch is eaten standing at their booth or post and it usually consists of pizza, sandwiches, or easy-to-eat take-out fare from neighborhood restaurants. Unless it is a very slow day or a special occasion, workers generally do not leave the floor to eat. Throughout the Wall

Street neighborhood, scores of restaurants, delis, and takeaway shops cater to the needs of the trading floors. Delivery people are not allowed on the floor, and in recent years, because of security concerns, they are not even permitted to enter the NYSE building. This has given rise to an interesting ritual as every day about noon hundreds of delivery people swarm around the side entrance of the NYSE. A worker from the booth or the post that placed the order leaves the chaos inside on the floor to confront the chaos outside as thongs of delivery people clamor to exchange food for money. Once they have secured their group's lunch, they bring it back triumphantly to their colleagues. In a manner more reminiscent of college dorm life than a world-class financial institution, empty pizza boxes, used Chinese food containers, and sandwich wrappers soon litter the prestigious floor. By the time the closing bell sounds at 4:00 P.M., the remains of takeaway food, combined with scraps of paper from thousands of completed trades, present a true challenge for the NYSE's cleaning crews.

THE COMMODITIES MARKETS

In addition to the NYSE, Smithsonian researchers interviewed traders at New York's two major commodity markets—The Mercantile Exchange or "The Merc" (now renamed NYMEX), and the New York Board of Trade or NYBOT, which is frequently referred to by its nickname, "Coffee, Sugar, and Cocoa." Like the NYSE, both are also open outcry markets with long histories and distinctive cultures of their own. Unlike the NYSE, they deal not in shares of a company, but rather in buying, selling, and trading "futures" of actual goods. While trading at the NYSE has evolved a system of moving from post to post through an intricately arranged floor pattern, trading at the commodities markets is conducted in centralized "trading pits." These "pits" or "rings" are actual circles some ten feet diameter. Each commodity has its own ring, which is encircled by several tiers of elevated bleachers on which, at peak times, scores of traders will stand facing each other and shouting out their buy and sell orders. It's sort of a concentrated, centrally focused version of the NYSE, and it is *extremely* loud. As one Merc trader told us:

> It's a difficult physical situation. You're trading in a ring where there's a lot of volume. There's a lot of pushing and shoving, on top of holding orders, fielding orders, making sure you didn't lose anything in your hand. Good hand/eye coordination. Good sense of hearing—although a lot of people lose their hearing. My hearing is still intact. My voice is great, too, I have a strong voice in the rings—but recently, in the last

ten years, if I trade for a full two or three days, I have to stop for a day. Plus, I like to sing. I took voice lessons to protect my voice—actually, for brokering not for singing. . . . Posture lessons, too, it's important to work out every day.[31]

Although the New York commodity markets are large, they are dwarfed by the ones in Chicago, where up to 500 or 600 traders are sometimes involved.[32] Nevertheless, with as many as 200 or 250 traders sometimes standing around the ring, how can participants possibly keep things straight? Gary Lapayover, one of our key informants at The Merc, credited training and experience:

> Your ears, after a while, get attuned to it. I can go in there and have a conversation with you and pick out certain months or quotes. It's not always that fast [busy], it depends on the period of time. As a matter of fact, I think a lot of times now it is slower. . . . It is more intense in the very busy period, but when I was younger, we used to trade all day long at the same pace and at the end of the day [you would] just drop. And you'd lose five to six pounds a day—besides your voice.[33]

The Merc traces its roots back to The Butter and Egg Exchange, which was established by New York dairy merchants in 1872 to facilitate and regulate the selling of milk and later eggs. In 1882, as products traded expanded to include canned goods, poultry, and dried fruits, the organization changed its name to The New York Mercantile Exchange (known later as NYMEX). Other exchanges also flourished in New York in the late-nineteenth and early-twentieth centuries and some of these eventually merged with NYMEX. For example, in 1933, the National Metal Exchange, the Rubber Exchange of New York, the National Raw Silk Exchange, and the New York Hide Exchange merged to form the COMEX, which in turn, merged with NYMEX in 1994.[34] Today, NYMEX/COMEX has separate trading pits for aluminum, coal, copper, crude oil, electricity, gas, gold, heating oil, natural gas, palladium, platinum, propane, silver, and uranium.

The third exchange that we studied in 2000/2001 was the NYBOT. NYBOT originated as the New York Cotton Exchange in 1870, and was the setting for the 1983 film *Trading Places*. After the destruction of its World Trade Center headquarters in 2001, it relocated to rented quarters in The Merc's new building at the northern end of the lower Manhattan's World Financial Center in 2003. Today, the NYBOT maintains trading rings for cotton and orange juice, as well as coffee, sugar, cocoa, and ethanol, but with more and more trading being done electronically, its future is not at all certain.[35]

There are three primary types of traders on the commodity exchanges: The first are brokers, who "execute" buy and sell orders called in by clients. Then there are "locals," traders who trade for themselves. And then there are people who are both brokers and locals, who are referred to as "dual traders." Some concentrate in a single market—say, crude oil, or palladium at The Merc or coffee at the NYBOT. Others go from one ring to another:

> There are some that do, especially on this floor because there are certain types of trades they do in oil called "crack spreads"—where it's a relationship between gasoline and/or heating oil and crude oil. . . . So they jump from ring to ring, sometimes. By and large, most of the people stay in one ring now. Guys used to move around a little more, but the competition is much greater than ever. . . . Even though more money can be made, there are also more people trading. When I started, there were very few independent brokers, almost everybody [worked for a] business. Now, there are many, many more people trading for their own accounts [i.e., locals] than people trading for customers.[36]

On the commodity exchanges, many of the seats are held and worked by families. Some firms can boast of three or four generations of traders on The Merc or NYBOT. The rapid increase in the number of seats over the past thirty years prompted many longtime traders to reflect on how much their workplace had changed:

> On the NYMEX floor there are seven hundred and something memberships; about 640 active traders. At the COMEX, I think there is about the same number. That's huge! When I started [ca.1970], there were sixty brokers. There were four hundred seats, but only about sixty brokers. There weren't more than two hundred people in the whole building. . . . Everybody knew everybody. You might not *talk* to some of them, but there was just this group of folks, and everybody knew everyone else. Now you can't know everybody.[37]

Like a few blocks away at the NYSE, to trade on the commodity exchanges, you must buy a seat, and like the number of members, the price of these seats has gone up tremendously in recent years. When we were recording interviews in 2001, one of The Merc traders, who had joined in the 1970s, told us with amazement that a Merc seat had just been sold for over a hundred thousand dollars:

They've basically gone up six-fold. And it's not only that . . . right now it's anywhere from eight to twelve thousand dollars to rent a seat for a month. When I started out, I think my first month was three or four hundred dollars a month. The Exchange was much smaller at the time—we didn't have a gasoline contract. We may have just started gasoline. Crude oil wasn't in existence; natural gas wasn't even a gleam in our eye at that point. The options markets for the energies didn't exist. So the lower [seat] price was much more justified. We've come a long way.[38]

Although buying a seat on the commodities exchanges is still far cheaper than on the NYSE, according to Merc trader Hess, traditional apprenticeship and avenues for advancement also have changed:

When I first started out, you were a clerk for six months, a year, two years, and then you were automatically a broker. The unfortunate thing that has happened in the last probably ten years is the price of admission has gone up so much—both the price of the seats and [seat] rentals—that it has excluded your average clerk from ever getting into the ring. . . . If you're going to lease a seat, and you're paying anywhere from ten to twelve thousand dollars a month, you also have to maintain fifty thousand dollars in your account—in cash! In addition to the money, you need to trade if you don't own a seat. So unless you have a rich daddy, it's kind of cost prohibitive. And you're now seeing clerks who are almost professional clerks. Normally, if you were a clerk more than a year or two, there was something wrong with you: You did not want to [trade], or you were so phobic you didn't want to get into the ring. . . . The goal was to be a broker; you didn't want to be a clerk all your life. What was the point? You weren't going to make the big money.[39]

LIFE IN THE TRADING PIT

The commodity rings are incredibly loud, but information somehow must be conveyed to and from the brokers' booths, which are located on the perimeter of the trading room, to the trader in the middle of the floor.[40] At some point in the distant past, the commodity markets developed a system of hand signals to communicate back and forth across the pit and to and from the booths. (Some historians claim it originated at the Wall Street Curb Market, as a way for curbside traders to communicate with their offices located on the upper stories of the surrounding buildings.) Today, although this traditional communications system is being replaced by handheld electronic devices, it is still used from time to time, especially at Coffee, Sugar, and Cocoa. Moreover, one trader told us, "some firms will have their own signals 'cause you don't want everyone else knowing your signals. It was mostly the clerks."[41]

Like the NYSE, the commodity exchanges have also developed their own occupational jargon and symbols. For example, an interesting letter code arose around the buying and selling of futures. Lapayover explained it to us:

> There's that whole system of letters which is very simple, [but] nobody has ever been able to explain how they derived it. It's universal in the futures industry, except for a few letters . . . [and] there were certain letters that they left out. . . . I'll give you all of them: There's January—January is "F"; "G" is February; "H" is March. There is no "I," because they might confuse that with a [numeral] one. "J" is April; "K" is May; June is "M." Of course, January, June, and July, [could be confusing], so July is an "N"; August is a "Q." They left "O" out because it looked like a quantity. No "P"—I don't know why. "U" is September. An upside down "V" is October. Oh, I know why! If you write a "u" fast, it could be a "v," so you'd do it [upside down] and that would be October. "X" is November; and "Z" was December. These are the futures months, and they're universal—New York, Chicago. Who made them? Nobody's ever known why they picked this way. They've just [always] been.[42]

At the time of our interviews, after a trader has made a purchase or sale in The Merc's rings, the note cards detailing the filled orders were then tossed—thrown, really—into the center of the pit, where yellow-jacketed clerks employed by The Merc, and surrounded by netting to help catch the shower of notes, first stamped them to confirm the time received, and entered them as official transactions into their computers.

CONGRATULATIONS, IT'S YOURS!: TAKING DELIVERY

A basic difference between the NYSE and the commodities markets is that on the former, customers are buying and selling shares in a company, while on the commodities markets, they are trading in actual goods and futures—"creating a market" and establishing price by trying to forecast the future price and availability of a commodity. You can make or lose money in either market, but if you misjudge on the commodities markets, you may have to take delivery of the goods! As Merc trader Hess, who trades in the heating oil ring, explained:

Futures expire—heating oils, all the oils, will trade on a month-to-month basis. We trade basically eighteen straight months out [i.e., in advance]. And we even trade some crude oil out five or seven years. A futures contract expires, in the oils, it expires on the last day of the month. So, if you "take a position" anytime before then, you have the opportunity to get out of the position . . . by the final minute, by the final second of the month. If you do not "liquidate your position" [i.e., sell the commodity], whether "long" or "short," then you're signaling to the Exchange that you're going to *take possession* or "make delivery" of that underlying commodity.

So, if you're long on heating oil and you don't get out of your position, or liquidate that position, then you are a "consumer"—or someone that's actually going to take *physical* delivery of that commodity. . . . You've got to make arrangements with the opposing seller to take forty-two thousand gallons of heating oil. And that's all New York harbor delivery! And that's all very succinctly [stated] and detailed exactly, our delivery process. If it's not, then the contract will never be a success.

In the metals it's a little different—we have something called "First Notice Day" and you're alerted by your clearing house exchange that you have to get out. It's not as much of a crisis if you don't get out of your metal position, because you can EFP [Exchange Futures for Physicals] it. . . . But if you're long or short heating oil or crude oil, it's a major problem . . . because you've got to take delivery or make delivery of a lot of stuff. And it has happened, not to all of us, but it's happened to me on occasion. And you're really scrambling and you have to pay up. It costs you quite a bit of money.[43]

We asked if the ultimate goal was to deliver the goods. "No," he said, "that's not the goal. Probably 98 percent of all futures contracts are not delivered." Instead, the ultimate goal of the futures market is really to establish price. "That's what the market does. The advantage that we have is the neutrality and the price exposure—something that the whole world can see."[44]

As daunting as it might be to have a tanker filled with natural gas delivered practically to your doorstep, and despite the generally serious atmosphere at the commodities markets, there seems to be a fair amount of camaraderie, joking, and touches of levity. For example, as on the NYSE, pit traders all wear different colored jackets and badges, but in addition to their official numbers, Merc badges often carry a person's nickname. Merc trader Hess ("Hess") told us about the time "I was down in Sanibel Island with my wife," and he met a fellow trader, one that he knew well from the floor:

And I wanted to introduce her, and I just kind of said, "ah, ah"… I didn't know the guy's name . . . I felt like such an idiot. I was introducing his badge! And there are people who only know me as "Hess"—they don't know my first name. . . . We get to pick [our badge names]. This guy may be a carpenter and [pick] like "Hammer" . . . So basically you can pick any symbol that you would like, as long as no one else has it, or is too close [to another's].[45]

Merc trader Lapayover, another of the Smithsonian's key informants, has the badge name "Zero," and has been known to wear polka-dotted jackets. He takes some credit for diversifying the jackets that are worn in the rings:

When I started . . . everyone wore a beige jacket—a tanish, khaki-colored, which the Exchange provided if you paid a service, and you'd go pick them up in the back. Actually, I was one of the people who started doing colors. . . . The Exchange stopped providing the service—they were doing badly after we had a default; they couldn't provide the laundry. We started all getting [our own] jackets, but they're still plain. There were about three or four companies—all dark blue. Then we started to get a little nuttier. One year, when I took over and I was running the business as a baby, as a twenty-five-year old, I came in with white jackets, all white. . . . And then another company . . . they had red and white, another company got yellow, and another company got lime green. And that's how it built. And you had to have a tie, although they didn't make you wear it, because [The Merc] was always more relaxed than the New York Stock Exchange. I don't know what happens there, but I know on this floor you learn right away, "Don't call me Mr. Lapayover," call me "Gary." "Mr. Lapayover" wastes time. If you need to talk to me, it's "Gary"! Everything was first name, even to the wealthiest guys.[46]

We asked Hess, one of the dual traders, to walk us through what his trading day was like on The Merc. The description he gave us reflects how, despite the relatively short hours he spent in the trading ring, the amount of work-related time he put in each in day was enormous:

When I get up in the morning, I'll put some music on, try to chill out a little bit. I will check in. If I'm in my apartment in the city, I do have an Access machine; it accesses our overnight trading system. I'll check all the markets, our markets—both the metals and the energy markets—and see exactly where the prices are and what the ranges have been overnight. I'll also check to see whether any of my orders—I occasionally trade [for myself, as a local]—to see if any of those were executed. . . . If I'm going to come to the gym and workout in the morning, I'll get up at 5:30 A.M. and leave fifteen, twenty minutes later. I'm a kind of a low maintenance guy, so I get dressed and leave. Otherwise, I'll put Bloomberg on and check and see what the world's been doing. If I don't go the gym, I take a shower and I usually leave around 7:00. I live uptown on the East Side and I'll take the subway downtown, get down to the floor around a quarter-to-eight. Once again, just check and see where the markets are trading at the moment—the energy markets and the metal markets.

And then I will hang around and trade, or usually execute orders in platinum, palladium. Palladium opens up at 8:10; Platinum at 8:20.[47] I don't trade it a lot anymore; I used to trade it quite extensively. Then I'll wait for the Crude Oil market to open up at 9:45; natural gas opens up at 9:30—See where those prices are; see where those markets are trading. Then I'll physically get into the pit at 9:50 in Heating Oil and trade for most of the day—usually the first hour, hour-and-a-half is busy. I'll sometimes take a break and see if I have any phone calls.[48]

We asked him what he liked best about trading.

Every day is unique. Basically, as traders, we have no idea how much money we're going to make or lose when we enter the door in the morning. Some days are hectic and crazy; other days are quite boring and I get to read the *[New York] Times* and the *[Wall Street] Journal*. Those are the days we *don't* want—we want the days to be busy. Each day has an ebb and a flow to it. I've been trading for such a long time that some days you know, "Look, it's just not in the cards today." Either it's you, or it's the markets, whatever, the environment. Other days it's a real struggle, you make money and it's a struggle or you lose money and it's a struggle. And then there's days where everything flows really well and most of your trades are mostly successful. Those are the days that we all relish and look forward to.[49]

Even when thing are "flowing really well," fellow Merc trader Joe Cicchetti told us, "The lifestyle of being a trader is tough":

Depends what of kind of trader you are—big or small; whether you're trading all the time; a day trader or a position trader—many different aspects. Stress level and aggression level differ with the individuals. Being a broker, the job is very difficult—filling and order taking, cancellations and executions. Not to mention the physical aspect of actually yelling in the ring to buy and sell. The stress of potential errors: Like buying fifteen when the guy said to buy twenty. Or buying when he thought he bought—now you've *both* bought and you have a problem. . . . In this business, the customer comes first, so when there's a problem and there's any money involved, the broker has to take the loss, not the customer.[50]

Like The Merc, those dealing in commodities and futures on the NYBOT have to master a complex world of trading in "front months" and "back months," and in calculating how to make money on "spreads," "switchers," "straddles," and "butterflies." And, as trader Tony DeMarco reminded us, "you're doing that under a lot of pressure. You've got to do it quick—you've got customers on the line waiting for their fills."[51] When we first interviewed DeMarco in 2001, the Coffee Exchange where he worked in his family's firm was just beginning to "go electronic." He was looking forward to the changes, especially the improvements it would bring to record keeping:

We're not electronic yet. . . . We're trying to preserve it, but a lot of technology is trying to work its way into our workplace. They're trying to get us to use the handhelds. You've got to punch in all the trades. It goes right into the system, [then] it will go right into the clearing house![52]

Interviewing traders, even those who voiced complaints and concerns, we heard a lot of variations of "I like the excitement." NYSE trader Bill Bertsch, summed it up nicely: "A lot of jobs don't have excitement, but here every single day is totally different. It's instant gratification—unlike a lot of other businesses."[53] "You have to like trading," another added, and you should at least be able to tolerate your colleagues because ultimately, "You spend more time with your fellow workers than you do with your family, friends, and spouse or otherwise."[54]

THOSE OTHER EXCHANGES: FLOOR TRADERS ON FLOOR TRADERS

Despite being located only a few blocks from each other, each of the exchanges has developed a distinctive culture of its own. Although the surnames of many senior NYSE brokerage house partners often suggest the multi-generational involvement of upper-class Anglo-American families, most floor traders come from middle- and lower-middle class white ethnic backgrounds. Different ethnic groups predominate on the different exchanges. Rather than attending Ivy League schools, many of those traders who did go to college received their education at solid but not flashy local New York schools such as Fordham, Pace, Long Island University, or the City University of New York (CUNY) system, which includes schools such as CCNY, Brooklyn College, and University on the Corner of Lexington Avenue ("UCLA"), which is better known as Baruch College. Many never completed college, some started directly after high school as a clerk or page and worked their way up through the exchanges. Richard Grasso, who served as president of the NYSE from 1995 to 2003, is a case in point. After graduating from a public high school in Queens, he began his career as a page on the NYSE trading floor and from there, worked his way up to the top of the ladder.

The majority of the workforce is still male and overwhelmingly white, but an increasing number of women as well as black, Latino, and Asian workers are now employed on Wall Street. To their credit, all the exchanges support training, education, and outreach efforts to encourage diversification of their work forces, but much remains to be done.[55] The gender barrier was technically broken in 1945, when women were admitted to the NYSE floor during World War II to fill manpower shortages. However, most of those women worked as telephone operators and clerks—certainly not as traders. In 1967, trader Muriel Siebert made international headlines when she became the first woman to buy a seat on the NYSE.

Given how physically close the exchanges are to one another, we found the lack of knowledge about and communication between the individual exchanges surprising. Most of the commodity traders had visited the NYSE, possibly because for many years it offered a well-known public exhibit and tour; however, most NYSE workers had never visited either The Merc or the NYBOT. We asked some of our NYSE interviewees how much they had to do with other exchanges or traders. They responded by telling us that the Wall Street community was hard to define, but that the NYSE, NYBOT, and NYMEX were all separate communities. However, lack of first-hand knowledge didn't inhibit our interviewees from offering their insights and opinions about what went on elsewhere on Wall Street. (We were, after all, dealing with New Yorkers.)

More than a few commodity traders voiced the opinion that NYSE traders looked down on them because they were trading goods and futures, rather than shares. As one Merc trader told us:

That other thing you asked—the stock exchanges to future exchanges? We were always the stepchildren of Wall Street. We were like the dirty—really, truly. There wasn't the élan, there wasn't the sophistication, and there wasn't the glamour or the aura. So we were always the stepchild. . . . For example, we called them "runners," plain and simple, [NYSE] called them "'pages," so there was a little more elegance.[56]

Another Merc trader explained it this way:

Obviously, NYSE is Blue Chip[57]—there is a different culture there. . . . The shirt and tie set—I'm not going to say stuffy, but it's a different atmosphere, totally different than the commodity atmosphere, which is living life at the edge. It's like NASCAR. Cars are all moving at the same time and then, all of a sudden, one stops and everybody bangs up into it. That's commodities in general. . . . They don't always move that way; it can look like Daytona—you sit there and watch it all day for five hundred laps. But sometimes, it is crash and burn, so there is a difference.[58]

NYSE members seem to waver back and forth between dismissing charges that they're snobby and being very proud to work at an internationally recognized and prestigious institution. Nevertheless, they willingly admit that reality does not always match assumptions. Standard & Poor's analyst Sam Stovall responded with a story about his father when we asked him about this topic:

A lot of what people think about Wall Street is purely misperception. It's a business. My father when he was first started at the NYSE was invited to lunch with a major executive at E. F. Hutton. And Pop thought: "Oh, this is going to be great. I'm going to get driven in a limousine up to one of these fancy luncheon clubs." And as they were heading down the elevator, the guy turns to my father and says: "You have a [subway] token, don't you?"[59]

Merc trade Lapayover estimated that 99 percent of the members on his exchange were New Yorkers. "When I started in the seventies," he told us, "there were pejorative terms for every exchange. The Merc was "Delancey Street"—all Jews. Well, mostly, not all."[60]

We asked who referred to them as Delancey Street.

The other three exchanges. Well, it was "Little Italy," the exchange where you can't get in if your name doesn't have a vowel on the end, which is the Coffee, Sugar and Cocoa Exchange. "The Irish Exchange" was cotton and orange juice. (It was mostly cotton, and it merged with orange juice a little later.) And the COMEX was more of a blend—they had everything in COMEX. But The Merc was the Jewish exchange; Coffee-Sugar was the Italian exchange. And it still exists. If you look at the membership roles [of the] New York Board of Trade, you'll be fascinated by the fact that still probably 75 percent of the names are Italian.[61]

Both the NYSE and Commodities members voiced some reservations about the newer exchanges, especially the online computer-driven NASDAQ:

NASDAQ is like an old Dodge City. . . . It's in its infancy; it's new. . . . I'm not saying it's not governed properly, that's not what I mean by Dodge City. But you've got the shoot-'em-up guys, you've got big shooters, you've got young players, you've got kids who don't have much risk—they can really make a difference. I know many people, even some that I've trained myself, who are very, very successful young men in their twenties and thirties. They superseded what we've done in twenty, thirty years.[62]

HOW TO BE A FLOOR TRADER: WORKING ON THE EXCHANGE FLOOR 101

Because of the complexity of what takes place on the exchanges, one subject that always elicited a great deal of response was "How did you learn to be a trader?" The recurring theme in most of the stories was the real sense of fear and panic that the novices experienced. (And that they remembered vividly even five or six decades later.) DeMarco's experience was typical, even though he had grown up around his family's NYBOT coffee brokerage business:

First day? Yeah, forget about it! I was sweating. "Can I go to the bathroom?" Scared the shit out of you! Plus, your father's screaming at you like you're an idiot—just to make things a little easier on you. My father was pretty wild—one of the best traders down there, but . . . there was a group of traders in his day and it was really something to see! It was no mercy. It wasn't like: "OK, you'll get that right the next time." Pretty crazy! So you learn from the fear of god how to do it right. And not everybody can do it. I would have trouble doing [it by the] book 'cause I didn't learn that way. I didn't go in the ring working the book all the time. I went in just learning how to trade myself and make money as a local—doing the straddles, trying to scalp the points between the switches, buy one month, sell another—and do it at a profit.[63]

Based on his experiences, NYSE's Bertsch had this advice for new traders:

> One thing that you do as a rookie in the business, you make sure everyone knows you're a rookie. "I'm new to the business, could you repeat that please?" You always repeat the orders to make sure you've got them right. . . . The people who play like they know what they're doing, usually don't make it because other people assume they know what they're doing and start killing the business with pretty complicated order flows. Then there's an error, and then there's bad blood. It's in your best interest to say, "I don't understand, I'm a rookie, I'd be happy to hand it over to somebody." . . . And if you do make an error and it's *your* fault, the other important thing is to just stand up for it right away. "I made a mistake, made an error, what can we do?"[64]

After the initial shock, most pages, clerks, and traders begin to acclimate themselves to their work environment relatively quickly. Standard & Poor's analyst Stovall, who began his career as a floor trader at the Merc, recalled his own experience:

> When I first went down there and heard all the screaming and yelling, I said "how can anybody make heads or tails out of this place?" And then, within a short period of time, I could have my back to the ring and could tell you who's bidding, who's offering what monthly contracts. And whether—based on the tone of the voice and who they were—whether there was any kind of size [i.e., volume] behind the request for bid and offer.[65]

"I used to take notes," Lapayover told us:

> Yeah, it didn't make sense, but I would have my little notebook . . . like a homework assignment and I would write things down. 'Cause I'd walk out and go: "Hey, Paul, you got a sell order?" He'd go, "It's a BUY order!" And I'd go, "Oh, sorry!" I didn't know *anything*! So I had a book. . . . I wrote everything down and would go home and study it.[66]

As Bertsch pointed out to us, sometimes the most important thing a novice page, clerk, or trader could do was admit he or she had done something wrong:

> This was one of my lessons that I learned, being pretty green. I had a bad . . . situation: A customer called with instructions, with an order, which we followed to a tee. But that was not what they were supposed to do, and the customer didn't recall giving those instructions! Now, we tape our phones, so technically, I could go back to the phone tape and replay it to the person. So I said, "Listen, you didn't give me those instructions. I'll play you the tape if you want." That was a BIG mistake! That person let their boss know what I had said; boss got on phone and let me have it: "Who do you think you are? You never told me your phones are recorded." "Listen," I said, "it was a rookie mistake; I should never have said it." And right after I said that he said: "Fine." And that was that. . . . The customers can yell and tell me I'm an idiot, but then the bell rings and the slate's clean.[67]

There are many multi-generational trading families on all the Wall Street exchanges, but some young employees find their way to the trading floors by happenstance. Cashin got into the NYSE through a friend of his uncle:

> My family knew nothing of Wall Street; in fact, my uncle was a bartender. And it was someone in the bar who suggested [I apply] and gave him the name of Thompson, McKinnon & Company—an old firm, which is now out of business.[68] I came in June of 1959 and I was hired for thirty-nine dollars a week, which I thought was adequate. When my first boss was looking at [my paperwork], he said, "There's a mistake in your pay. Nobody would be working for this." And I said, "No, I am."[69]

Luck, and a supportive and generous mentor, were what started Joe Cicchetti's career as a floor trader at The Merc. "Kid like me who grew up on 116th Street in Harlem? It was a far cry from the Mercantile Exchange. The family was proud . . . the opportunity to trade was a big thing. This is a good story:

> I was made a broker right before I turned twenty-one. A little ahead of time—you had to be twenty-one, but they needed to have me in the ring and I guess they facilitated the situation. I had to go through training, but I had already been there for two, three, four years, so I had my badge given

to me. . . . I was in the ring about six months, executing orders like crazy. Years ago there was a basic education/testing system and the Head of the [Education] Committee came to me and said, "Joe, we never tested you about whether you should be in the ring, should be a broker or not." And I turned around and said, "Well, do it quickly because I have too many orders here; I don't have time to fuss around with this test." He says, "Joe, how long do you have to notice an error on the board?" And I says, "An error? I have zero money! I cannot afford an error. I do not make them!" He turns around and goes, "You're in."[70]

Others already knew a bit about the markets before they started. A Merc trader told us that when he was a teenager he was "always interested in gambling, playing cards, shooting marbles—and always interested in stocks." He started trading when he was sixteen—"my father co-signed a stock account for me." He "tried to get an internship on American Stock Exchange one summer, but it didn't work out." However, once enrolled in a downtown Manhattan college he made a friend whose uncle worked at The Merc, and who had given his nephew a job. Curious about what his friend was doing, "I visited him on his first or second day," and

I spent one day down here, and I said, "You got to get me a job, this is for us." A couple of months later, he was able to find me a job from a local who needed a clerk. . . . And I worked for him full time, this broker, and continued to go to school part time. . . . A year and a half later, I became a broker . . . I've been a broker ever since.[71]

Before the introduction of computers and the major expansion of the market in the late 1970s, some aspects of floor trading were very different. There are few traders left who remember the 1930s or 1940s; however, we spoke with quite a few, especially on the NYSE, who recalled the 1950s and 1960s. Despite the occasional twinges of nostalgia, most agreed that the stress and anxiety were just as intense during their early years on the NYSE—although there were more slow periods in between the busy ones to cushion the frenzy. Many of the skills they had to master and tasks they had to perform have long since disappeared. Cashin remembered starting out as a "quote boy":

In those days, we didn't have all the electronics. If somebody out in Scranton wanted to know what the quote was, what the market was in AT&T stock— was it a ninety bid, offered at ninety and a half, for example? There were no

Trader leans on a 'hitching post' to study state-of-the-art electronics suspended from 'bonnets' ringing individual trading posts on the floor of the NYSE . PHOTO BY EIGHTFISH/THE IMAGE BANK COLLECTION/GETTY IMAGES.

Quotron machines, no ILXs, none of those things. No CNBC to quickly turn to. So the brokers in the office at Thompson McKinnon . . . would wire in, if they were out in Scranton, and ask for a quote in AT&T. That [slip of paper] would then be put in a long conveyor belt—if I can describe them correctly—they were belts, but they had slots in them so you would drop in a piece of paper; and they had little bank stops. . . . If my desk were here, the conveyor belt went along side, there would be a stop in the rake that was for the quote boy. And [the slip] would come and they would pile up here, and that's how I would know [what to look up]. . . . Almost every large order room would have this . . . [otherwise] you'd have so many pages, that people would start bumping into each other.

So I would have a phone—rotary dial—and if it were AT&T there would be a specific number. And I would pick it up and dial [AT&T] and some lovely young lady—because they were almost always young ladies at the other end—would say, "AT&T is presently ninety bid, offered at ninety and a quarter." I would reach over to the far conveyor belt, which was going back the other way, [note down the price] and it would get back [to the trader] and be called to the guy [in Scranton]. Very slow, painstaking process. And it was considered state of the art at the time! . . . The transformation that I have seen in the forty years that I have been in the business![72]

Andrew Blum, who later became Chairman of the Bond Market Association, started out at the NYSE as a board boy in 1951 at thirty-five dollars a week:

> My job was to change the ink in the Dow Jones machine and the board tape every morning and every night, which was sort of a sloppy job. . . . The ink was sort of thick and turned you violet. If you got it on yourself, you couldn't get it off. . . . I think my dry-cleaning bill was more expensive than what I made every week.
>
> All the customers' men had, like, little bells, and they'll get the order, and hit the bell. And I'll run over and look at it, see whether it was a listed order or an OTC [over the counter], or called in, bond order, or mutual fund. And I would take it to the appropriate window to see that it got executed. It was sort of interesting. If somebody wanted a sandwich or something, I went out and got it.[73]

In addition to the drama of high-power trading, young workers occasionally got to see sobering reflections of life and death on the floor of the exchange. One NYSE trader remembered a bizarre incident that reinforced the "business is business" attitude that sometimes took hold during a particularly busy market:

> I must have been in my first job, maybe for four years—It had to be the late sixties when the volume really started to shake up, maybe sixty-eight or sixty-nine. The volume really started exploding on Wall Street and one day we were really very busy. And by then, I was head order clerk and I traded the smallest of stocks for the manager—who had been very busy because we were just about to go out of business, no thanks to me. But I noticed a little bit of hubbub down, about half way down . . . near the entrance [by] the bond trading area. And there was . . . an older gentleman, white hair, very distinguished, always wore the white collars, and blue shirts, and spats. His name was Mr. Kelly. He was partner of this firm, and he worked on the bond desk, doing I know not what. But he was there everyday and he sat upright and, you know, fine. And there was a bit of a hubbub, [but nothing stopped]. And later on in the day, passing by, I was going to the men's room or something, and noticed that Mr.

Kelly was *covered* by a sheet and slumped over on his desk. He had passed away! He had a heart attack. But they didn't want to interrupt the trading day and they were sort of trading *over* him![74]

After spending time as a page or a clerk, some young men were designated by their firms to become brokers. Years ago, this was done in a very traditional manner:

When you were about to become a new broker, you'll be assigned to a mentor. . . . You'll watch him trade first. Then, in your first several trades, he will watch and make sure that you're doing things right. The problem [is] you have to make sure that the mentor is not in any conflict of interest with what's going on with the kid. "You've got it to buy; I have it to sell. So just pay up." That would be such a conflict of interest as to be abhorrent. So that rather raucous test of mettle has been replaced by far more structured mentoring.[75]

Despite the odds, most people learned to adapt. Cicchetti told us that this happens surprisingly quickly on The Merc:

You can watch new people looking scared, and after two weeks, that's gone. I'm not saying that you get streetwise, but you get *exchange wise.* And if you don't know, someone will tell you. The education process happens almost by default because everyone's money is involved. It's not to anyone's benefit to have someone not functioning at their best level.[76]

HAZING RITUALS AND PRACTICAL JOKES

As in many other specialized professions, we documented numerous tales of hazing and practical joking on the floors of all the exchanges. Some of these were done to teach and test novice employees. Some were done to let newcomers know what hierarchies existed at the workplace, outline the parameters of acceptable professional and social behavior, or reinforce group cohesion. And some were done to relieve tension or lessen boredom or just because someone had an inspired idea. Everyone we spoke to agreed that these sorts of high jinks used to be much more common in "the old days" before the pace of the market and the volume of trades increased so markedly.

"You can't do many of those old, almost initiation things that they used to do when I came on," Cashin told us, before relating the tale of a particularly elaborate hazing routine that was done during the 1960s with some frequency on the floor of the NYSE to "test the mettle" of new traders:

> If you're going to be dealing with somebody for millions of dollars, you better be sure he's not going to have a nervous breakdown the first time something happens. What they would do in the old days is they would have an imaginary stock—"Coney Island Sand" or something like that. And, of course, you would be relatively new to the game. . . . And [the prank was done] with the aid and assistance of all the people who were involved with the new broker's firm, [so] there would be no harm to anybody. So to start out, they [the other traders at your booth] would send for whoever the "big guy" was at the [novice's] firm and, say, "Arthur Cashin had just begun as a neophyte." They would tell the big guy at the desk [upstairs or away from the floor] and he would say: "Alright, get the new guy in here and let me talk to him on the phone." And he would tell me: "Coney Island Sand—there's big news coming out on the stock. It's running up. This is our most important client. I want you to run out [to the floor] and buy five or ten thousand shares. And make sure you get us a good price. This is your first test!"
>
> Now, unbeknownst to me, or whoever the neophyte would be, everybody was in on it. And when I was called in [to the booth], the clerk or one of the other representatives of the firm would give the high sign [to the other floor traders]: "He's on the phone now." And when I would leave . . . they would say "Coney Island Sand is being traded at 12K." So, I would go over to Post 12, Section K, to see the stock that I hadn't really noticed before. And by then, there would be this crowd of usually somewhat senior brokers standing there bidding up this fictitious stock. [They'd be yelling] "thirty for 100"; then "thirty and a half" for it!—It would be as if it was being taken over! So, now a neophyte broker comes in, and My God! This thing's going up like a rocket! And because everybody's tentative when they begin, instead of my saying: "Take 'em" or whatever [and offer] thirty and a half for it—well, it would trade at thirty-one. How did that happen? I'd [offer] thirty-one for it, and it traded at thirty-one and a half—then thirty-two, thirty-three, thirty-five, thirty-six! And the [neophyte] broker might try to push his way through the crowd and they would be less than thoroughly gentle in pushing back: "Out of the way, son, I'm really buying this stock here!" So, now there would be great anxiety—"Oh boy, where am I going? [My career] is going to end right here." And [his boss] would call him back in while the crowd was officially trading and say: "Well, did you buy any?"

"No." "Oh my god! I don't know what we're going to do with the client! Well, thank god, I found another guy while you were *missing* the market in there. Now we've got a seller. If you couldn't *buy* 'em, at least go in and *sell* it!"

So now, all pre-arranged, he would head back [to the post]. And they are collapsing this fictitious stock back down to *below* thirty. He doesn't have a buy order anymore, and it's gone. . . . He gets there and it's at thirty-six, thirty-four—and so within a brief period of time, his skill set seems to have failed him in both directions! What could have happened? And then, assuming—'cause they certainly didn't want anybody to have a heart attack—how well his mettle stood up, they would do something silly; like somebody would cut his tie or rip his shirt as a sign: "OK son, now you've learned how tough this could be. And you learned how tough this could be *without* costing you or your client any money. Now, remember from now on how you're supposed to do this and don't cost anybody any money!"[77]

So hazing was used to mentor incoming traders? we asked. "Yes," said Cashin, "but certainly you don't find it at the Harvard Business School!"[78]

Cutting ties or ripping shirts seemed to be a fairly common rite of initiation for new traders at the NYSE. Museum of American Financial History (now Museum of American Finance) curator Meg Ventrudo was told that they "actually used to cut shirt sleeves off. And when you made your first big trade, they'd snip your tie and hand you the other half of it! . . . I think when they take your shirt off it's called 'fleecing the lambs.'"[79]

The pace of the market is so much faster now that only a few old-timers remember lazy mid-summer days when trading was so slow that water gun fights occasionally broke out on the floor of the NYSE. A lot of nonsense is remembered with fondness usually reserved for one's college fraternity. And as in all workplaces, no matter how serious, sometimes run-of-the-mill silliness just breaks out. Among the many stories we collected about the trading floor, a few of our favorites from the prestigious NYSE include:

It would be the middle of summer and all of a sudden everyone would start screaming, "It's snowing in NY! It's snowing in NY!" I was about fourteen, and I would look out the window: "It's not snowing!" And I'd look down and they had put baby powder all over my shoes. . . . They'd get older people as well. Who did it? You would never know.[80]

One that used to be done often—not now because of technology—they used to have card punchers. Someone would be there and punch the holes in the cards [to confirm a trade], and put it in the machine, and the machine would read them. There were devices that held the cards—metal something or other. . . . And they had a specialist book—which is now electronic—that also had heavy metal plates. When someone was out late the previous night, they would drop plates behind them and the person would jump so high and be so miserable. It echoes, clanks, and rings in your ears.[81]

There's an odd tradition—and I don't know exactly when it occurs, if it's triple witching or whatever—But around 3:20 people start yelping. And they yelp slowly. Then, as 3:33 comes up, everyone's going crazy! That happens rarely, maybe once a quarter. And I haven't figured out what the deal is. Don't know who starts it. You just hear it from afar. Someone "yips" and it builds . . . I'm sure it's on Fridays, but I'm not sure exactly when it happens. First, when you hear it, you think what are these people doing? Then you're there for a year and you find yourself yelping away, too.[82]

Another thing is the tomahawk chop: There's a specialist on the floor by the name of Earl Ellis and he's from Texas. Definitely a little bit of the prankster. I'm sure there's a story about why everyone does it, but ever since I've been there, they would start [singing] "E-a-r-l." And the whole place would do it. Half the floor of the NYSE singing "E-a-r-l![83]

Although it seems to be a far less common occurrence in recent years, the floor of the NYSE would occasionally erupt in song. The 1890s hit *Wait Till the Sun Shines, Nellie* seems to have been a favorite, but when the market breaks through barriers, the floor has also been known to launch into a chorus of *Happy Days are Here Again*.[84] Some longtime members also recalled that in the distant past, before the visitors' gallery was enclosed in glass, "there was a railing, and women were up there with skirts, and sometimes you could see a little more of their legs than they'd planned, and there were a group of songs for that, too." Interestingly, none of the men could recall a single one of those songs when asked by the female folklorist doing the interview.[85]

Pranks were often justified as a way "to prevent people from getting too caught up in themselves. Very dangerous in this business!" one senior NYSE trader told us. "A lot of experienced professionals," he continued, "all learn that no one is smarter than the tape; no one's smarter than the market. We've seen geniuses come and go. I always get nervous when somebody says, 'that's the smartest man on Wall Street.' 'Cause I've heard it so many times, and his face keeps changing."[86] Pranks pulled on the floor of the NYSE to keep hot-shot egos in check include:

> They put signs on your back: Someone will walk around with "Kick me." They'll make these little paper stirrups and tape them to their heels. So someone will walk by [and] they're going "Yeh-ha!" Then they'll put half of a knife stuck to a piece of paper so it looks like the guy got stabbed in the back. Or a shark's fin—"duh, duh, duh, duh" [sings theme from *Jaws*]. You don't figure it out until there's plenty of people making enough noise and then: "Alright, get it off my back." Good stuff![87]

> They'll put a paperclip on a paperclip chain on the back of your floor jacket—a lot of the jackets are mesh because it's just so hot—You'll put a paperclip on somebody's chain of paperclips and there will be something tied to the end, and the guy will just walk around the floor not knowing and everyone will make a comment to him.[88]

Other practical jokes are played with the specific goal of teaching or reinforcing group values and cohesion. For example:

> One of our young guys was involved in a stock. He thought he was a big guy because there weren't a lot of players in that stock and he was one of them. So I put a little note on his back saying: "God, I'm *the* player in stock XYZ. *And I really love the stock!*" And everyone's coming up to him and saying, "So, I heard you really like XYZ?" . . . And he's like, "Yeah, I really do like the stock. I think this is a good buy here." He knows something's up, but he doesn't know why people keep asking him. We're talking random people, people who he's never met before in his life.[89]

Years ago there used to be teletype machines that punched out "these tiny little yellow pieces of paper, that used to pile up in a basket. . . . And [on rainy days] when people came in with rather fanciful umbrellas . . . somebody might go by and put one or two handfuls of these paper punches in. So when you walked out thinking, 'Don't I look grand in my Brooks Brothers suite?,' and you'd put up your umbrella, open it, and this rain of yellow pieces of paper would fall out."[90]

Another well-remembered prank involved a rather pretentious trader who carried a walking stick to work, which he would leave in the corner of his booth. Every day over the course of several weeks, his colleagues would surreptitiously sand a quarter of an inch of wood off the end of his stick, leading him to wonder if he was growing taller.[91]

But perhaps our favorite story was of the NYSE trader who, in an era when all men wore hats, took to sporting a white straw bowler to work one summer, which he carefully hung each morning on the hat rack in his booth. At this time, the Financial District was filled with hat shops, and his colleagues, anxious of make a point about his growing pomposity, duly noted the maker and the man's hat size, and then went out and purchased half a dozen hats in decreasing quarter-sizes. Each week, the trader's hat would be discretely switched for an identical, albeit slightly smaller replacement. As his hat(s) started riding up higher and higher on his head, he began to notice something odd, only be assured by his colleagues that his head was swelling.[92]

RISK, CHANCE, AND SPECULATION

"There is no great secret in fortune making," noted nineteenth-century Wall Street investor and legendary miser Hetty Green, is reputed to have said, "All you have to do is buy cheap and sell dear, act with thrift and shrewdness, and be persistent."[93] Wall Street traders are sensitive to the fact that to many people, what they do for a living seems to go against the grain of the Puritan ethic. They know that some would criticize them for reaping significant financial rewards from the labor of others. However, the brokers who earn commissions on sales of financial paper see themselves differently. They believe they are one of the essential wheels that keep the machinery of capitalism running. Their exchanges, they contend, create and maintain a central marketplace at which reliable quotes and equal public access ensure a "level playing field" for all who wish to invest in securities. As one futures trader told us:

> The futures exchange is what America is about. This is capitalism in its purest form. And this is American because it doesn't matter where you come from. It helps to have money, but you don't have to . . . I started out with nothing.[94]

The recognition that their livelihood is dependent on public trust explains why all the exchanges, as well as the government regulatory agencies that closely monitor them, are so sensitive and usually react so forcefully to charges of "insider trading." Insider trading would seriously tilt the levelness of the playing field.

Most traders frame their approach to their daily work in terms of risk, risk aversion, and risk assessment, and most vehemently refute the idea that floor trading is in any way related to gambling. (On an initial visit to the NYSE floor, a Smithsonian researcher made the mistake of jokingly remarking to a floor official that in their different colored floor jackets, the traders reminded her of race track teams. "That's gambling," the horrified guide told her, "this isn't.") Because it seemed to be such a fundamental part of their daily work, we asked the traders to tell us their feelings about risk.

"There's a mix of people on the NYMEX exchange floor," Lapayover said, personally:

> I hate gambling, I hate losing. I never gamble. . . . There are some guys who are very conservative, and there are others who are, like, "Give me action." Lots of people like action. Give me action? Don't you get enough action here during the day? You trade all day, then you're flying out [and] you're going to Atlantic City! A bunch of [Merc] guys took limos to the Kentucky Derby! . . . There's not enough action or hours in the day for whatever speculating they want to do?[95]

On the other hand, another Merc trader told us:

> You've got to have a feel for gambling to some degree. I shouldn't say gambling—it's calculated risk. But you have to have a feel for that. You've got to be able to take losses—I mean, it's sometimes hard that you're going to walk out of here with less money than you walked in with. Ah, a love of trading! . . . You know, it's interesting: there's lots of times where you get tired of what you do—and you say: "I haven't helped anybody in the world. I haven't done anything, other than hopefully feathered my own pocket," but not everybody can be an EMT and save the world. From a philosophical point, I think of that all the time: Why am I doing this? I ought to be a chef, because I can create something—and I like to cook! If I had to do it over again, I would consider being a chef. But you have to have a kind of a love for the business, because there's many times—sometimes numerous times during the day—when you hear somebody go: "I hate this place!"[96]

"You have to go on gut feelings," explained another. "If 'ten' is knowing everything and 'one' is knowing nothing, you've got to make a decision starting at 'four' and be done by 'six.' Because otherwise, if you wait till ten, everything is full valued. . . . Like they say: "Use history as a guide, but don't dare use it as Gospel. And in some cases, you don't want to use it at all!"[97]

Over the past two centuries, the Wall Street exchanges have had their ups and downs. Where the public tends to use terms like "crashes" and "panics," today Wall Street prefers to refer to these as "market corrections." One of the best known stories about Wall Street concerns the number of suicides that followed the Stock Market Crash of 1929. Our interviewers anticipated collecting lots of oral histories about to this seismic economic correction. Instead, we were repeatedly informed that this was an urban legend—that there were no suicides among Wall Street workers. "Not here," people said, "we're used to market fluctuations." "Because it was such a horrible event," historian Ventrudo conjectured, "everyone likes there to be some kind of dramatization around the event. . . . Perhaps unlucky investors in small town America did away with themselves after 1929, but Wall Street workers need to be made of stronger stuff." And anyways, "there's always another trading day."[98]

NYBOT coffee trader DeMarco explained that there is a fine line between investing and accepting a certain amount of risk, and letting ego and gambling get the upper hand:

> A lot of times, it's just a fifty-fifty shot and you've got to have the guts to go in there and take that shot. There are the technical theories and all this stuff. People do charts and they follow numbers—but that's all out the window once [the market] blows through all those numbers. Now you're back to "Where's your discipline?" You can't get carried away with saying, "I know where [the market's] going to go." A lot of ego goes in there and it kills more people. . . . People don't want to give up. And they get into that gambling. A lot of people can't ever get enough. They get greedy, and greed will really ruin your day. . . . You can do well here, but you also can do terrible. But a lot of businesses are that way.[99]

Lapayover pointed out that most of the traders on the commodity markets are quite young—many still in their twenties and thirties. We asked if traders became more cautious with age or were there just more young traders because the older ones did well enough to retire after a number of years? There didn't seem to be a yes or no answer, but he did offer this cautionary tale:

> This is one of the only businesses in the world where it doesn't matter how hard you work. You can work harder than you ever worked before in your life and go home with less money than you started. That's a very alien concept to anyone. You know: "I think I just worked the hardest day in my life"—You're tired, drained, physically beat up, mentally tortured—and have

less than you started with! . . . [But] the other side of it is you can make money that you couldn't make anyplace else. If you're decent, [you work] four or five hours a day . . . you can make anything, *anything!* That's attractive. And remember, I said you have to have an ego. So nobody comes in without some ego. So that's the other part of it. This is instant gratification.[100]

Our final word comes from Cicchetti, a floor trader from The Merc, who shared with us his philosophy about trading and how he keeps his work in perspective:

It's a business. But I have the attitude that I play it like a game. There are rules. You play the rules. When you're wrong, you protect yourself; when you're right, you take advantage of it. That's the game. . . . You try to be light-hearted about it. Everybody gets emotional. . . . They make mistakes—we all do that. . . . Learning to manage the psychological aspect is paramount in learning how to trade.[101]

"I HAVE A SYSTEM"

To have a successful career on the exchanges, individuals must have a high tolerance for risk, but that doesn't mean that traders don't try to control risk by learning as much as they can about the products they are buying and selling, understanding their competitors, and keeping informed about the world around them. Although research and analysis play a major part on Wall Street, there are so many variables that most traders have their own systems to predict what the markets will do.

Zweig, a respected Wall Street reporter and financial writer for such leading journals as *Money*, offered some interesting insights into the culture of Wall Street:

When you first become the kind of journalist I am, you think investing is driven by economics—because that's what everybody tells you. And it takes you a while—an embarrassingly long time—to figure out that that's not true. Investing has nothing to do with economics. It's the last thing that drives investing. Investing is driven by two things: history and psychology. And if you spend all your time trying to figure out the economics of investing, you might as well put your money under a mattress.[102]

When asked if there were guiding philosophies behind his decisions to buy and sell, Merc trader Hess reflected for a minute and then told us:

> You know, a lot of us on the floor just scout. As soon as I buy, I'm ready to sell. As soon as I sell, I'm ready to buy—and I keep that perspective. . . . I don't think you should pyramid a bad position. In other words, if [they] buy it at thirty and it goes to twenty, they'll buy more, and then they'll buy it even, and then they'll buy all the way down. . . . I don't believe in pyramiding a bad position. I'll pyramid a good position, obviously. I'll buy something at ten, and I'll buy some at thirty, and I'll buy some at forty, on the way up. 'Cause I'm kind of playing with my own profits. But I don't think you should pyramid a bad position. Just the kind of things that I've gone by.[103]

There are two kinds of traders, he explained:

> Anyone that is a trader looks [either] at "fundamentals" or "technicals." Fundamentals are basically what's happening in the market. Technicals would be looking at charts and mechanically trying to determine future price. Fundamentals—you'd just read on a company; what its sales are; what its profits are; what its inventory levels are. And we all watch the news—you know, what OPEC is doing, since they've obviously been quite influential in the oil markets over the last few years. Technical analysis . . . is where you look for patterns and you try to predict the future. I guess the average broker is a technical *and* a fundamental trader. He basically has charts in his head, because he's watching the market on an almost second, to minute, to hourly basis. And he knows where the flow and the ebb is, too.
>
> Sometimes it works out; sometimes, it doesn't. . . . Some people do spend a lot of time going over their stuff. I've found that that wasn't really that necessary. And if I was trading longer term, then technical analysis would be more worthwhile, but since I don't—most of us kind of trade on the seat of our pants. We buy and sell, and we're bullish and bearish numerous times all within the same day.[104]

Stovall of Standard & Poor's told us a great story about his younger years as a floor trader and how he determined whether to buy or sell by carefully watching and understanding the personal mannerisms of a fellow trader in The Merc's heating oil pit:

For nine months I worked on the floor of The Merc Exchange in the heating oil pit. You have two kinds of traders: the institutional traders representing the oil firms; and then you had the independents or locals—they were willing to accept the risk to create this marketplace. One of these locals would always stand on the top of the ring holding his elbow, flicking the [order] card with his teeth, and then tick back and forth like a metronome. If he was ticking back and forth slowly, he was on the right side of the market, and it was doing what he thought it was going to be doing—so he was just sitting. If he ticked back and forth rapidly, we knew he was either long or short and the market was going against him.[105]

Of course, all this creates a great deal of tension and sometimes everyone in the chain "gets beat up." Many traders see themselves "at the end of the food chain":

> If the institutional customer has a problem, they're going to yell at the sales trader; if the sales trader is getting yelled at, he's going to yell at the [floor] trader. If the floor broker's yelled at, he's going to yell at the clerk. Now, the only person the clerk can yell at is the broker, but the clerk is a subordinate to the broker. So, if the broker messed up . . . the clerk still takes it! Sometimes the broker will get on the phone and say, "Listen, I made a mistake." But nine times out of ten, it's that clerk that takes the brunt of the screaming and yelling. So [getting beat up] literally means someone's not happy. Unfortunate, but it's reality.[106]

As Zweig wisely cautioned during one of our interviews, "There are long periods where people in the markets take validation from what's happening around them and start to believe they have a system."[107] People do make a lot of money on Wall Street, but as folklorists we noticed that the stories of Wall Street followed a similar pattern to stories about immigration to the United States: the narratives people were anxious to tell us invariably celebrated success. We rarely heard about traders or investors who did poorly on the exchanges. One Wall Streeter summed it up nicely:

> The returns on venture capital over a protracted period of time—Is it very attractive? You're damn right it is! But is it a two-times or three-times [increase] every year? Not a chance! You hear about the grand slam home runs, but you don't hear about the guys who struck out.[108]

TRUST AND ETHICS

He who sells what isn't his'n/Must buy it back or go to prison.
Bears make money, bulls make money, but pigs don't make money.
—traditional Wall Street sayings

Folklorists are particularly interested in oral culture. One of the most impressive things we learned by speaking to so many Wall Street workers was that even in an occupation that is rapidly incorporating some of the world's most advanced technology, the spoken word is still paramount. In the culture of Wall Street, a verbal understanding between traders remains absolute and final. Without this mutual understanding, the open outcry system would be impossible. Trust and "being as good as one's word" remains the touchstone upon which the Wall Street markets are grounded. Cashin was particularly eloquent on the importance of verbal agreements:

Well, let's go back to a couple of simple things. . . . I go into a trading crowd and change a partial ownership—which is a share—or let's say fifty thousand shares of something. I could be trading five million, ten million, twelve million dollars worth of ownership in a viable business. There's no lawyer standing behind me. There's no accountant standing behind me. There's not even a notary. I don't give you a piece of paper, or a contract. I look in your eye and I say "Sold!" And you say, "Bought!" And we both walk away from each other.[109]

If there are disputes, they are promptly dealt with by "floor officials." Cashin is a senior trading-floor official on the NYSE: "It's an honor, I suppose, but it's a lot of work if you do it right. Every day somebody comes up to me and says: 'I have this client complaint.' . . . And you go and you investigate it whether it's one hundred shares or ten thousand, because, after *trust* is lost in this place, the game is over. Why would you come here?"

As I like to point out to people, when you see on the floor of this exchange paper changing hands, that's when something *hasn't* occurred. That's when I can't buy "Telephone" at the price my client asked me to buy it. It's still too high. And I have another client who wants me to go to IBM, now! And so I will go, either to another broker or to the specialist, and say: "Here, this is for my good client. If it gets to that price, buy it. I will give you a commission, a partial share." And it will cost that client no more; it comes out of my operating.[110]

Cashin sees the trading floor as a great equalizer. More than anything else, a trader must stand by his verbal commitments.

> Say there's a fellow named Bob, who dislikes me vehemently and I can't stand him. And when we see each other walk down the street, I cross the block to get away from him, 'cause I don't even want to nod at him. But if he's good for his word, he has integrity, his trades stand up, he belongs here as much as the next guy does. I don't have to date his daughter and he doesn't have to date mine. We don't have to socialize. Trade, and I know it's there. It's the only way you can sleep at night knowing there are millions and millions of dollars lying out there verbally [committed] that have to be resolved.
>
> I'll tell you a quick story about that. . . . If I am someone's friend for many years, I'm still an agent for a client—somebody I never met. But I promised them that I would get them the fairest price and the best price possible. And my friend is an agent for someone else. And because we do our job, I will compete with him, try and out-think him, try and play a little chess game, a little bridge game, a little whatever with his head, to try and do a little better for my client. . . . It's like football: for three hours on a Sunday, he's paid to make me look foolish, and I'm paid to make a fool out of him on behalf of our fans, the people who pay us. And hopefully, at the end of the game, whoever is victorious can turn to the loser and say, "Good game, would you come by the house?"[111]

"You have to understand the frailty of this business," he concluded. "I don't only have to be good at what I do, I have to worry about you. And, God forbid, you go out of business! That contract I had with you lapses. Your clients would have to worry about you falling apart; my clients would have to worry about why the other side of that trade is not clearing."[112]

Absolute trust that verbal agreements are being made in good faith and will be strictly enforced is essential to the continuation of open outcry trading. As NYSE trader James Jacobson explained, the very first thing his grandfather, the floor trader Benjamin Jacobson, taught him was: "When you come down to this institution, your word is your bond. All contracts are done orally. It's not like a real estate deal where you sign things. You're forgiven mistakes, but you'll never be forgiven [the] mistake of lying."[113]

THE FUTURE

> It's like standing in front of a tidal wave—you know it's coming and you
> act accordingly. —Bill Bertsch

The Smithsonian Wall Street interviews were conducted at what proved to be a pivotal moment in the history of Wall Street. The open outcry system was still the heart of the Wall Street exchanges, but change was in the air. Almost everyone interviewed spoke at great length about how the Internet, online Internet trading, and other forms of new technology would impact the trading floors. It wasn't simply that traders were reluctant to learn new skills; rather, they realized that this technology might reorder or even eliminate the face-to-face social and professional world in which they had always operated.

Although many looked forward to aspects of technology that would relieve them of mundane tasks, especially those related to routine record keeping, open outcry still had numerous defenders. Merc trader Hess explained at great length how open outcry allows for "that emotional negotiation where electronic trading doesn't."

> Sometimes, it's kind of a cat and mouse game. Do I lift [raise] the offer? Do I wait for the bid? Do I try to get my bid in if sometimes I'm better off saving that ten points? . . . But what if I don't, and the market rallies and I miss the opportunity to buy it?
>
> The other thing that I think the open outcry brings that an electronic system doesn't is the "market makers"—the people like myself. I also handle orders and . . . I trade for my own account. We provide the liquidity. When the markets get real volatile, or even when they're not, we're the ones that actually add the grease to the market. If the market's thirty [bid at] forty and nobody's budging, somebody thinks it's going to go higher. They'll lift that offer for the customer that wants to sell it. And without that, I don't think the markets would be as liquid. I think they'll be even more volatile.
>
> When there was some crisis in the stock market, some of the over-the-counter (OTC) brokers and some of the NASDQ guys just didn't pick up their phones. Well, we're *always* there making markets. Now the bid and offers may get wider; obviously, we're not a shooting gallery. But I think that that's a critical aspect that the guys and women making their living on the floor provide that liquidity and tempering some of that volatility.[114]

But others we interviewed acknowledged that for investors who are not on The Street, open outcry and the trading floors can be mysterious and frustrating. "Before the Crash of 1987," journalist Zweig, pointed out,

> The only way you could buy a stock was to telephone your broker. The broker would then put you on hold or call you back with a trade confirmation. Then three to seven days later, you would get this thing in the mail that said you bought one hundred shares at this price. And then, if you wanted to sell, you had to go through the same thing all over again. . . . There were pieces of paper at every step of the way. The speed had not really changed since the 1880s. It was no faster to trade a stock in 1985 than it was in 1885.[115]

"Not too long ago on the COMEX," Hess told us, "before they had some sort of electronic system, each clerk would literally go to another clerk—and this would be in a big room one floor down in Four World Trade Center—and they would go to the opposing broker and physically check each trade: 'OK, I bought these four lots, those four lots.' Every half hour they would get a new sheet, and that's how they physically matched them up!"[116]

Despite the technical advantages, Zweig cautioned us that the introduction of direct electronic trading through the Internet, which began to gain popularity in the late 1990s, also has some major drawbacks:

> By enabling people to coalesce into ad hoc interest groups—in chat rooms and bulletin boards devoted to certain stocks—it creates almost a teenage pack mentality. There are things you'll do when there are other people around that you won't dream of doing by yourself. . . . And in these Internet chat rooms, it meant buying a stock you've never heard of, that was just letters: "QXP—I don't know what it is, but it's great! It doubled! And Moe over here says it's going to triple." So you have what psychologists call "sensation-seeking" or "thrill-seeking" behavior. People were getting an odd, virtual high from hanging out with each other, and making money, and driving these stocks up without having a clue about what they were doing. . . . It's clear that people are much more *rapidly* informed than they had been, but far from clear that they're *better* informed.[117]

On the other hand, being physically at the center of the trading floor, which used to be a major advantage for brokers, might actually limit a trader's access to information. As Cashin pointed out:

I've had this discussion with the Securities Exchange Commission (SEC) in the past because we all have old thoughts locked in. The SEC said, "You're on the floor, that's a great advantage. That's time and place priority." And I said, "Not anymore, because that information is flashing out there instantly to everybody. Plus the fact they have TV sets, they have CNN, CNBC, Fox, whatever. They've got a zillion things throwing information to them upstairs that I don't necessarily have access to [on the floor]." Now, I am not claiming some naive innocence about the whole thing—there are advantages [in being] at the spot of trade, depending on how it's done.[118]

Despite some reservations, many traders seemed hopeful and excited about the opportunities technological innovation might offer to them and their exchanges. As Hess of The Merc noted:

Right now, we basically do our business the way it has been done for 150 years. It's all open outcry. We wave arms, we yell, we scream—our trading pads are obviously different and our compliance is a lot different, [and] our order trail is much more refined and accurate than it was even ten years ago. The U.S. is basically the last bastion of "open outcry" [futures trading] right now. . . . So the world looks like it's moving towards electronic.

The way [The Merc does] business now, a customer will call his broker, the broker will have to call the floor. Or else [the order] comes in on a wire and it's either called on the floor or a machine spits out the order on the floor. Then that's stamped, taken to the broker. The broker fills it, gives it back to the clerk; the clerk then reports the "fill back," and the customer eventually gets it back. And it's a long process. What we want to do is ultimately have a trader—it could be a day trader, let's say that an individual sitting in California—[who] wants to buy one lot of heating oil. He'll punch that in. The broker's handheld [device], nanoseconds later, will say "buy one heating." . . . He'll buy it. Punch in the opposing broker, punch in the price. As he punches the price in, the customer on the other [computer line] is instantly getting his fill back. Times and sales can always be matched up because as soon as he executes it, we've got the order trail and the price reporting. So that could match up. It can clear instantly through the clearing system. Doesn't have to be recorded, doesn't have to be settled at the end of the day. Boom, it's all done![119]

"There's an old saying on Wall Street," Stovall told us: "There are two emotions that drive stock prices: fear and greed. What's fun is that with computers, because things happen so quickly, and because there is so much, too much, information out there, I think people experience both fear and greed at the exact same moment!"[120]

EPILOGUE

Several months after the completion of our interviews and the participation of many of those quoted in this chapter in the 2001 Smithsonian Folklife Festival, the landscape of Wall Street was seriously disrupted by a terrorist attack on the Twin Towers of the World Trade Center. Located on the western edge of the Financial District, the World Trade Center was targeted for destruction precisely because it was the symbolic representation of Wall Street and the American capitalist system. The psychological impact of September 11 on Wall Streeters was enormous, especially since a huge proportion of the almost 2,800 New Yorkers murdered in the attacks worked in the financial community. It was not unusual for financial workers who survived, even those who did not work at World Trade, to lose scores of co-workers, friends, competitors, and acquaintances.

In the immediate aftermath of the attacks, all the exchanges were closed for days. The floor of the NYBOT, which had been located underneath the South Tower at Four World Trade, was gone, the AMEX was damaged, and when The Merc opened the following week, it had to bring in workers to its riverside headquarters by ferry because it was virtually inaccessible by land. More than fifty thousand financial workers were displaced. Diana Henriques, a financial reporter for *The New York Times*, conveyed the mood of the Street when she noted:

> There wasn't a person with whom I work . . . who did not have a Rolodex that was not scattered with people who had been lost. The firms that had survived had scattered; we did not know how to reach them. The simple job of calling up four sources and writing a story became a monumental task because of the diaspora that followed those events.[121]

Yet, remarkably, one-by-one, the trading floors regrouped and reopened. On November 15, scarcely two months after the momentous events of September 11, our colleagues at the Museum of American Financial History (now Museum of American Finance), a Smithsonian Affiliate, in collaboration with the Smithsonian Institution, invited Wall Street workers to a forum at the U.S. Custom House a few blocks south of the still smoldering World Trade Center. The event, titled "Always Another Trading Day: Endurance and Optimism in the Culture and History of Wall Street," was not so much a forum as a community gathering. It gave financial workers—from floor clerks to leading CEOs—a chance to reflect on the culture and history of The Street and to celebrate the occupational pride and traditions that united them. It was the first cultural event in lower Manhattan following the attacks, and one of the first in anyone's memory that included traders and financial workers from all the exchanges. "Our goal this afternoon," began Museum director Brian Thompson, "is to step back from two months of day-to-day getting by and, together, take a longer term view, steeped in the history, the culture, and the strength of our community."[122]

Brief remarks were offered by luminaries from all the exchanges, leading financiers, community leaders, and Harry Poulakalos, the owner of Harry's of Hanover Square, a favorite local restaurant. Two of the most eloquent speakers were reporters. Financial reporter Henriques from *The New York Times* told the audience that the recent events had caused her and her fellow business reporters to take a deeper look at the concept of Wall Street as an occupational community, and she expressed surprise at what she found.

> I think business reporters were unexpectedly affected because . . . it was not principally a business story. Obviously, the impact of this on business—on the nation's financial markets—was compelling and an immense story. . . . But it was clear that, in a way, perceptions had shifted from making money to assessing those deeper bonds of community that held firms together. I was struck by the instantaneous departure of ruthlessness in the conversations I had with people. I was struck by an interesting shift in competitiveness that occurred, literally, overnight: people almost competing to see how generous they could be, instead of how successful they could be. People competing to see how kind they could be to rivals and to competitors, rather than how much more market share they could get. It's really been an amazing thing to watch as a financial writer; and as an amateur business historian, I can't wait to see how it turns out.[123]

Speaker Zweig, senior columnist for *Money* Magazine, who had been an important informant and advisor for the Smithsonian project, took a longer term, more historical perspective. After recounting previous fires, disasters, and disruptions that had challenged Wall Street over the centuries, he predicted that:

The people who on September 11, and September 12, and September 13 were saying on CNN, and on CNBC, and on MSNBC, and all the other electronic media, words like, "everything has changed," "nothing will ever be the same again," are almost all certainly wrong. . . . Wall Street will not only survive, it will thrive, and it will prevail.[124]

The determination and resiliency demonstrated by the financial workers who gathered that day in the Customs House seem to have been well founded. Despite the many pundits who predicted that the disaster would mean the end of the physical concentration of financial services in lower Manhattan, many of the hardest hit financial firms resolutely remained downtown or returned as soon as their facilities were repaired or new space was acquired. It is still too early to assess what the long-term impact of this tragedy will be on the culture of the trading floors and exchanges throughout New York's Financial District; but if nothing else, it seems to have underscored and reinforced a sense of shared community among the workers of Wall Street.

ACKNOWLEDGMENTS AND CREDITS

T HE SMITHSONIAN Institution's New York City Project, which culminated with the New York City at the Smithsonian exhibition at the 2001 Smithsonian Folklife Festival in Washington, D.C., also included numerous related conferences, concerts, forums, lectures, ceremonies, and public events in New York and Washington. These events, as well as subsequent films, recordings, and publications based on documentation generated by the project, were produced by the Smithsonian Center for Folklife and Cultural Heritage in collaboration with New York's Center for Traditional Music and Dance, City Lore: The New York Center for Urban Culture, the Museum of American Financial History (now the Museum of American Finance), and numerous other cultural institutions throughout the five boroughs.

This extensive, multi-faceted project would have not been possible without the support and guidance of a remarkable coalition of funders, civic and cultural leaders, politicians, scholars, experts, dedicated individuals, and colleagues, and this book would be incomplete without acknowledging their profound contributions.

Major funding came from the New York City Council, Howard P. Milstein, and the New York Stock Exchange. Major support was provided by Amtrak, Con Edison, the Recording Industries Music Performance Trust Funds, and Arthur Pacheco. Major contributors included the New York Community Trust, the Durst Foundation, May & Samuel Rudin Family Foundation, Leonard Litwin, and Bernard Mendik. Additional donors include Stephen and Judy Gluckstern, Emigrant Savings Bank, and Jeffrey Gural.

The Smithsonian thanks members of the New York City Project's Leadership Committee for their support, especially committee co-chairs, Senator Daniel Patrick Moynihan and Elizabeth Moynihan and corporate chairman Howard P. Milstein. Other leadership committee members included John H. Biggs of TIAA-CREF, Joyce Bove of the New York Community Trust, Kitty Carlisle Hart of the New York State Council on the Arts, Robert B. Catell of Keyspan Energy, Schuyler Chapin of the New York City Department of Cultural Affairs, Michael Clark of the Citizen's Committee for New York City, journalist Walter Cronkite, Clive Davis of Arista Records, actor Ossie Davis of Emmalyn II Production Company, Douglas Durst of The Durst Organization, Osborn Elliott of the Citizen's Committee for New York City, Charles A. Gargano of Empire State Development, Arthur Gelb of the *New York Times* College Scholarship Program, Judith O'Conner Gluckstern of the Lucky Star Foundation, Commissioner Raymond W. Kelly, of the New York City Police Department, Nathan Leventhal of Lincoln Center for the Performing Arts, Inc., Harold O. Levy of the New York City Schools, Edward Lewis of Essence Communications, Earle I. Mack, Chairman Emeritus of the New York State Council on the Arts, Eugene R. McGrath of Consolidated Edison Company of New York Inc., Robert Morgenthau, District Attorney of New York County, Lester Morse of The Lester Morse Company, Arthur J. Pacheco of Bear Stearns, Libby Pataki, First Lady of New York State, Peter J. Powers of Powers Global Strategies, Al Roker of Al Roker Productions, Inc., Howard J. Rubenstein of Rubenstein Associates, Inc., Lew Rudin, of the Association for a Better New York, Richard J. Schwartz, Chair of the New York State Council on the Arts, Martin E. Segal of the New York International Festival of the Arts, Commissioner Henry Stern of the City of New York Parks & Recreation Department, Arthur O. Sulzberger, Jr. of the *New York Times*, author and journalist Calvin Trillin, the Honorable Peter F. Vallone, Speaker of the New York City Council, Mike Wallace, Senior Correspondent of *60 Minutes*, John Wang of the Asian American Business Development Center, and Tim Zagat of NYC & Company.

CONTENT ADVISORS, COLLABORATORS, AND FIELDWORKERS

In addition to the Leadership Committee, the project was greatly assisted by an equally distinguished advisory committee. Its members, drawn from cultural organizations and educational institutions throughout the city, included Ruth Abram, from the Lower East Side Tenement Museum, Gladys Pena Acosta from RAICES, Ray Allen from the American Studies Program at Brooklyn College/CUNY, Gage Averill from the Music Department at New York University, Fatima Bercht from *El Museo del Barrio*, Melody Capote from the Caribbean Culture Center/African Diaspora Institute, Barbara Cohen-Stratyner from the New York Public Library for the Performing Arts at Lincoln Center, food historian Cara De Silver, Miriam De Uriarte from *El Museo del Barrio*, Howard Dodson from the New York Public Library's Schomburg Center for Research in Black Culture, Sharon E. Dunn from the New York City Board of Education, Juan Flores from the Black and Puerto Rican Studies Department, Hunter College/CUNY, Laura Hansen from Place Matters at the Municipal Art Society, John Haworth, from the Smithsonian's National Museum of the American Indian, Ellie Hisama from the Institute for Studies in American Music at Brooklyn College/CUNY, Barbara Kirshenblatt-Gimblett from the Performance Studies Department at New York University, Lea Krauss from The New York Community Trust, Susana Torruella Leval from *El Museo del Barrio*, Robert MacDonald from the Museum of the City of New York, Fay Chew Matsuda from the Museum of Chinese in the Americas, Ethel Raim from the Center for Traditional Music and Dance, Jan Seidler Ramirez from the New-York Historical Society, Frances A. Resheske from the Consolidated Edison Company, Joseph Sciorra, from the Calandra Italian American Institute at Queens College, Gabrielle Shubert from the New York Transit Museum, Pravina Shukla from the Folklore Department at Indiana University, John Kuo Wei Tchen from the Asian/Pacific/American Studies Program and Institute at New York University, Brian Thompson from the Museum of American Financial History (Museum of American Finance); Michael Wallace from the History Department at the Graduate Center/City University of New York, Steve Wheeler, Archivist of the New York Stock Exchange, Theodora Yoshikani from the American Museum of Natural History, and Steve Zeitlin from City Lore: The Center for Urban Culture. Photographer Martha Cooper merits special thanks and acknowledgement for generously allowing us to use of her magnificent images to enrich all phases of the project.

Assistance with both the interview and production phases of the 2001 Smithsonian Folklife Festival were facilitated by the cooperation of organizations and individuals too numerous to mention, but we would like recognize the exceptional contributions of Terry Marone and Actors' Equity Association, Coney Island Bagels and Bialys, Barbara Matera and Barbara Matera, Ltd., The Citizen Committee for New York City, Bob Kelly, Local 28 of the Sheet Metal Workers International Association, the Metropolitan Transportation Authority, Museum of American Financial History (Museum of American Finance), New York City Department of Transportation, New York City Transit Authority, New-York Historical Society, New York Mercantile Exchange, New York Stock Exchange, New York Transit Museum, Robert Baron and the New York State Council on the Arts, Nino Novellino and Costume Armour, Andrew Rosenwach and the Rosenwach Group, Inc., Russ & Daughters, and Tats Cru.

Finally, this book would not have been possible without the dedication, savvy, and professionalism of the fieldworkers who walked the streets, rode the subways, and occasionally braved the ferry to interview this amazingly constellation of knowledgeable New Yorkers. Fieldworkers involved in the Smithsonian New York City Project included Jerald Albarelli, Ray Allen, Emily Botein, Lori Branston, Kathleen Condon, Martha Cooper, Amanda Dargan, Andrew Davis, Tony DeNonno, Sonia Estreich, Makale Faber, Kwali Fabes, Michael Greene, Laura Hansen, Annie Hauck-Lawson, Marion Jacobson, Denise Lynch, Elena Martinez, Cathy Ragland, Ethel Raim, Henry Sapoznik, Roberta Singer, Les Slater, Scott Spencer, Brian Thompson, Kay Turner, Tom Van Buren, Meg Ventrudo, Yu-Cheng Wang, Bill Westerman, Lois Wilken, and Steve Zeitlin. Special thanks also goes to Smithsonian Center for Folklife and Cultural Heritage Director Richard Kurin and Smithsonian Folklife Festival Director Diana Parker for their support and encouragement of the New York City Project from its inception to its actualization as a large and complex event; to the Smithsonian's New York City Festival staff members Arlene Reiniger, Stephen Kidd, and Dorey Butter, who oversaw the day-to-day tasks that made the exhibition a reality; to Director of Development Josh Silver; to New York Project Smithsonian interns Wai Kwan Chung, Matthew Closter, Erica Davis, Erin Forbes, Amy Morros, and Helen Veit; and to the rest of the remarkable Smithsonian and Smithsonian Folkways staff who contributed to the success of this undertaking.

For assistance with the preparation of this manuscript, the author would like to thank readers Kristin Aguilera, Ray Allen, Dorey Butter, Arlene Reiniger, and Meg Ventrudo. Thanks also to Ginger Strader and the helpful staff of the Smithsonian Institution Scholarly Press for their help and guidance in bringing this project to fruition. I also want to acknowledge the vital contributions of the late Caroline Newman at Smithsonian Press, who provided the author with critical support and greatly appreciated encouragement. Lastly, for shepherding the manuscript into print, I want to thank the staff at Rowman & Littlefield, including acquisition editor Jack Meinhardt, production editor Elaine McGarraugh, assistant editor Marissa Parks, and copyeditor Claudia Frigo. Any errors are, of course, entirely my own and not a reflection of their valiant efforts.

Ultimately, the profoundest thanks are owed to the hundreds of New Yorkers who took time from their busy lives to share their stories, knowledge, and insights with us, and by doing so, allowed us to make their understandings of New York City at the turn of the twenty-first century a permanent part of our national record.

Appendix

New York City Project:
Guide to Recorded Interviews

T HE QUOTES found throughout this book come from two main sources. The majority of quotes are transcriptions of oral interviews recorded by Smithsonian researchers or researchers from sister cultural organizations collaborating with the Smithsonian on the New York City Project. These recordings were made between 1999 and 2001 in "the field," which in this case consisted of various locations throughout the five boroughs. Individuals and groups were interviewed in their offices, workshops, homes, places of business, and the occasional corner coffee shop. Documentation was done primarily on audiocassette tape. Footnotes throughout the text reference individual tapes by year and tape accession number. The abbreviation "CFCH" is used for the Smithsonian Institution's Center for Folklife and Cultural Heritage. By consulting the "Interview Tape Log—Field Interviews" list, readers can ascertain the name of the interviewee and the interviewer. For example, CFCH, 1999:1 refers to a taped interview with Terry Marone of Actors' Equity done by the author in 1999.

Other quotes are transcribed from audiocassette recordings made by Smithsonian staff at the 2001 Smithsonian Folklife Festival, which took place on the National Mall in Washington, D.C., between June 27 and July 8, 2001. At the festival, many of the more than two hundred New York participants took part in scheduled "narrative sessions" held on festival stages in front of audiences that ranged from several dozen to several hundred museum visitors. These panel discussions on prearranged topics were led by a folklorist/moderator, who posed questions to the panelists and helped field questions from the audience. Scores of panel discussions were presented and recorded during the course of the festival. Transcriptions from eleven particularly relevant narrative session tapes, each given a separate letter designation from A to K, are included in this text and noted as CFCH/Festival. By consulting the Interview Tape Log—Festival Interviews list, readers can ascertain the names of those involved and the date of the discussion. For example, CFCH/Festival, Tape A actually refers to Audiocassette FP-2001-CT-0166, which was recorded on June 27, 2001 (referenced as 6/27/2001) on one of the program's narrative stages. The panel, titled "Backstage Stories," featured participants Susan Spain, Janice Lorraine, Monique Midgette, and interviewer Andrew Davis.

Both sets of documentary materials, the field tapes and the festival tapes, are housed at the Ralph Rinzler Folklife Archives and Collections at the Smithsonian Institution's Center for Folklife and Cultural Heritage in Washington, D.C. For further information, researchers and others wishing to access the tapes should contact the center's archivists.

INTERVIEW TAPE LOG—FIELD INTERVIEWS: AUDIOCASSETTES RECORDED IN NEW YORK CITY

Center for Folklife and Cultural Heritage. New York City Project 1999–2001. Audiocassette 1999:1. Terry Marone, Actors' Equity. Interviewed by Nancy Groce. Smithsonian Institution, Washington, D.C.

Center for Folklife and Cultural Heritage. New York City Project 1999–2001. Audiocassette 1999:2. Helen Guditas, Broadway Theatre Institute. Interviewed by Nancy Groce. Smithsonian Institution, Washington, D.C.

Center for Folklife and Cultural Heritage. New York City Project 1999–2001. Audiocassette 1999:3. Michael Clark, Citizens' Committee for New York City. Interviewed by Nancy Groce. Smithsonian Institution, Washington, D.C.

Center for Folklife and Cultural Heritage. New York City Project 1999–2001. Audiocassette 1999:4. Tony DeMarco, Irish music session. Interviewed by Nancy Groce. Smithsonian Institution, Washington, D.C.

Center for Folklife and Cultural Heritage. New York City Project 1999–2001. Audiocassette 1999:5. Brian Thompson and Meg Ventrudo, Museum of

American Financial History. Interviewed by Nancy Groce. Smithsonian Institution, Washington, D.C.

Center for Folklife and Cultural Heritage. New York City Project 1999–2001. Audiocassette 1999:6. John Kret, Official Guide. New York Stock Exchange. Interviewed by Nancy Groce. Smithsonian Institution, Washington, D.C.

Center for Folklife and Cultural Heritage. New York City Project 1999–2001. Audiocassette 1999:7. Olga Koutcherova, Choir director. Greenpoint Russian Orthodox Cathedral. Interviewed by Nancy Groce. Smithsonian Institution, Washington, D.C.

Center for Folklife and Cultural Heritage. New York City Project 1999–2001. Audiocassette 1999:8. John Herzog, Museum of American Financial History. Interviewed by Nancy Groce. Smithsonian Institution, Washington, D.C.

Center for Folklife and Cultural Heritage. New York City Project 1999–2001. Audiocassette 1999:9. Ramnarine Sasenarine, Indo-Caribbean musician. Interviewed by Nancy Groce. Smithsonian Institution, Washington, D.C.

Center for Folklife and Cultural Heritage. New York City Project 1999–2001. Audiocassette 1999:10. Barney Greengrass, Owner's Barney Greengrass: "The Sturgeon King." Interviewed by Nancy Groce. Smithsonian Institution, Washington, D.C.

Center for Folklife and Cultural Heritage. New York City Project 1999–2001. Audiocassette 1999:11. John Loftgren. Theatrical Stage Employees, Local 1-IAISE. Interviewed by Nancy Groce. Smithsonian Institution, Washington, D.C.

Center for Folklife and Cultural Heritage. New York City Project 1999–2001. Audiocassette 1999:12. Charles Sachs, Curator, New York Transit Museum. Interviewed by Nancy Groce. Smithsonian Institution, Washington, D.C.

Center for Folklife and Cultural Heritage. New York City Project 1999–2001. Audiocassette 1999:13. Ziegfeld Follies Club. Interviewed by Nancy Groce. Smithsonian Institution, Washington, D.C.

Center for Folklife and Cultural Heritage. New York City Project 1999–2001. Audiocassette 1999:14. Jean Alexander, West Indian American Day Carnival Association. Interviewed by Nancy Groce. Smithsonian Institution, Washington, D.C.

Center for Folklife and Cultural Heritage. New York City Project 1999–2001. Audiocassette 1999:15. Barbara Matera, Barbara Matera, Ltd. Interviewed by Nancy Groce. Smithsonian Institution, Washington, D.C.

Center for Folklife and Cultural Heritage. New York City Project 1999–2001. Audiocassette 1999:16. Ruth Nerken, acting coach at Broadway Brunch

Club. Interviewed by Nancy Groce. Smithsonian Institution, Washington, D.C.

Center for Folklife and Cultural Heritage. New York City Project 1999–2001. Audiocassette 1999:17. Gypsy Robe ceremony at opening of *Fascinating Rhythm*. Recorded by Nancy Groce. Smithsonian Institution, Washington, D.C.

Center for Folklife and Cultural Heritage. New York City Project 1999–2001. Audiocassette 1999:18. Gina Higginbotham, Director, Music Under New York. Interviewed by Nancy Groce. Smithsonian Institution, Washington, D.C.

Center for Folklife and Cultural Heritage. New York City Project 1999–2001. Audiocassette 2000:1. Vincent Buchanan, Arthur D. Cashing, Jr., and Leopold Korins, New York Stock Exchange Luncheon Club. Interviewed by Nancy Groce. Smithsonian Institution, Washington, D.C.

Center for Folklife and Cultural Heritage. New York City Project 1999–2001. Audiocassette 2000:2. Gary Lapayover, New York Mercantile Exchange. Interviewed by Nancy Groce. Smithsonian Institution, Washington, D.C.

Center for Folklife and Cultural Heritage. New York City Project 1999–2001. Audiocassette 2000:3. Riley Jones Cohen, actor. Interviewed by Nancy Groce. Smithsonian Institution, Washington, D.C.

Center for Folklife and Cultural Heritage. New York City Project 1999–2001. Audiocassette 2000:4A, 4B. Andrew Blum, Bond Market Association. Interviewed by Nancy Groce. Smithsonian Institution, Washington, D.C.

Center for Folklife and Cultural Heritage. New York City Project 1999–2001. Audiocassette 2000:5. Estee Adoram, Manager, Comedy Cellar. Interviewed by Nancy Groce. Smithsonian Institution, Washington, D.C.

Center for Folklife and Cultural Heritage. New York City Project 1999–2001. Audiocassette 2000:6. Sam Chwat, New York Speech Improvement Services. Interviewed by Nancy Groce. Smithsonian Institution, Washington, D.C.

Center for Folklife and Cultural Heritage. New York City Project 1999–2001. Audiocassette 2000:7. Comedians, Comedy Cellar. Interviewed by Nancy Groce. Smithsonian Institution, Washington, D.C.

Center for Folklife and Cultural Heritage. New York City Project 1999–2001. Audiocassette 2000:8. Mark Federman, Russ & Daughters. Interviewed by Annie Hauck-Lawson. Smithsonian Institution, Washington, D.C.

Center for Folklife and Cultural Heritage. New York City Project 1999–2001. Audiocassette 2000:9. Jeff Holtermann, Holtermann's Bakery. Interviewed by Annie Hauck-Lawson. Smithsonian Institution, Washington, D.C.

Center for Folklife and Cultural Heritage. New York City Project 1999–2001. Audiocassette 2000:10. Steve Ross: Coney Island Bagels & Bialys. Interviewed by Annie Hauck-Lawson. Smithsonian Institution, Washington, D.C.

Center for Folklife and Cultural Heritage. New York City Project 1999–2001. Audiocassette 2000:11. Gary Brouwer, Broadway milliner. Interviewed by Nancy Groce. Smithsonian Institution, Washington, D.C.

Center for Folklife and Cultural Heritage. New York City Project 1999–2001. Audiocassette 2000:12. Ernie Smith, Penn & Fletcher. Interviewed by Marion Jacobson. Smithsonian Institution, Washington, D.C.

Center for Folklife and Cultural Heritage. New York City Project 1999–2001. Audiocassette 2000:13. Woody Shelp, Broadway milliner. Interviewed by Marion Jacobson. Smithsonian Institution, Washington, D.C.

Center for Folklife and Cultural Heritage. New York City Project 1999–2001. Audiocassette 2000:14. Deborah Skell, fashion designer. Interviewed by Marion Jacobson. Smithsonian Institution, Washington, D.C.

Center for Folklife and Cultural Heritage. New York City Project 1999–2001. Audiocassette 2000:15. Michael Steward-Former, window dresser, Dell Roostein. Interviewed by Marion Jacobson. Smithsonian Institution, Washington, D.C.

Center for Folklife and Cultural Heritage. New York City Project 1999–2001. Audiocassette 2000:16. Michael Mators, window dresser. Interviewed by Marion Jacobson. Smithsonian Institution, Washington, D.C.

Center for Folklife and Cultural Heritage. New York City Project 1999–2001. Audiocassette 2000:17. Carol Barnhart, mannequin maker. Interviewed by Marion Jacobson. Smithsonian Institution, Washington, D.C.

Center for Folklife and Cultural Heritage. New York City Project 1999–2001. Audiocassette 2000:18. Barry Lederer, fashion show sound designer. Interviewed by Marion Jacobson. Smithsonian Institution, Washington, D.C.

Center for Folklife and Cultural Heritage. New York City Project 1999–2001. Audiocassette 2000:19. Tom Beebe, window dresser. Interviewed by Marion Jacobson. Smithsonian Institution, Washington, D.C.

Center for Folklife and Cultural Heritage. New York City Project 1999–2001. Audiocassette 2000:20A, 20B. Andrew Rosenwach and employees, Rosenwach Water Tanks. Interviewed by Kathleen Condon. Smithsonian Institution, Washington, D.C.

Center for Folklife and Cultural Heritage. New York City Project 1999–2001. Audiocassette 2000:21. Ralph Jennings, station manager, WFUV. Interviewed by Nancy Groce. Smithsonian Institution, Washington, D.C.

Center for Folklife and Cultural Heritage. New York City Project 1999–2001. Audiocassettes and videocassettes 2000:22. Wall Street workers, Harry's of Hanover Square dinner. Interviewed by Nancy Groce. Smithsonian Institution, Washington, D.C.

Center for Folklife and Cultural Heritage. New York City Project 1999–2001. Audiocassette 2000:23. Lemont "Leo" Oluwale Haskins, street chess player. Interviewed by Makale Faber. Smithsonian Institution, Washington, D.C.

Center for Folklife and Cultural Heritage. New York City Project 1999–2001. Audiocassette 2000:24. Imad Khachan, Chess Forum. Interviewed by Makale Faber. Smithsonian Institution, Washington, D.C.

Center for Folklife and Cultural Heritage. New York City Project 1999–2001. Audiocassette 2000:25. Chris Macks, Chess Forum. Interviewed by Makale Faber. Smithsonian Institution, Washington, D.C.

Center for Folklife and Cultural Heritage. New York City Project 1999–2001. Audiocassette 2000:26. Jonathan Zachary, street chess player. Interviewed by Makale Faber. Smithsonian Institution, Washington, D.C.

Center for Folklife and Cultural Heritage. New York City Project 1999–2001. Audiocassette 2000:27. Poseidon Bakery. Interviewed by Annie Hauck-Lawson. Smithsonian Institution, Washington, D.C.

Center for Folklife and Cultural Heritage. New York City Project 1999–2001. Audiocassette 2000:28. Norma Jean Darden, African American restaurant owner (Spoonbreads) and food expert. Interviewed by Annie Hauck-Lawson. Smithsonian Institution, Washington, D.C.

Center for Folklife and Cultural Heritage. New York City Project 1999–2001. Audiocassette 2000:29. Sal Batolomeo, Rosario's Pizza. Interviewed by Annie Hauck-Lawson. Smithsonian Institution, Washington, D.C.

Center for Folklife and Cultural Heritage. New York City Project 1999–2001. Audiocassette 2000:30. Evergreen Chinese Restaurant chefs. Interviewed by Annie Hauck-Lawson. Smithsonian Institution, Washington, D.C.

Center for Folklife and Cultural Heritage. New York City Project 1999–2001. Audiocassette 2000:31. Tats Cru, muralists: Wilfredo "Bio" Feliciano; Hector "Nicer" Nazario; and Sotero "BG183" Ortiz. Interviewed by Elena Martinez. Smithsonian Institution, Washington, D.C.

Center for Folklife and Cultural Heritage. New York City Project 1999–2001. Audiocassette 2000:32. Torin Reid, train operator, Metropolitan Transit Authority. Interviewed by Steve Zeitlin. Smithsonian Institution, Washington, D.C.

Center for Folklife and Cultural Heritage. New York City Project 1999–2001. Audiocassette 2000:33. New York Talkers. Interviewed by Steve Zeitlin. Smithsonian Institution, Washington, D.C.

Center for Folklife and Cultural Heritage. New York City Project 1999–2001. Audiocassette 2000:34. Nicholas Maldarelli, Sheet Metal Workers International Association, Local Union No. 28, Metropolitan New York and Long Island. Interviewed by Elena Martinez. Smithsonian Institution, Washington, D.C.

Center for Folklife and Cultural Heritage. New York City Project 1999–2001. Audiocassette 2000:35. Chico Garcia, muralist. Interviewed by Elena Martinez. Smithsonian Institution, Washington, D.C.

Center for Folklife and Cultural Heritage. New York City Project 1999–2001. Audiocassette 2000:36. Shenyar Chaudhry, Pakistani kite maker and flyer. Interviewed by City Lore staff. Smithsonian Institution, Washington, D.C.

Center for Folklife and Cultural Heritage. New York City Project 1999–2001. Audiocassette (mirco) 2000:37. Sandra Lane, train operator, Metropolitan Transit Authority. Interviewed by Steve Zeitlin. Smithsonian Institution, Washington, D.C.

Center for Folklife and Cultural Heritage. New York City Project 1999–2001. Audiocassette 2000:38. Nino Novellino, Costume Armour, Inc. Interviewed by Andrew Davis. Smithsonian Institution, Washington, D.C.

Center for Folklife and Cultural Heritage. New York City Project 1999–2001. Audiocassette 2000:39. Bob Kelly, Bob Kelly Wig Creations. Interviewed by Andrew Davis. Smithsonian Institution, Washington, D.C.

Center for Folklife and Cultural Heritage. New York City Project 1999–2001. Audiocassette 2000:40. David Rosenberg, I Weiss & Sons, theatrical curtains. Interviewed by Cathleen Pagl. Smithsonian Institution, Washington, D.C.

Center for Folklife and Cultural Heritage. New York City Project 1999–2001. Audiocassette 2000:41. Joe Haneman, parade organizer. Interviewed by Nancy Groce. Smithsonian Institution, Washington, D.C.

Center for Folklife and Cultural Heritage. New York City Project 1999–2001. Audiocassette 2000:42. Kevin McCarthy, New York Police Department bagpiper. Interviewed by Scott Spencer. Smithsonian Institution, Washington, D.C.

Center for Folklife and Cultural Heritage. New York City Project 1999–2001. Audiocassette 2000:43. Sergeant John Tansey, New York Police Department bagpiper. Interviewed by Scott Spencer. Smithsonian Institution, Washington, D.C.

Center for Folklife and Cultural Heritage. New York City Project 1999–2001. Audiocassette 2000:44. Richard Baratz, Wall Street Bank note and stock certificate engraver and caricaturist for Sardi's restaurant. Interviewed by Kay Turner. Smithsonian Institution, Washington, D.C.

Center for Folklife and Cultural Heritage. New York City Project 1999–2001. Audiocassette 2000:45. Arthur Cashin, New York Stock Exchange. Interviewed by Kay Turner. Smithsonian Institution, Washington, D.C.

Center for Folklife and Cultural Heritage. New York City Project 1999–2001. Audiocassette 2000:46. David Granger, New York Stock Exchange. Interviewed by Kay Turner. Smithsonian Institution, Washington, D.C.

Center for Folklife and Cultural Heritage. New York City Project 1999–2001. Audiocassette 2000:47. Joe Cicchetti, New York Mercantile Exchange. Interviewed by Kay Turner. Smithsonian Institution, Washington, D.C.

Center for Folklife and Cultural Heritage. New York City Project 1999–2001. Audiocassette 2001:1. Scott Hess, New York Mercantile Exchange. Interviewed by Kay Turner. Smithsonian Institution, Washington, D.C.

Center for Folklife and Cultural Heritage. New York City Project 1999–2001. Audiocassette 2001:2. Anthony "Tony" DeMarco, New York Board of Trade. Interviewed by Kay Turner. Smithsonian Institution, Washington, D.C.

Center for Folklife and Cultural Heritage. New York City Project 1999–2001. Audiocassette 2001:3. Tod Bertsch, New York Stock Exchange. Interviewed by Kay Turner. Smithsonian Institution, Washington, D.C.

Center for Folklife and Cultural Heritage. New York City Project 1999–2001. Audiocassette 2001:4. Karen Hackett, New York Stock Exchange. Interviewed by Kay Turner. Smithsonian Institution, Washington, D.C.

Center for Folklife and Cultural Heritage. New York City Project 1999–2001. Audiocassette 2001:5. Michael LaBranche, New York Stock Exchange. Interviewed by Kay Turner. Smithsonian Institution, Washington, D.C.

Center for Folklife and Cultural Heritage. New York City Project 1999–2001. Audiocassette 2001:6. Jason Zweig, *Money* Magazine. Interviewed by Kay Turner. Smithsonian Institution, Washington, D.C.

Center for Folklife and Cultural Heritage. New York City Project 1999–2001. Audiocassette 2001:7. John Herzog, Herzog, Heine, Geduld. Interviewed by Kay Turner. Smithsonian Institution, Washington, D.C.

Center for Folklife and Cultural Heritage. New York City Project 1999–2001. Audiocassette 2001:8. Sam Stovall, Standard & Poor's. Interviewed by Kay Turner. Smithsonian Institution, Washington, D.C.

Center for Folklife and Cultural Heritage. New York City Project 1999–2001. Audiocassette 2001:9. Mike Geoghan, New York Mercantile

Exchange. Interviewed by Kay Turner. Smithsonian Institution, Washington, D.C.

Center for Folklife and Cultural Heritage. New York City Project 1999–2001. Audiocassette 2001:10. Madeline Boyd, New York Mercantile Exchange. Interviewed by Kay Turner. Smithsonian Institution, Washington, D.C.

Center for Folklife and Cultural Heritage. New York City Project 1999–2001. Audiocassette 2001:11. (See also 2001:15.) Myron Kandel, CNN Senior Financial Editor, CNN-FM. Interviewed by Kay Turner. Smithsonian Institution, Washington, D.C.

Center for Folklife and Cultural Heritage. New York City Project 1999–2001. Audiocassette 2001:12. Joe Gabriel, New York Stock Exchange Facilities Manager. Interviewed by Kay Turner. Smithsonian Institution, Washington, D.C.

Center for Folklife and Cultural Heritage. New York City Project 1999–2001. Audiocassette 2001:13. James Jacobson, New York Stock Exchange. Interviewed by Kay Turner. Smithsonian Institution, Washington, D.C.

Center for Folklife and Cultural Heritage. New York City Project 1999–2001. Audiocassette 2001:14. Bill Bertsch, Wall Street trader. Interviewed by Kay Turner. Smithsonian Institution, Washington, D.C.

Center for Folklife and Cultural Heritage. New York City Project 1999–2001. Audiocassette 2001:15. Myron Kandel, CNN Senior Financial Editor, CNN-FM. (Also see 2001:11) Interviewed by Kay Turner. Smithsonian Institution, Washington, D.C.

Center for Folklife and Cultural Heritage. New York City Project 1999–2001. Audiocassette 2001:16. Michel Marks, New York Mercantile Exchange. Interviewed by Kay Turner. Smithsonian Institution, Washington, D.C.

Center for Folklife and Cultural Heritage. New York City Project 1999–2001. Audiocassette 2001:17. Interviewed by Yu-Cheng Wang, Chinese herbalist. Smithsonian Institution, Washington, D.C.

Center for Folklife and Cultural Heritage. New York City Project 1999–2001. Audiocassette 2001:18. Rabbis Baumgarten and Pape, matzoth makers. Interviewed by Annie Hauck-Lawson. Smithsonian Institution, Washington, D.C.

Center for Folklife and Cultural Heritage. New York City Project 1999–2001. Audiocassette 2001:19. Edie Cowan, Broadway choreography, director, and gypsy. Interviewed by Nancy Groce. Smithsonian Institution, Washington, D.C.

INTERVIEW TAPE LOG—FESTIVAL INTERVIEWS: AUDIOCASSETTES RECORDED AT THE 2001 SMITHSONIAN FOLKLIFE FESTIVAL

Tape A. Center for Folklife and Cultural Heritage. New York City Festival Program. Audiocassette FP-2001-CT-0166. (6/27/2001) "Backstage Stories." Participants: Susan Spain, Janice Lorraine, Monique Midgette. Interviewed by Andrew Davis. Smithsonian Institution, Washington, D.C.

Tape B. Center for Folklife and Cultural Heritage. New York City Festival Program. Audiocassette FP-2001-CT-1067. (6/28/2001) "Gypsy Robe Presentation Ceremony." Participants: Terry Marone, Tom Miller, Mary Lou Westerfield. Interviewed by Dwight Blocker Bowers and Andrew Davis.

Tape C. Center for Folklife and Cultural Heritage. New York City Festival Program. Audiocassette FP-2001-CT-1067. (6/28/2001) "Backstage Broadway: Gypsy Tales." Participants: Don Brodie, Edie Cowan Terry Marone, Mary Lu, Tom Rocco. Interviewed by Andrew Davis. (Session recorded on B-side of Tape B.)

Tape D. Center for Folklife and Cultural Heritage. New York City Festival Program. Audiocassette FP-2001-CT- 0169. (6/29/2001) "Broadway Costumes—Barbara Matera." Participants: Judy Adamson, Josephine Spano, Pat Sullivan. Interviewed by Andrew Davis.

Tape E. Center for Folklife and Cultural Heritage. New York City Festival Program. Audiocassette FP-2001-CT-0102. (6/29/2001) "Subway Stories." Participants: Bruce Alexander, Sandra Lane, Tony Palombella, Torin Reid. Interviewed by Steve Zeitlin.

Tape F. Center for Folklife and Cultural Heritage. New York City Festival Program. Audiocassette FP-2001-CT-0103. (6/29/2001) "Subway Stories." Participants: Bruce Alexander, Sandra Lane, Tony Palombella, Torin Reid. Interviewed by Steve Zeitlin.

Tape G. Center for Folklife and Cultural Heritage. New York City Festival Program. Audiocassette FP-2001-CT-0104. (6/30/2001) "Water Towers." Participants: John DeGeorge, Wilson Felix, Kenny Lewis, Andrew Rosenwach, Joe Syczky, Charles Zimmerman. Interviewed by Kathleen Condon.

Tape H. Center for Folklife and Cultural Heritage. New York City Festival Program. Audiocassette FP-2001-CT-0105. (6/30/2001) "Water Towers." Participants: John DeGeorge, Wilson Felix, Kenny Lewis, Andrew Rosenwach, Joe Syczky, Charles Zimmerman. Interviewed by Kathleen Condon.

Tape I. Center for Folklife and Cultural Heritage. New York City Festival Program. Audiocassette FP-2001-CT-0109. (7/1/2001) "Transit Tales." Participants: Bruce Alexander, Sandra Lane, Tony Palombella, Torin Reid. Interviewed by Steve Zeitlin.

Tape J. Center for Folklife and Cultural Heritage. New York City Festival Program. Audiocassette FP-2001-CT-0118. (7/5/2001) "Transit Tales." (Continuation of session on Tape I.) Participant: Bruce Alexander, Sandra Lane, Tony Palombella, Torin Reid. Interviewed by Kathleen Condon.

Tape K. Center for Folklife and Cultural Heritage. New York City Festival Program. Audiocassette FP-2001-CT-0126. (7/8/2001) "Backstage Broadway." Participants: Gary Brouwer, Linda Rice, Scott Sliger. Interviewed by Emily Botein.

Notes

PREFACE

1. New York author Washington Irving first used the term *Gotham* for New York in 1807 in his magazine *Salmagundi*. The original Gotham (Anglo-Saxon for "goat town") was a village near Nottingham in the English Midlands whose citizens pretended to be fools to avoid being taxed by King John. Irving was trying to make a sarcastic point about some of the pretentious, foolish people around him, but New Yorkers liked the term and enthusiastically adopted the nickname. See Kenneth T. Jackson, ed., *The Encyclopedia of New York City* (New Haven, CT: Yale University Press, 1995), 475.

2. For a list of the many fieldworkers, advisors, and supporters whose dedication, guidance, and hard work made the Smithsonian's New York City Project possible, please see the Acknowledgments and Credits, 201–2.

3. For an overview of the fieldwork on which this text is based and an explanation of how quotes taken from Smithsonian field recordings are referenced, see the Appendix—New York City Project: Guide to Recorded Interviews, p. 207–8.

INTRODUCTION

1. An increasing amount of research is being done on Dutch New York. For an excellent recent study that reveals how much Dutch New Amsterdam differed from its English neighbors, see Russell Shorto, *The Island at the Center for the World: The Epic Story of Dutch Manhattan and the Forgotten Colony that Shaped America* (New York: Doubleday, 2004). See also Edwin G. Burrows and Mike Wallace's authoritative *Gotham: A History of New York City to 1898* (New York: Oxford University Press, 1999), 27–77.
2. See 2000 U.S. Census, http://factfinder.census.gov/home/saff/main.html?_lang=en.
3. Kenneth T. Jackson, ed., *Encyclopedia of New York City* (New Haven, CT: Yale University Press, 1995), 112. For more in-depth discussion of New York's early African American community, see Thelma Willis Foote, *Black and White Manhattan: The History of Racial Formation in Colonial New York City* (New York: Oxford University Press, 2004).
4. The term *folklife* has also gained currency among academic and public sector folklorists. Many scholars believe it connotes a wider area of interest than "lore," which has historically prioritized sayings, proverbs, narratives, and other forms of orally transmitted traditional culture. Folklife, they contend, does a better job of indicating the inclusion of traditional beliefs, behaviors, and three-dimensional cultural expressions such as traditional architecture, cooking, or crafts. In truth, many folklorists use the terms interchangeably.
5. John Loftgren, conversation with the author, April 23, 1999.

CHAPTER 1

1. Today, the term *applied folklore* is often used interchangeably with *public sector folklore* to indicate a project that takes place outside the academy and usually involves public programming or cultural education. Applied folklore was initially used to indicate the study and use of traditional culture to ameliorate real-world problems (e.g., to improve quality of life, educate audiences, or bridge cultural divisions). Unlike "pure" academic research, which exists for its own sake, applied folklorists frequently employ the materials they collect for a specific purpose. The term was introduced by folklorist Benjamin Botkin in the late 1930s, who hoped that projects, like the collection and dissemination of oral histories from former slaves by the New Deal Federal Writers' Project, with which he was involved, would improve race relations.
2. This text features interviews with many, but by no means all, of the occupational workers involved with the Smithsonian's New York City Project. The documented stories of an equal number of those interviewed by the project—musicians, community storytellers, urban game specialists, garment workers, window dressers, home cooks, dialecticians, mannequin makers, community radio announcers, the staff of Amateur Night at the Apollo, and others—are not included in this publication and

await their own, well-deserved studies. For a complete list of all recorded interviews, see the Appendix, 207.

3. Folklore's bias toward rural culture is discussed herein, but this might be a good place to note folklorist Archie Green's insight that "To this day, folklorists go to 'the field' . . . where they engage in 'fieldwork.' Obviously, we do not chop cotton, nor do we grub potatoes; yet we invest the word fieldwork with talismanic meaning, as if corn tassels decorated our tape recorders." Archie Green, "Industrial Lore: A Bibliographic-Semantic Query," in Working Americans: Contemporary Approaches to Occupational Folklore, *Western Folklore*, 37:3 (1978), 213.

4. The term *folk-lore* was coined by the British antiquarian and writer William John Thoms (1803–1885) in an 1846 letter to the *Athenaeum*. Thoms suggested that his Anglo-Saxon compound term be used in lieu of less precise phrases such as *popular antiquities* or *popular literature*.

5. For example, in 1888 the British folklorist Alfred Nutt noted: "We are 'civilized men'; the vast majority of our fellows are in this sense not civilized. Using the word very roughly, the Murri, the Maori, the Aztec, the Dorsetshire hind, may all be said to be in a 'primitive' stage, and the study of man in such a stage is folk-lore." Alfred Nutt, "Folk-Lore Terminology," *The Folk-Lore Journal* 2:10 (October 1884), 312.

6. See Newell's description of collecting a version of the thirteenth-century ballad "Little Sir Hugh" (Child 155) from African American children playing in the Manhattan streets and then tracing it back to a young Irish American girl living in a "hut" near Central Park, who had learned it from her mother. William Wells Newell, *Games and Songs of American Children* (New York: Harper and Brothers, 1883; Reprint; New York: Dover, 1963), 75.

7. Those interested in an outstanding example of early urban or occupational documentation are urged to consult Henry Mayhew's 1851 classic *London Labour and the London Poor*. Mayhew, an investigatory journalist, set out to document the lower rungs of London society. His study remains an unparalleled landmark in urban ethnology, both because of the scope of occupations included and the excellence of his interviews. Initially published in three volumes, it has been republished numerous times, including in an excellent condensed version edited by Peter Quennell. See Henry Mayhew, *Mayhew's London: Being Selections from "London Labour and the London Poor,"* edited by Peter Quennell (London: Spring Books, 1969).

8. Jerrold Hirsch, "Folklore in the Making: B. A. Botkin," *Journal of American Folklore* 100:395 (June–March, 1987), 3.

9. Benjamin Botkin, ed., *New York City Folklore: Legends, Tall Takes, Anecdotes, Stories, Sagas, Heroes and Characters, Customs, Traditions and Sayings* (New York: Random House, 1956), xvii.

10. In 1928, Botkin introduced the term *folk-say* to cover his expanded interests. Despite his promotion of folk-say in his academic and popular publications, it never caught on and is rarely used today. See B. A. Botkin, "Folk-Say and Folklore," *American Speech* 6:6 (August 1931), 404–6.

11. Hirsch, "Folklore in the Making: B. A. Botkin," 23.

12. Bruce Jackson, "Benjamin A. Botkin (1901–1975)," *Journal of American Folklore* 89:351 (Jan.–Mar. 1976), 1.

13. Benjamin A. Botkin, ed., *A Treasury of American Folklore: Stories, Ballads and Traditions of the People* (New York: Crown Publisher, 1944).

14. Benjamin A. Botkin, ed., *Sidewalks of America: Folklore, Legends, Sagas, Traditions, Customs, Songs, Stories, and Sayings of City Folk* (Indianapolis: The Bobbs-Merrill Company, Inc., 1954), vii.

15. See Archie Green, "Industrial Lore: A Bibliographic-Semantic Query," 237.

16. Ellen Stekert, Foreword to *The Urban Experience and Folk Traditions.* edited by C. Américo Paredes and Ellen J. Stekert (Austin: University of Texas Press, 1971), 11.

17. Martin Laba, "Urban Folklore: A Behavioral Approach," *Western Folklore* 38:3 (1979), 158.

18. Laba, "Urban Folklore," 158–59.

19. Barbara Kirshenblatt-Gimblett, "The Future of Folklore Studies in America: The Urban Frontier," *Folklore Forum* 16:2 (1983), 179–80.

20. Kirshenblatt-Gimblett, "The Future of Folklore Studies in America," 180.

21. The New York State Council on the Arts (NYSCA) established a folklore coordinator's position in 1980, which expanded into a Folk Arts Program in 1985. Folklorist Robert Baron has guided NYSCA folk arts funding since its inception.

22. The New York Folklore Society (NYFS) itself was established in 1944. A membership organization primarily focused on upstate New York, its goal, as co-founder Louis Jones stated, was "'to plow back' into the community the folklore collected by scholars and lay people throughout the state." NYFS published the respected journal *New York Folklore Quarterly* through 1974, and later the equally influential journal *New York Folklore*. Today, it continues in its role as one of the leading folklore organizations in the United States and publishes *Voices: Journal of New York Folklore*. For further information visit www.nyfolklore.org.

23. The core group of the New York City Chapter included Deborah Autorino, Robert Baron, Brunhilde Biebuyck, Martha Cooper, Faye Ginsburg, Nancy Groce, Reginetta Haboucha, Lee Haring, Flora S. Kaplan, Barbara Kirshenblatt-Gimblett, Barbro Klein, Allen Walker Read, Lyn Tiefenbacher, Eleanor Wachs, Gerald Warshaver, and Yael Zerubavel, among others.

24. Conference announcement, 1979. Author's collection.

25. Speakers at the 1979 conference including folklorists Gerald Davis, Richard Dorson, Henry Glassie, Kenneth Goldstein, Bruce Jackson, Barbara Kirshenblatt-Gimblett, Barbro Klein, Alan Lomax, John Szwed, and Robert Ferris Thompson; ethnomusicologists Salwa El-Shawan, Adelaide Reyes-Schramm, and Mark Slobin; as well as dozens of prominent journalists, sociologists, historians, and politicians.

26. For example, City Lore's study of children's folklore resulted in Amanda Dargan and Steve Zeitlin's excellent book, *City Play* (New Brunswick: Rutgers University Press,

1990). Also an oral history of New York transit workers served as the basis of Sally Charnow and Steve Zeitlin's *I've Been Working on the Subway* (Brooklyn: New York Transit Museum, 1992).

27. For additional information on City Lore, visit www.citylore.org/.

28. The Balkan Arts Center changed its name to the Ethnic Folk Arts Center in the 1980s, then to the Center for Traditional Music and Dance (CTMD) in the mid-1990s. For additional information, visit www.ctmd.org.

29. Among CTMD's many accomplishments, its work with older Irish master musicians and dancers led to the formation of the acclaimed Irish supergroup Cherish the Ladies. CTMD programming also stimulated a revival of interest in Jewish klezmer music and led to "second careers" for many of its master performers.

30. CTMD prides itself as being among the great proponents in the United States of what the late folklorist Alan Lomax called "Cultural Equity"—the right of every community or ethnic group to express and sustain its distinctive cultural heritage. Conversation with Ethel Raim, 2008.

31. Robert S. McCarl, Jr., "Occupational Folklife: A Theoretical Hypothesis" in Working Americans: Contemporary Approaches to Occupational Folklife, *Western Folklore* 37:3 (1978), 145.

32. Green, "Industrial Lore: A Bibliographic-Semantic Query," 214.

33. William Allen, Charles Ware, and Lucy McKim Garrison, *Slave Songs of the United States* (New York: A. Simpson & Co., 1867).

34. Fletcher S. Bassett, *Legends and Superstitions of the Sea and of Sailors* (Chicago: Belford, Clarke, 1885).

35. For an excellent overview of the study of occupational folklore in the United States, see Green's excellent article "Industrial Lore."

36. Green, "Industrial Lore," 215.

37. George Korson, *Songs and Ballads of the Anthracite Miner* (New York: Hitchcock, 1927).

38. Green, "Industrial Lore," 215.

39. See Botkin, *Sidewalks of America*.

40. For a complete list of Festival programs, see *Smithsonian Festival of American Folklife Program Books, 1971–1976* (Washington, D.C.: Smithsonian Institution, 1971–1976). The "Archives of Occupational Folklife" with over six hundred hours of audiocassettes documenting these festival programs are housed at the Smithsonian Center for Folklife and Cultural Heritage's Rinzler Archive.

41. Other notable exceptions included George Carney's 1982 festival program on pipeline workers; Jack Santino's 1983 program on aviation workers; and Sam Schrager's 1986 program on trial lawyers. Important studies generated by these festival programs include Jack Santino and Paul Wagner's 1982 documentary film *Miles of Smiles: The Untold Story of the Black Pullman Porter*, and Santino's subsequent book *Miles of Smiles, Years of Struggle: Stories of Black Pullman Porters* (Urbana: University of Illinois Press, 1989); Robert McCarl, *The District of*

Columbia Fire Fighters' Project: A Case Study in Occupational Folklife (Washington, D.C.: Smithsonian Institution Press, 1985); and Sam Schrager, *The Trial Lawyer's Art* (Philadelphia: Temple University Press, 1999).

42. Studs Terkel, *Working: People Talk about What They Do All Day and How They Feel about What They Do* (New York: Pantheon Books, 1974).

43. Alan Dundes and Carl R. Pagter, eds., *Work Hard and You Shall Be Rewarded: Urban Folklore from the Paperwork Empire* (Bloomington: Indiana University Press, 1975).

44. An exception was the groundbreaking 1986 Smithsonian Folklife Festival program on trial lawyers curated by Sam Schrager. His book, based in part on festival research, details this fascinating study. See: Schrager, *The Trial Lawyer's Art.*

45. C. Kurt Dewhurst, "The Arts of Working: Manipulating the Urban Work Environment," *Western Folklore* 43:3 (July 1984), 193.

46. Green, a leading scholar in the field of occupational folklore, introduced the term *laborlore,* which is also used by many contemporary folklorists.

47. Throughout the field, folklore has been supplemented or replaced by *folklife.* This is reflected by departmental name changes at universities and at major institutions, such as the Smithsonian, which now has a "Center for Folklife and Cultural Heritage," and the Library Congress, which houses the "American Folklife Center."

48. McCarl defined *technique* as "the 'working knowledge' (what you need to know to do the job) of any work group . . . passed from one worker to another through imitation and instruction, it begins to reveal a pattern of interactions that is unique to that particular group and almost invisible to the outside observer." McCarl, "Occupational Folklife," 148, 158.

49. Ethnomusicologists have been particularly active in documenting New York City's musical cultures. For a general introduction to research in New York City, see Ray Allen and Nancy Groce, "Folk and Traditional Music in New York State," Special Issue, *New York Folklore* 14: 3–4 (Summer–Fall, 1988); and *New York City: Global Beat of the Boroughs* (Smithsonian Folkways Recordings: SFW40493, 2001), a double-CD sampler of ethnic traditions of New York released in connection with the 2001 Smithsonian Folklife Festival program.

CHAPTER 2

1. Actors refer to non-musical plays as "legitimate" or "legit" theater, but few know that the phrase dates back to 1662 when King Charles II of England gave his official "Patent" or "Charter" to two London theaters—Covent Garden and Drury Lane—granting them certain rights and privileges. Both theaters specialized in dramatic plays, such as those of William Shakespeare, which included little by way of singing, dancing, or general spectacle. By the early nineteenth century, the term "legit theater" was widely used by actors of the "old school," who wanted to make sure

audiences knew they weren't involved with those new low-rent musical comedies, farces, or reviews.

2. CFCH, 2001:19.

3. Edward B. Marks, *They All Had Glamour: From the Swedish Nightingale to the Naked Lady* (New York: J. Messner, Inc., 1944), 1–12.

4. CFCH/Festival, Tape K.

5. CFCH, 2001:19.

6. CFCH, 1999:2.

7. CFCH, 1999:1.

8. CFCH, 2001:19.

9. CFCH, 1999:16.

10. CFCH, 1999:16.

11. CFCH/Festival, Tape A.

12. CFCH/Festival, Tape A.

13. In 1880, Bush Electric Light Company, one of several competing concerns that were trying to demonstrate the advantages of electric street lights, talked city officials into letting them illuminate what was then the heart of Manhattan's theater district, Broadway between 14th Street and 34th Street. New Yorkers were soon calling that stretch of Broadway "The Great White Way." The nickname stuck, although people now use it to describe Times Square, not Union Square.

14. CFCH/Festival, Tape A.

15. CFCH/Festival, Tape A.

16. CFCH/Festival, Tape A.

17. For information on Actors' Equity, visit www.actorsequity.org.

18. CFCH/Festival, Tape A.

19. CFCH/Festival, Tape A.

20. CFCH, 2000:3.

21. CFCH, 2001:19.

22. CFCH/Festival, Tape C.

23. CFCH, 2001:19. Fortunately, in this case the show was *Little Shop of Horrors,* which went on to enjoy a healthy Off-Broadway run before moving uptown for an extended stay on Broadway.

24. CFCH, 2001:19.

25. CFCH, 2001:19.

26. CFCH/Festival, Tape C.

27. CFCH/Festival, Tape C.

28. CFCH, 1999:1.

29. CFCH, 2001:19.

30. CFCH, 2001:19.

31. CFCH, 1999:1.

32. CFCH, 1999:1.

33. CFCH, 1999:17.

34. CFCH, 1999:15.

35. CFCH/Festival, Tape K.

36. CFCH: 2000:11.

37. CFCH/Festival, Tape K.

38. CFCH, 1999:15.

39. CFCH/Festival, Tape K.

40. CFCH, 1999:15.

41. CFCH, 2000:38.

42. Matera was interviewed at her Manhattan atelier by the author on September 1, 1999. See CFCH, 1999:15. The Smithsonian thanks the late Matera and her colleagues at Barbara Matera, Ltd., for their assistance and cooperation. Special thanks to Matera employees and costume makers Judy Adamson, Jarred Aswegan, Polly Kinney, Josephine Spano, and Patricia Sullivan for coming to Washington to participate in the 2001 Smithsonian Folklife Festival.

43. CFCH, 1999:15.

44. CFCH, 1999:15.

45. CFCH, 1999:15.

46. CFCH, 1999:15.

47. CFCH, 1999:15.

48. Gray Brouwer was interviewed by the author at his atelier on August 8, 2000. See CFCH, 2000:11. Also see Marion Jacobson's interview with Woody Shelp, CFCH, 2000:13. The Smithsonian thanks Brouwer and Tom Schneider for their advice and guidance on the theatrical millinery display and for coming to Washington to participate in the 2001 Smithsonian Folklife Festival.

49. CFCH, 2000:11.

50. CFCH, 2000:11.

51. CFCH/Festival, Tape K.

52. CFCH, 2000:11.

53. CFCH, 2000:11.

54. CFCH, 2000:39. Bob Kelly was interviewed at his Times Square shop by folklorist and theater historian Andrew Davis on November 7, 2000. The Smithsonian thanks Kelly for his assistance and support of the New York City Project and the 2001 Smithsonian Folklife Festival.

55. CFCH, 2000:39.

56. CFCH, 2000:39.

57. CFCH, 2000:39.

58. CFCH, 2000:39.

59. CFCH, 2000:39.

60. CFCH, 2000:39.

61. CFCH, 2000:39.

62. CFCH/Festival, Tape K.

63. CFCH/Festival, Tape K.
64. CFCH/Festival, Tape K.
65. CFCH/Festival, Tape K.
66. CFCH/Festival, Tape K.
67. Linda Rice, conversation with author, Fall 2001.
68. CFCH/Festival, Tape K.
69. Linda Rice, conversation with author, Fall 2001.
70. CFCH/Festival, Tape K.
71. Nino Novellino and members of his staff were interviewed at his Hudson Valley atelier by folklorist and theater historian Andrew Davis on November 13, 2000. See CFCH, 2000:38. The Smithsonian thanks Novellino for his assistance and support, and Costume Armour staff members Brian Healy, Peter Ray, Brian Wolfe, and Leslie Wolfe for coming to Washington to participate in the 2001 Festival Program.
72. CFCH, 2000:38.
73. CFCH, 2001:19.
74. CFCH, 2001:19.
75. CFCH/Festival, Tape K.
76. CFCH/Festival, Tape K.
77. John Loftgren was interviewed by the author in a Chinese restaurant in Times Square between an afternoon rehearsal and evening show on April 23, 1999. See CFCH, 1999:11.
78. CFCH, 1999:11.
79. CFCH, 1999:11.
80. CFCH, 1999:11.
81. CFCH, 1999:11.
82. CFCH, 1999:11.
83. CFCH, 1999:11.
84. CFCH/Festival, Tape K.
85. CFCH/Festival, Tape K.
86. CFCH/Festival, Tape K.
87. CFCH, 1999:16.

CHAPTER 3

1. For an excellent study of New York City graffiti, see Martha Cooper and Henry Chalfant, *Subway Art* (New York: Henry Holt & Company, 1984). See also Tony Silver and Henry Chalfant's classic 1983 documentary film, *Style Wars*.
2. For a discussion on controversies surrounding graffiti, see Joe Austin, *Taking the Train: How Graffiti Art Became an Urban Crisis in New York City* (New York: Columbia University Press, 2001).

3. See Steve Hager, *Hip-Hop: The Illustrated History of Break Dancing, Rap Music and Graffiti* (New York: St. Martin's Press, 1984).

4. For example, see Tony Marcano, "Tats Cru Wins Coca-Cola Account," *New York Times*, April 16, 1995.

5. This profile is based on an interview conducted by folklorist Elena Martinez of City Lore on August 3, 2000, at the Tats Cru workshop in the Bronx. CFCH, 2000:31. The Smithsonian thanks Tats Cru both for the interview and for participating in the 2001 Smithsonian Folklife Festival in Washington, D.C.

6. CFCH, 2000:31.

7. CFCH, 2000:31.

8. CFCH, 2000:31.

9. CFCH, 2000:31.

10. CFCH, 2000:31.

11. CFCH, 2000:31.

12. See Austin, *Taking the Train*.

13. For an excellent study of the memorial wall movement, see Martha Cooper and Joseph Sciorra, *R.I.P.: Memorial Wall Art* (New York: Henry Holt & Co., 1994).

14. CFCH, 2000:31.

15. CFCH, 2000:31.

16. CFCH, 2000:31.

17. CFCH, 2000:31.

18. For an interesting article about how New Yorkers memorialized the World Trade Center, see Kay Turner, "Here Was New York," *Voices: Journal of New York Folklore* 33:2–4 (Winter 2007), 24–30.

19. CFCH, 2000:31.

20. CFCH, 2000:31.

21. CFCH, 2000:31. For further information on Tats Cru, visit their website: www.themuralkings.com.

CHAPTER 4

1. For the history of the Local 28, see www.smwialu28.org/history.

2. CFCH, 2000:34.

3. Elena Martinez's interview with Nicholas Maldarelli took place on September 20, 2000 at the Local 28 Apprentice School in Jamaica, Queens. See CFCH, 2000:34. The Smithsonian thanks Local 28 and Maldarelli for their cooperation, and union members George Andrucki, Stan Bernstein, Robin Delk, Maldarelli, Leah Rambo, Thomas Schlitz, George Treanor, and Arthur Tyburski, for coming to Washington to enthusiastically participate in the 2001 Smithsonian Folklife Festival.

4. CFCH, 2000:34.

5. CFCH, 2000:34.
6. See www.smwialu28.org/index28.html.
7. CFCH, 2000:34.
8. CFCH, 2000:34.
9. CFCH, 2000:34.
10. CFCH, 2000:34.
11. CFCH, 2000:34.
12. For an excellent recent study on tin men and the history and traditions of the tin smith-ing craft, see: Archie Green, *Tin Men* (Urbana: University of Illinois Press, 2002).
13. CFCH, 2000:34.
14. CFCH, 2000:34.
15. In 1975, a federal district court found the Local 28 guilty of racial discrimination in violation of Title VII of the Civil Rights Act of 1964. The court established a 29 percent minority membership goal and ordered the union to implement proce-dures to meet the goal. In 1982 and 1983, the union was found guilty of civil con-tempt for disobeying the court orders and ordered that the goal be met by August 1987. See: The Oyez Project, *Local 28 v. EEOC*, 478 U.S. 421 (1986), www.oyez.org/cases/1980-1989/1985/1985_84_1656/.
16. CFCH, 2000:34.
17. CFCH, 2000:34.

CHAPTER 5

1. The subway map is the most commonly used guide to the city. The current subway map was designed by Michael Hertz of Merrick, Long Island. Introduced in 1998, it replaced Hertz's 1979 map, which, in turn, replaced a very stylized 1970 subway map designed by Massimo Vignelli. Vignelli's map won praise from designers, but it was widely disliked by New Yorkers, who found it confusing. Subway maps are distributed for free at token booths throughout the subway system.
2. CFCH, 2000:37.
3. This chapter is based primarily on interviews conducted for the Smithsonian in New York by folklorist Steve Zeitlin of City Lore: The Center for Urban Culture, and audiocassette tape recordings of public discussions at the 2001 Smithsonian Folklife Festival in Washington, D.C. The Smithsonian thanks the Metropolitan Transit Authority and the New York Transit Museum and their staffs for their sup-port and assistance. We are especially grateful to MTA employees Bruce Alexander, Chris Creed, Anthony Palombella, Torin Reid, and the late Sandra Lane for their enthusiastic participation in the 2001 Smithsonian Folklife Festival.
4. CFCH, 2000:32.
5. Because of the large influx of women into the system in recent years, the official term has been changed to "train operator," but many of the workers, both male and

female, who joined the MTA before the 1990s continue to refer to themselves as "motormen."

6. CFCH, 2000:32.
7. CFCH, 2000:32.
8. CFCH, 2000:37.
9. CFCH, 2000:37.
10. CFCH, 2000:32.
11. CFCH, 2000:32.
12. CFCH, 2000:32.
13. CFCH, 2000:32.
14. CFCH, 2000:32.
15. CFCH/Festival, Tape I.
16. CFCH: 2000:32.
17. For more information about the art work in New York City subways, visit the MTA's "Arts for Transit" web page: www.mta.info/mta/aft/about/.
18. CFCH, 2000:32.
19. CFCH/Festival, Tape I.
20. CFCH, 2000:32.
21. CFCH/Festival, Tape I.
22. CFCH/Festival, Tape I.
23. CFCH/Festival, Tape I.
24. CFCH/Festival, Tape I.
25. CFCH/Festival, Tape I.
26. CFCH/Festival, Tape J.
27. CFCH/Festival, Tape J.
28. CFCH/Festival, Tape J.
29. CFCH, 2000:37.
30. CFCH/Festival, Tape J.
31. Brian Sharkey, MTA motorman in conversation with author.
32. CFCH/Festival, Tape F.
33. CFCH/Festival, Tape F.
34. CFCH/Festival, Tape E and CFCH/Festival, Tape I.
35. CFCH/Festival, Tape E.
36. CFCH/Festival, Tape E.
37. CFCH/Festival, Tape E.
38. CFCH, 2000:32.
39. CFCH/Festival, Tape E and CFCH/Festival, Tape J.
40. CFCH/Festival, Tape J.
41. CFCH/Festival, Tape E.
42. CFCH/Festival, Tape J.
43. CFCH/Festival, Tape E.
44. CFCH, 2000:32.

45. CFCH, 2000:32 and CFCH/Festival, Tape J.
46. CFCH/Festival, Tape J.
47. CFCH/Festival, Tape J.
48. CFCH/Festival, Tape J.
49. CFCH/Festival, Tape E and CFCH/Festival, Tape J.
50. CFCH/Festival, Tape J.
51. CFCH/Festival, Tape J.
52. CFCH/Festival, Tape J.
53. CFCH/Festival, Tape J.
54. CFCH/Festival, Tape J.
55. CFCH/Festival, Tape E and CFCH/Festival, Tape I.
56. CFCH, 2000:37.
57. CFCH/Festival, Tape J.
58. CFCH/Festival, Tape J.
59. CFCH/Festival, Tape J.
60. CFCH/Festival, Tape J.
61. CFCH/Festival, Tape E and CFCH/Festival, Tape I.
62. For an interview with Music Under New York coordinator Gina Higginbotham, see CFCH, 1999:18.
63. The *erhu* is a long-necked Chinese bowed fiddle.
64. They are a major step forward from the "saxophone terrorist" of the 1980s. For several years, subway riders had to endure an excruciatingly bad tenor sax player who would burst into cars and play until people gave him money to stop.
65. CFCH/Festival, Tape E.
66. CFCH/Festival, Tape E.
67. CFCH, 2000:32.
68. CFCH, 2000:32.
69. The homeless people documented in Jennifer Toth's 1993 book *Mole People* were not subway residents, but instead lived in Amtrak tunnels under Grand Central Terminal and Pennsylvania Station and along the West Side Drive. Toth noted that they preferred train to subway tunnels because Amtrak had less traffic.
70. CFCH/Festival, Tape F.
71. CFCH/Festival, Tape E.
72. CFCH/Festival, Tape E.
73. CFCH/Festival, Tape E.
74. CFCH, 2000:37.
75. CFCH, 2000:32.
76. CFCH, 2000:37.
77. CFCH/Festival, Tape E.
78. See "Breaking the Routine: Voice of the Subway," *New York Times*, January 15, 1987.
79. CFCH, 2000:37.

80. CFCH/Festival, Tape E.
81. CFCH/Festival, Tape E.
82. CFCH, 2000:37.
83. CFCH, 2000:37.
84. CFCH/Festival, Tape J.
85. CFCH/Festival, Tape F.
86. CFCH, 2000:37.
87. CFCH, 2000:37.
88. CFCH, 2000:32.

CHAPTER 6

1. This chapter is based on interviews conducted for the Smithsonian in New York City by folklorist Steve Zeitlin of City Lore: The Center for Urban Culture, as well as audiocassette tape recordings of public discussions at the 2001 Smithsonian Folklife Festival in Washington, D.C. See CFCH/Festival, Tapes E, F, I, and J. The Smithsonian thanks the Metropolitan Transit Authority for their support, and particularly Tony Palombella for his cooperation and participation in the 2001 Smithsonian Folklife Festival.
2. CFCH/Festival, Tape F.
3. CFCH/Festival, Tape E.
4. CFCH/Festival, Tape F.
5. CFCH/Festival, Tape F.
6. CFCH/Festival, Tape F.
7. CFCH/Festival, Tape F.

CHAPTER 7

1. This profile is based on fieldwork and interview tapes recorded by folklorist Kathleen Condon at the Rosenwach workshops in Long Island City, Queens and Greenpoint, Brooklyn, a rooftop on West 75th Street in Manhattan, and at several public narrative sessions during the 2001 Smithsonian Folklife Festival in Washington, D.C. Those interviewed include Anthony Aviles, David Bonilla, William Bush, Adonis "CJ" Cegisman, Ryszard Danielewski, Wilson Felix, John DeGeorge, Kenneth Lewis, Akir Mactume, Roger Martinez, Robert Olecki, Andrew Rosenwach, and Charles Zimmerman. The Smithsonian thanks the staff and management of Rosenwach Tank Company, Inc., for their cooperation and support as well as for their enthusiastic participation in the 2001 Smithsonian Folklife Festival.
2. Artesian wells are named after the town of Artois in northern France, where these types of pressure-driven wells were developed.
3. CFCH, 2000:20A.
4. CFCH, 2000:20A.

5. CFCH, 2000:20A.
6. CFCH, 2000:20A.
7. CFCH, 2000:20A.
8. CFCH, 2000:20A.
9. CFCH, 2000:20A.
10. CFCH, 2000:20A.
11. CFCH, 2000:20A.
12. CFCH, 2000:20A.
13. CFCH, 2000:20A.
14. CFCH, 2000:20A.
15. CFCH, 2000:20A.
16. CFCH, 2000:20A.
17. CFCH, 2000:20A.
18. CFCH, 2000:20B.
19. CFCH, 2000:20B.
20. CFCH, 2000:20A.
21. CFCH, 2000:20A.
22. CFCH, 2000:20A.
23. CFCH, 2000:20A.
24. CFCH, 2000:20A.
25. CFCH, 2000:20A.
26. CFCH, 2000:20A.
27. CFCH, 2000:20A.
28. CFCH, 2000:20A.
29. CFCH, 2000:20A.
30. CFCH, 2000:20B.
31. CFCH, 2000:20B.
32. CFCH, 2000:20A.
33. CFCH, 2000:20A.
34. CFCH, 2000:20A.
35. CFCH, 2000:20A.
36. CFCH, 2000:20B.
37. CFCH, 2000:20B.
38. CFCH, 2000:20B.
39. CFCH, 2000:20B.
40. CFCH, 2000:20B.

CHAPTER 8

1. This interview with Mark Federman was recorded by Annie Hauck-Lawson of Brooklyn College on September 9, 2000, during field research for the Smithsonian Folklife Festival. Federman was also recorded several times at the 2001 Smithsonian

Folklife Festival in Washington, D.C., during discussions on the narrative stages. All quotes in this chapter are drawn from audiocassette interview tape CFCH, 2000:8. The Smithsonian thanks Federman and Herman Vargas for participating in the 2001 Festival, and all the employees of Russ & Daughters for their interest and support of the New York City Project.

2. Since this interview took place in 2000, Federman's nephew Josh Russ Tupper and his daughter Niki Russ Federman have both returned to work in the family business. Niki left a promising career in a West Coast art museum, but as she told the author during a recent conversation, she probably meets as many artists now in the shop as she did at her old institution. For more information on Russ & Daughters, visit their website at *www.russanddaughters.com.*

CHAPTER 9

1. All quotes in this chapter are drawn from audiocassette interview tape CFCH, 2000:10. Food historian and fieldworker Annie Hauck-Lawson recorded this interview with Steve Ross in Brooklyn, New York, on March 12, 2000. The Smithsonian thanks Coney Island Bagels & Bialys, Ross and members of the Ross family, including his father Donald and mother Esta, for their interest in and support of the Smithsonian New York City Project and for their participation in the 2001 Smithsonian Folklife Festival in Washington, D.C.

CHAPTER 10

1. The Smithsonian Institution thanks the New York Stock Exchange, the New York Board of Trade, and the New York Mercantile Exchange, as well as individuals throughout the Financial District for their help with our research and for their support and cooperation in presenting a major program on Wall Street as part of the 2001 Smithsonian Folklife Festival. Most of the Smithsonian Wall Street interviews were conducted by folklorist Kay Turner, with supplementary interviews and assistance from Brian Thompson, Kristin Aguilera, and Meg Ventrudo from the Museum of American Financial History (Museum of American Finance). Interview tapes are now housed in the Ralph Rinzler Archives at the Center for Folklife and Cultural Heritage at the Smithsonian Institution.

   Participants in the Wall Street area of the 2001 Smithsonian Folklife Festival included Richard Anderson, Jr., Richard Anderson, Sr., Richard Baratz, Madeline Boyd, Victoria Chukwuka, Joseph Cicchetti, Tony DeMarco, Joe Gabriel, Michael Geoghan, John Herzog, Scott Hess, Myron Kandel, Michael LaBranche, Gary Lapayover, Michel Marks, Mark Tomasko, Nancy Norton Tomasko, Steve Wheeler, and Jason Zweig.

2. To date, very little ethnographic research has been done on financial workers. Rosemary O. Joyce's 1982 article "Wall Street Wags: Uses of Humor in the Financial

Community" in *Western Folklore*, while interesting, is primarily focused on stock and bond salesmen in Columbus, Ohio.

3. Charles Henry Dow (1851–1902) and Edward Davis Jones (1856–1920) began issuing economic news bulletins—or as they called them, "flimsies"—in 1882 from a small basement office at 15 Wall Street. Their average of key industrial stocks first appeared in 1884. Although neither man was trained as a journalist, Dow went on to found the *Wall Street Journal.*

4. For an excellent recent history of Dutch New York, see Russell Shorto, *The Island at the Center for the World: The Epic Story of Dutch Manhattan and the Forgotten Colony that Shaped America* (New York: Doubleday, 2004). See also, Edwin G. Burrows and Mike Wallace, *Gotham: A History of New York City to 1898* (New York: Oxford University Press, 1999).

5. During the American Revolution, the Continental Congress paid its expenses by issuing script known as "continentals," and in the uncertain times that followed, the phrase "not worth a continental" became synonymous with *worthless.* To settle their debts, New York merchants turned to more stable European currencies, including a type of coin known as the *thaler,* which was minted by several countries. The thaler, which was pronounced "tholler" or "dollar," later gave its name to American currency. The Spanish *thaler* coin was milled to be dividable into eight smaller "bits"—literally "pieces of eight"—each worth twelve and a half cents. (This is also where the slang term "two-bits," for a quarter of a dollar, originated.) The idea of an eighth being the smallest or base unit became deeply ingrained in the traditions of the New York financial community, and stocks on the New York Stock Exchange continued to be traded in eighths until 2001! Many Wall Street traders were upset when the eighths, and later sixteenth or "teennies" as they were affectionately called, were replaced by modern decimalization. And of course, the "ticker tape" had to be redesigned.

6. Arthur Cashin, *A View of Wall Street from the Seventh Floor* (Lyme, Conn.: Greenwich Publishing Group, Inc., 1999), 31–32. For more extensive information on Duer, and his impact on American history, see Francis James Roberts, "*The King of the Alley": William Duer: Politician, Entrepreneur, and Speculator, 1768–1799* (Philadelphia: American Philosophical Society, 1992).

7. For information on both the tree and the Agreement, see Cashin, *A View of Wall Street from the Seventh Floor*, 32.

8. CFCH, 2000:01.

9. For a historic overview of Wall Street, see Charles R. Geisst, *100 Years of Wall Street* (New York: McGraw-Hill, 2000); and John Steele Gordon, *The Great Game: The Emergence of Wall Street as a World Power, 1653–2000* (New York: Scribner, 1999).

10. Curb brokers were not always the most reliable or honest of brokers. In fact, in 1857 the term "guttersnipe" was coined to describe the less reputable of them.

11. For information on the history of gold trading, see Tom Kalinke, "Sleepless in New York: Evening Hours at the Exchange," *Financial History* (2005), available at www. financialhistory.org/.

12. In 2007, NYBOT became a wholly owned subsidiary of the Intercontinental Exchange (ICE).

13. CFCH, 2001:1.

14. CFCH, 2000:47.

15. Because the goal of our project was to document the occupational culture of the trading floors, we will not attempt to offer explanations for all of the financial terms mentioned in this chapter. Readers seeking more detailed information are encouraged to visit the excellent websites maintained by each of the featured exchanges.

16. In 2007, the impact of electronic trading on the NYSE was reflected by the closing of the Blue Room and the Expanded Blue Room and the consolidation of the remaining traders in The Main Room and The Garage. See "NYSE's Trading Floor to Shrink Further," *Reuters,* September 13, 2007.

17. CFCH, 2001:12. A "two-dollar broker" is an old term that referred to a small trader who executed orders as an agent for other firms. At one time, they were paid two dollars for every order they executed.

18. CFCH, 2000:45.

19. CFCH, 2001:12.

20. DOT stands for "Designated Order Turnaround" system, an electronic order-routing system that has since been superseded by Super DOT.

21. CFCH, 2001:6.

22. See www.nyse.com.

23. CFCH, 2001:3.

24. An alphabetical list of the stocks being traded on "The Big Board" is the source of the term "Listed Stocks."

25. CFCH, 1999:5.

26. CFCH, 2000:45.

27. CFCH, 2000:1.

28. CFCH, 2001:3. Until recently, the information traded on the floor was sent to backroom typists to be typed and entered into the records, but most floor traders now use electronic devises they refer to simply as "handhelds."

29. CFCH, 2001:3.

30. CFCH, 2000:1.

31. CFCH, 2000:47.

32. In March 2008, NYMEX accepted a purchase offer from CME Group, the parent company of the Chicago Mercantile Exchange and the Chicago Board of Trade. It is too soon to tell what impact this will ultimately have on the NYMEX and its culture.

33. CFCH, 2000:2.

34. For additional information on NYMEX, see www.nymex.com/index.aspx.

35. In January 2007, the NYBOT was purchased by Intercontinental Exchange (ICE). Since then, rumors that its floor trading will be discontinued have continued to

surface. See Zachery Kouse, "NYBOT-TOMS Out. No Future for Futures: Pits to Close in 2008," *New York Post*, October 22, 2007.

36. CFCH, 2000:2.
37. CFCH, 2000:2.
38. CFCH, 2001:1.
39. CFCH, 2001:1.
40. Rapid communication was always an important factor on The Street. In the early days, young page boys, known as "runners," were employed to rush messages and paper transactions between Wall Street offices. A semaphore system using flags was established between Wall Street and Philadelphia as early as the 1830s; a little later, homing pigeons were pressed into service. And when the telegraph appeared in the mid-1840s, stock traders immediately made use of the new technology. The stock ticker, invented by Edward A. Calahan in 1867, was an outgrowth of the telegraph. It was designed to print out stock prices on a continuous strip of paper tape. Suddenly, information from the exchange floors could be transmitted almost instantly to brokers throughout the country.

    The first Ticker Tape Parade occurred spontaneously in 1886 when excited Wall Street workers, inspired by the passing of a giant parade celebrating the inauguration of the Statue of Liberty, began throwing whatever they could lay their hands on out of their windows, which overlooked the parade's route through lower Manhattan.

41. CFCH, 2001:2.
42. CFCH, 2000:2.
43. CFCH, 2001:1.
44. CFCH, 2001:1.
45. CFCH, 2001:1.
46. CFCH, 2000:2.
47. NYMEX pits have staggered opening times.
48. CFCH, 2001:1.
49. CFCH, 2001:1.
50. CFCH, 2000:47.
51. CFCH, 2001:2.
52. CFCH, 2001:2.
53. CFCH, 2001:14.
54. CFCH, 2001:1.
55. See Tim McLaughlin, "Top Wall Street Jobs Still Elude Women, Minorities," *Reuters,* December 27, 2006.
56. CFCH, 2000:2.
57. "Blue Chip" is used to refer to stocks issued by stable, well-respected firms. The term comes from gambling casinos, where the highest value counters ("chips") were usually colored blue. Dow Jones' employee Oliver Gingold is credited with introducing the term on The Street ca. 1923.

58. CFCH, 2000:47.

59. CFCH, 2001:8.

60. CFCH, 2000:2. Delancey Street is one of the main arteries on Manhattan's Lower East Side. It runs through the heart of what used to be a heavily Jewish neighborhood.

61. CFCH, 2000:2.

62. CFCH, 2000:47.

63. CFCH, 2001:2.

64. CFCH, 2001:3.

65. CFCH, 2001:8.

66. CFCH, 2000:2.

67. CFCH, 2001:3.

68. Several of our informants suggested that someone could do a wonderful "verbal archeology" of Wall Street by tracing firm names through the mergers, acquisitions, and splits over the course of the last two hundred years.

69. CFCH, 2000:45.

70. CFCH, 2000:47.

71. CFCH, 2001:1.

72. CFCH, 2000:45.

73. CFCH, 2000:4.

74. CFCH, 2000:1.

75. CFCH, 2000:45.

76. CFCH, 2000:47.

77. CFCH, 2000:45.

78. CFCH, 2000:45.

79. CFCH, 1999:5.

80. CFCH, 2001:3.

81. CFCH, 2001:3.

82. CFCH, 2001:3.

83. CFCH, 2001:3.

84. CFCH, 2000:1.

85. CFCH, 2000:1.

86. CFCH, 2000:1.

87. CFCH, 2001:3.

88. CFCH, 2001:3.

89. CFCH, 2001:3.

90. CFCH, 2000:1.

91. Conversations with author. March, 15, 1999.

92. Conversations with author. March, 15, 1999.

93. Henrietta "Hetty" Howland Robinson Green (1834–1916) was probably the wealthiest woman in the United States at the height of the Gilded Age and a major force on Wall Street. Stories of her canny trading and her miserly habits are still quoted on the Street.

 94. CFCH, 2000:2.
 95. CFCH, 2000:2.
 96. CFCH, 2001:1.
 97. CFCH, 2001:8.
 98. CFCH, 1999:5.
 99. CFCH, 2001:2.
100. CFCH, 2000:2.
101. CFCH, 2000:47.
102. CFCH, 2001:6.
103. CFCH, 2001:1.
104. CFCH, 2001:1.
105. CFCH, 2001:8.
106. CFCH, 2001:3.
107. CFCH, 2001:6.
108. CFCH, 2000:4.
109. CFCH, 2000:45.
110. CFCH, 2000:45.
111. CFCH, 2000:45.
112. CFCH, 2000:45.
113. CFCH, 2001:13.
114. CFCH, 2001:1.
115. CFCH, 2001:6.
116. CFCH, 2001:1.
117. CFCH, 2001:6.
118. CFCH, 2000:45.
119. CFCH, 2001:1.
120. CFCH, 2001:8.
121. Museum of American Finance, *Always Another Trading Day.* Transcript of forum.
122. Museum of American Finance, *Always Another Trading Day.* Transcript of forum.
123. Museum of American Finance, *Always Another Trading Day.* Transcript of forum.
124. Museum of American Finance, *Always Another Trading Day.* Transcript of forum.

BIBLIOGRAPHY

Abrahams, Roger D. "Towards a Sociological Theory of Folklore: Performing Services." In *Working Americans: Contemporary Approaches to Occupational Folklife*, Robert H. Byington, ed. Smithsonian Folklife Studies, No. 3. Los Angeles: California Folklore Society, 1978.

Ahearn, Charlie. *Wild Style*. (Film) First Run Features, 1982.

Allen, Ray, and Nancy Groce, eds. *Folk and Traditional Music in New York State*. Special Issue. *New York Folklore* 14 (Summer–Fall 1988): 3–4.

Allen, Ray, and Lois Wilcken, eds. *Island Sounds in the Global City: Caribbean Popular Music and Identity in New York*. Brooklyn: New York Folklore Society/Institute for Studies in American Music, Brooklyn College, 1998.

Austin, Joe. *Taking the Train: How Graffiti Art Became an Urban Crisis in New York City*. New York: Columbia University Press, 2001.

Bassett, Fletcher S. *Legends and Superstitions of the Sea and of Sailors*. Chicago: Belford, Clarke, 1885.

Botkin, Benjamin A. "Folk-Say and Folklore." *American Speech* 6:6 (August 1931): 404–6.

———. ed. *New York City Folklore: Legends, Tall Tales, Anecdotes, Stories, Sagas, Heroes and Characters, Customs, Traditions and Sayings*. New York: Random House, 1956.

————. ed. *Sidewalks of America: Folklore, Legends, Sagas, Traditions, Customs, Songs, Stories and Sayings of City Folk.* Indianapolis: Bobbs-Merrill Company, 1954.

————. ed. *A Treasury of American Folklore: Stories, Ballads and Traditions of the People.* New York: Crown Publishers, 1944.

Burrows, Edwin G., and Mike Wallace. *Gotham: A History of New York City to 1898.* New York: Oxford University Press, 1999.

Byington, Robert H. "Strategies for Collecting Occupational Folklife in Contemporary Urban/Industrial Contexts." In "Working Americans: Contemporary Approaches to Occupational Folklife." *Western Folklore* 37:3 (July 1978): 185–98.

Cashin, Arthur D., Jr. *A View of Wall Street from the Seventh Floor.* Prepared and Served by the Stock Exchange Luncheon Club. Lyme, Conn.: Greenwich Publishing Group, 1999.

Charnow, Sally, and Steve Zeitlin. *I've Been Working on the Subway.* Brooklyn: New York Transit Museum, 1992.

Cooper, Martha, and Henry Chalfant. *Subway Art.* New York: Henry Holt and Company, 1984.

Cooper, Martha, Henry Chalfant, and Joseph Sciorra. *R.I.P.: Memorial Wall Art.* New York: Henry Holt and Company, 1994.

Dargan, Amanda, and Steven Zeitlin. *City Play.* New Brunswick, NJ: Rutgers University Press, 1990.

Dewhurst, C. Kurt. "The Arts of Working: Manipulating the Urban Work Environment." *Western Folklore* 43:3 (July 1984): 192–202.

Dundes, Alan, and Carl R. Pagter, eds. *Work Hard and You Shall Be Rewarded: Urban Folklore from the Paperwork Empire.* Bloomington: Indiana University Press, 1975.

Foote, Thelma Wills. *Black and White Manhattan: The History of Racial Formation in Colonial New York City.* New York: Oxford University Press, 2004.

Geisst, Charles R. *100 Years of Wall Street.* New York: McGraw-Hill, 2000.

————. *Wall Street: A History.* New York: Oxford University Press, 1997.

Gordon, John Steele. *The Great Game: The Emergence of Wall Street as a World Power, 1653–2000.* New York: Scribner, 1999.

Green, Archie. "Industrial Lore: A Bibliographic-Semantic Query." In "Working Americans: Contemporary Approaches to Occupational Folklore." *Western Folklore* 37:3 (July 1978): 213–44.

————. *Tin Men.* Urbana: University of Illinois Press, 2002.

————. *Wobblies, Pile Butts, and Other Heroes: Laborlore Explorations.* Urbana: University of Illinois Press, 1993.

Groce, Nancy. *New York: Songs of the City.* New York: Watson-Guptill Publications, 1999.

Hager, Steve. *Hip-Hop: The Illustrated History of Break Dancing, Rap Music and Graffiti.* New York: St. Martin's Press, 1984.

Hirsch, Jerrold. "Folklore in the Making: B. A. Botkin." *Journal of American Folklore* 100:395 (January–March 1987): 3–38.

Jackson, Bruce. "Benjamin A. Botkin (1901–1975)." *Journal of American Folklore* 89:351 (1976): 1–6.

Jackson, Kenneth T., ed. *The Encyclopedia of New York City*. New Haven, Conn.: Yale University Press, 1995.

Joyce, Rosemary O. "Wall Street Wags: Uses of Humor in the Financial Community." *Western Folklore* 41:4 (October 1982): 292–303.

Kalinke, Tom. "Sleepless in New York: Evening Hours at the Exchange." *Financial History* 69 (2005): 22.

Kirshenblatt-Gimblett, Barbara. "The Future of Folklore Studies in America: The Urban Frontier." *Folklore Forum* 16:2 (1983): 175–234.

Korson, George. *Songs and Ballads of the Anthracite Miner*. New York: Hitchcock, 1927.

Laba, Martin. "Urban Folklore: A Behavioral Approach." *Western Folklore* 38:3 (July 1979): 158–69.

Marks, Edward B. *They All Had Glamour: From the Swedish Nightingale to the Naked Lady*. New York: J. Messner, 1944.

Mayhew, Henry. *Mayhew's London: Being Selections from "London Labour and the London Poor."* Peter Quennell, ed. London: Spring Books, 1969.

McCarl, Robert S., Jr. *The District of Columbia Fire Fighters' Project: A Case Study in Occupational Folklife*. Washington, D.C.: Smithsonian Institution Press, 1985.

———. "Occupational Folklife: A Theoretical Hypothesis." In "Working Americans: Contemporary Approaches to Occupational Folklife." *Western Folklore* 37:3 (July 1978): 145–60.

Miller, Ivor. *Aerosol Kingdom: Subway Painters in New York City*. Oxford: University Press of Mississippi, 2002.

Museum of American Financial History. *Always Another Trading Day: Endurance and Optimism in the Culture and History of Wall Street*. Transcript of forum. November 15, 2001. Available at www.financialhistory.org/MEDIA/nov15/nov15trans.htm.

Newell, William Wells. *Games and Songs of American Children*. New York: Harper and Brothers, 1883. Reprint, New York: Dover, 1963.

Nutt, Alfred. "Folk-Lore Terminology." *The Folk-Lore Journal* 2:10 (October 1884): 311–15.

Paredes, Americo, and Ellen J. Stekert, eds. *The Urban Experience and Folk Traditions*. Austin: University of Texas Press, 1971.

Roberts, Francis James. *"The King of the Alley": William Duer: Politician, Entrepreneur, and Speculator, 1768–1799*. Philadelphia: American Philosophical Society, 1992.

Santino, Jack. *Miles of Smiles, Years of Struggle: Stories of Black Pullman Porters*. Urbana: University of Illinois Press, 1989.

Santino, Jack, and Paul Wagner. *Miles of Smiles, Years of Struggle: The Untold Story of the Back Pullman Porter*. (Film) The Columbia Historical Society in cooperation with the Smithsonian Institution's Office of Folklife Programs. Benchmark Films, 1982.

Schrager, Sam. *The Trial Lawyer's Art.* Philadelphia: Temple University Press, 1999.

Sen, Amartya. *Identity and Violence: The Illusion of Destiny.* New York: W. W. Norton & Company, 2006.

Shorto, Russell. *The Island at the Center for the World: The Epic Story of Dutch Manhattan and the Forgotten Colony that Shaped America.* New York: Doubleday, 2004.

Silver, Tony, and Henry Chalfant. *Style Wars.* (Film) Public Art Film, 1983.

Smithsonian Center for Folklife and Cultural Heritage. *Thirty-fifth Annual Smithsonian Folklife Festival.* Washington, D.C.: Smithsonian Institution, 2001.

Smithsonian Folkways Recordings. *New York City: Global Beat of the Boroughs.* CD. SFW 40493. Washington, D.C.: Smithsonian Folkways Recordings, 2001.

Smithsonian Institution. *Smithsonian Festival of American Folklife Program Books.* 1971–2001. Washington, D.C.: Smithsonian Institution, 1971–2001.

Snyder, Robert W. *Transit Talk: New York's Bus and Subway Workers Tell Their Stories.* New York: The New York Transit Museum and New Brunswick: Rutgers University Press, 1997.

Sobel, Robert. *The Big Board: A History of the New York Stock Market.* Washington, D.C.: Beard Books, 2000.

Terkel, Studs. *Working: People Talk about What They Do All Day and How They Feel about What They Do.* New York: Pantheon Books, 1974.

Toth, Jennifer. *The Mole People: Life in the Tunnels beneath New York City.* Chicago: Chicago Review Press, 1993.

Turner, Kay. "Here Was New York." *Voices: Journal of New York Folklore* 33:2–4 (Fall–Winter 2007): 24–30.

Zimmerman, Jean. *The Women of the House: How a Colonial She-Merchant Built a Mansion, a Fortune, and a Dynasty.* Orlando, FL: Harcourt, 2006.

INDEX

ABOUT THE AUTHOR

NANCY GROCE is a folklorist, ethnomusicologist, and native New Yorker with wide-ranging interests in music, history, and culture. She holds a Ph.D. in American studies and has worked as the official Borough Folklorist for both Brooklyn and Staten Island. Her previous publications include *New York: Songs of the City*, a history of the city through song lyrics, as well as numerous other books and articles on the Big Apple.

Groce served as a curator at the Smithsonian Center for Folklife and Cultural Heritage for many years, where among other activities she directed the 2001 New York City exhibition at the renowned Smithsonian Folklife Festival. She also curated major Smithsonian Folklife Festival programs on Scotland (2003), Alberta (2006), and Northern Ireland (2007). Currently a Smithsonian Research Associate, she is a member of the staff of American Folklife Center at the Library of Congress.